First World War
and Army of Occupation
War Diary
France, Belgium and Germany

4 DIVISION

Headquarters, Branches and Services
General Staff
1 January 1915 - 30 April 1915

WO95/1441

The Naval & Military Press Ltd
www.nmarchive.com
Published in association with The National Archives

Published by

The Naval & Military Press Ltd

Unit 10 Ridgewood Industrial Park,

Uckfield, East Sussex,

TN22 5QE England

Tel: +44 (0) 1825 749494

www.naval-military-press.com

www.nmarchive.com

This diary has been reprinted in facsimile from the original. Any imperfections are inevitably reproduced and the quality may fall short of modern type and cartographic standards.

© **Crown Copyright**
Images reproduced by permission of The National Archives, London, England, 2015.

Contents

Document type	Place/Title	Date From	Date To
Heading	4th Division General Staff Jan-Mar 1915		
Heading	III Corps Second Army General Staff 4th Division January 1915		
War Diary	Nieppe	01/01/1915	31/01/1915
Miscellaneous	Works Reports		
Miscellaneous	3rd Army Corps.	01/01/1915	01/01/1915
Miscellaneous	Hdqrs. 3rd Corps	23/01/1915	23/01/1915
Miscellaneous	11th Brig section.	23/01/1915	23/01/1915
Miscellaneous	Weekly Report. Headquarters, 3rd Corps	29/01/1915	29/01/1915
Miscellaneous	Artillery Reports.		
Miscellaneous	G.S. C Arty Group.	25/01/1915	25/01/1915
Miscellaneous	G.S. North Arty Group.	26/01/1915	26/01/1915
War Diary	G.S.	27/01/1915	27/01/1915
Miscellaneous	Intelligence.		
Miscellaneous	Late Information.	25/01/1915	25/01/1915
Miscellaneous	4th Division.	26/01/1915	26/01/1915
Miscellaneous	Correspondence & Miscellaneous Papers.		
Miscellaneous	Correspondence On The Following Subjects Will Be Found In Box Marked "4th Division-Correspondence."		
Miscellaneous	11th Brig.	24/01/1915	24/01/1915
Miscellaneous	4th Division. Provisional Instructions For The Organization And Employment Of Grenadiers.	24/01/1915	24/01/1915
Miscellaneous	Volume II Introduction.		
Heading	III Corps Second Army General Staff 4th Division February 1915		
War Diary	Nieppe	01/02/1915	28/02/1915
Miscellaneous	Work Reports.		
Miscellaneous	Weekly Report. Hd. Qrs. 3rd Corps.	05/02/1914	05/02/1914
Miscellaneous	Weekly Report. Headquarers, 3rd Corps.	12/02/1915	12/02/1915
Miscellaneous	Appendix "A" State of Work on New Line of Defence on afternoon. 11/Feb/1915.	11/02/1915	11/02/1915
Miscellaneous	Appendix "B". Distribution-IV Division-Infantry.	10/02/1915	10/02/1915
Map	Frelinghien		
Miscellaneous	A Form. Messages And Signals.		
Map	Scale 12"=1. Mile.		
Map	St. Yves.		
Miscellaneous	Weekly Report. Headquarters, 3rd Corps.	19/02/1915	19/02/1915
Miscellaneous	Report on Work on 2nd (Supporting) Line.		
Miscellaneous	Weekly Report. 3rd Corps.	26/02/1915	26/02/1915
Miscellaneous	Report on 2nd (Divisional) Line of Defence.		
Miscellaneous	Appendix "A"		
Map	Frelinghien.		
Map	St Yves.		
Miscellaneous	Artillery Reports.		
Miscellaneous		06/02/1915	06/02/1915
Miscellaneous		08/02/1915	08/02/1915
Miscellaneous	G.S. 14 Arty	09/02/1915	09/02/1915
Miscellaneous	14th Bde		
Miscellaneous		14/02/1915	14/02/1915
Miscellaneous	32nd Bde		

Miscellaneous	Work done.	17/02/1915	17/02/1915
Miscellaneous	4 Div Arty	19/02/1915	19/02/1915
Miscellaneous	4 Div Arty	24/02/1914	24/02/1914
Miscellaneous	4 Div Arty	25/02/1915	25/02/1915
Miscellaneous	Distribution of Infantry.		
Miscellaneous	Distribution-Infantry 4th Division.		
Miscellaneous	Casualties.		
Miscellaneous	4th Division. Casualties-February 1915		
Miscellaneous	Correspondence.		
Miscellaneous	Correspondence On The Following Subjects Will Be Found In Box Marked "4th Division-Correspondence."		
Miscellaneous		14/03/1915	14/03/1915
Heading	Subject		
Heading	III Corps Second Army. War Diary General Staff 4th Division March 1915.		
Heading	War Diary March 1915		
War Diary	Nieppe.	01/03/1915	31/03/1915
Miscellaneous	Operation Orders		
Operation(al) Order(s)	Operation Order No. 20 by Maj-Gen. H.F.M. Wilson, CB, Commdg. 4th Divn.	14/03/1914	14/03/1914
Miscellaneous			
Operation(al) Order(s)	Operation Order No. 21 by Maj-Gen. H.F.M. Wilson, CB, Commdg. 4th Divn.	15/03/1915	15/03/1915
Miscellaneous			
Miscellaneous	4th. Div. No. A/84	18/03/1915	18/03/1915
Operation(al) Order(s)	3rd Corps Operation Order No. 45	19/03/1915	19/03/1915
Operation(al) Order(s)	Operation Order No. 22 by Maj-Gen. H.F.M. Wilson, C.B. Commdg. 4th Divn.	20/03/1915	20/03/1915
Miscellaneous	4th Division		
Miscellaneous	Artillery Reports		
Miscellaneous	G.S.	04/03/1915	04/03/1915
Miscellaneous	G.S.	05/03/1915	05/03/1915
Miscellaneous	G.S.	06/03/1915	06/03/1915
Miscellaneous	G.S.	07/03/1915	07/03/1915
Miscellaneous	G.S.	08/03/1915	08/03/1915
Miscellaneous	A Form. Messages And Signals.		
Miscellaneous	G.S.	09/03/1915	09/03/1915
Miscellaneous	A Form. Messages And Signals.		
Miscellaneous		21/03/1915	21/03/1915
Miscellaneous	A Form. Messages And Signals.		
Miscellaneous	A Form. Messages And Signals		
Miscellaneous	A Form. Messages And Signals.		
Miscellaneous	Progress Reports		
Miscellaneous	Weekly Report. 4th Div. No. GGG/28	05/03/1915	05/03/1915
Miscellaneous	Report on progress of work on 2nd line. February 4th.		
Miscellaneous			
Miscellaneous	Weekly Report. Right Sector. (12th Brigade)	12/03/1915	12/03/1915
Miscellaneous	Report on 2nd Line, 4th Division.		
Miscellaneous	Weekly Report.	19/03/1915	19/03/1915
Miscellaneous	4th Division. Report of Progress on Second Line.		
Diagram etc			
Miscellaneous	Weekly Report. 3rd Corps.	26/03/1915	26/03/1915
Miscellaneous	Summary of Information		
Miscellaneous	Orders for handing over stores, etc.		
Miscellaneous	First Army Summary of Information.	11/03/1915	11/03/1915

Miscellaneous	4th Division. Information 4th and 6th Divisions, 10th March, 1915	10/03/1915	10/03/1915
Miscellaneous	Information-4th and 6th Divisions, 10/11th March, 1915	11/03/1915	11/03/1915
Miscellaneous	Information-4th & 6th Divisions, 12th March, 1915	12/03/1915	12/03/1915
Miscellaneous	Information 4th Division. 13th March, 1915	13/03/1915	13/03/1915
Miscellaneous	Correspondence On The Following Subjects Will Be Found In Box Marked "4th Division-Correspondence."		
Map	St. Yves.		
Map	Frelinghien.		
Miscellaneous	Notes with Reference to Vermelles:	01/02/1915	01/02/1915
Map	Scale 2"=1. Mile.		
Miscellaneous	Notes with reference to Vermelles:	01/02/1915	01/02/1915
Map	Scale 2"=1. Mile.		
Map	St. Yves.		
Map	Belgium And Part Of France		
Miscellaneous	Translations.		
Miscellaneous	Belgium And France		
Map	Neuve-Eglise		
Map	Messines		
Miscellaneous	Translations.		
Miscellaneous	Belgium And France.		
Heading	G.S. 4th Div. Mar., 1915		
Map	Le Touquet & Frelinghien		
Heading	War Diary 4th Div April 1915 Appendix (A)		
Map	G.H.Q. 2nd Line IV Div.		
Map			
Miscellaneous	6 Div		
Miscellaneous	4th Div		
Map			
Heading	4th Division War Diaries General Staff April 1915		
Heading	War Diary 4 Div April 1915 Appendix (B)		
Heading	III Corps. Second Army. General Staff 4th Division April 1915		
War Diary	Nieppe	01/04/1915	02/04/1915
Miscellaneous	Casualties For The Months Of April & May 1915		
Miscellaneous	Weekly And Progress Reports.		
Miscellaneous	Weekly Report.	02/04/1915	02/04/1915
Miscellaneous	Progress Report on 2nd Line, 1st April, 1915	01/04/1915	01/04/1915
War Diary	Nieppe	03/04/1915	30/04/1915
Miscellaneous		08/04/1915	08/04/1915
Miscellaneous Diagram etc	Le Touquet Mine	08/04/1915	08/04/1915
Miscellaneous	To The Adjutant 2 Lancs Fus.	08/04/1915	08/04/1915
Miscellaneous	Subject-Report on Operations 9-4-1915-Explosion of Mine.	09/04/1915	09/04/1915
Miscellaneous	Operations At Le Touquet 9th April 1915 Explosion Of A Mine.	09/04/1915	09/04/1915
Miscellaneous	Explosion of Mine At Le Touquet.	09/04/1915	09/04/1915
Miscellaneous	4th Division.	09/04/1915	09/04/1915
Miscellaneous	4th Division.	10/04/1915	10/04/1915
Miscellaneous	3rd Corps.	22/04/1915	22/04/1915
Miscellaneous	12th Inf. Brig. (Right Sector).		
Miscellaneous	Table "A".		
Operation(al) Order(s)	Operation Order No. 24 by Maj. Gen. H.F.M. Wilson, C.B. Commdg. 4th Div.	14/04/1915	14/04/1915

Operation(al) Order(s)	Operation Order No. 25 by Maj. Gen. H.F.M. Wilson, C.B. Commdg. 4th Div.	20/04/1915	20/04/1915
Miscellaneous	Distribution of Infantry.		
Miscellaneous	4th Division. Distribution Of Infantry. Month of April.		
Miscellaneous	11th Inf. Brig. (Centre Sector)		
Operation(al) Order(s)	Operation Order No. 23 by Maj. Gen. H.F.M. Wilson, C.B. Commdg. 4th Div.	11/04/1915	11/04/1915
Miscellaneous	Divisional Operation Orders Nos. 23, 24 & 25		
Miscellaneous	Work Report.	23/04/1915	23/04/1915
Miscellaneous	4th Division. Progress Report-Supporting Line.	15/04/1915	15/04/1915
Miscellaneous	Left Sector.	16/04/1915	16/04/1915
Miscellaneous	Right Sector.		
Miscellaneous	3rd Corps.	16/04/1915	16/04/1915
Miscellaneous		09/04/1915	09/04/1915
Miscellaneous	4th Division. Progress Report-Supporting Line.		
Miscellaneous	Weekly Report.	09/04/1915	09/04/1915
Map			
Heading	War Diary HQ 4th Div April 1915. Appendix (C)		
Miscellaneous	4th Division. Casualties.		

4TH DIVISION

GENERAL STAFF

JAN - MAR 1915

III. Corps.
Second Army.

GENERAL STAFF

4.th DIVISION

JANUARY

1915

Note: The messages mentioned in the diary will be found in a separate box marked "messages."

Attached:

Work Reports.
Artillery Reports.
Intelligence.
Correspondence &
Misc. Papers.

War Diary - 1st January 1915.

NIEPPE.

              Wet afternoon and night.

Time	Entry	Ref
4-45 am	3rd Corps informed no change.	(G.1, H.32, BM.1/11&12)
7 am	5th and 6th Divisions report no change.	(G.651, G.20)
8-32 am	Brigades informed that an officer from H.Q. would come round on Tuesday and Friday to collect information re trenches.	G.2
8-50 am	3rd Corps report that they are trying to get pumps and flares asked for.	G.202
5-30 pm	Commander 2nd Army directs that informal understandings with enemy are to cease. Officers and N.C.O's allowing them are to brought before a Court Martial.	G.211
5-45 pm	The above message repeated f to all units and acknowledged to 3rd Corps.	G.7 GG.3
7-50 pm	3rd Corps informed left section of 10th Brig. received 50 shells and their right section a few shells. 12th Brig. H.Q. and H.Q. right section also shelled. 11th Brig. no change.	G.8
8-12 pm	5th Div. inform us that their trenches in Section A and B severely shelled by enemy to-day.	G.342

      Brigades asked to have ready tomorrow morning lists of recommendations for mention in despatches.

      Attached. Report of our and the enemy's doings during period 22nd to 31st December.

WAR DIARY.
January 2nd, 1915.

NIEPPE.

              Raining slightly most of the day and night.

4-50 am.   3rd Corps informed no change.   H/20,BM/1/11-2
                                                                                                 G/1.

7-50 am.   5th and 6th Divs report all quiet.   G/352,G/37

7-10 pm.   3/Corps informed some shelling against both sections 10th Brigade, otherwise all quiet.   GG/2.

7-30 pm.   5th and 6th Divs report no change.   G/43,G/69

10-0 pm.   3/Corps inform us there will be no Operation Orders tonight.   G/221.

War Diary - 3rd January 1915.

NIEPPE.

Wet day, fine night.

4-45 am.	3rd Corps informed - no change.	H.48, BM.1/11&12 and G.1
9-0 am	5th and 6th Divisions report no change.	G.695 & G.45
1-40 pm	5th Division report enemy at Douve Fe active during the night.	G.372
7-41 pm	3rd Corps informed left section of 10th Brig. more heavily shelled than usual. Right section also shelled with light guns. 11th and 12th Brigs. nothing to report.	H.49 BM.11/11 BM.11/12 GG.3
7-29 pm	5th Division report ½ all quiet, but trenches fairly heavily shelled during day.	G.380
7-18 pm	6th Div. report Houplines having been shelled, otherwise all quiet.	G.52
8 pm	3rd Corps issue no Operation Orders.	G.229

NIEPPE.   War Diary - 4th January 1915.

a.m.

    Rain during day - fine night.
4-45 3rd Corps informed - no change. (H.57, BM.1/11&12, G.1)
7-0   5th and 6th Divisions report no change. (G.237, G.58)
9-50 3rd Corps report Worcesters bayonetted 20 Germans   G.237
during night - Brigades informed.   G.2
10-25 27th Div. notify us that they are sending no more parties
of officers and N.C.O's to our trenches.   G.239
10-23 G.H.Q. ask Div. Staff Officer and a Staff Officer from
each Brigade to attend at St Omer tomorrow to witness
destruction of wire entanglements (by motor car) - Brigs.
informed.   G.3

p.m.
12-45 3rd Corps order that 6" guns of 8th Siege Battery should
go to 1st Corps - route and destination to be sent later.
One of the guns to be drawn by the caterpillar so as to make   G.243
comparison with ordinary tractor.   G.247
6-30 6th Div. report no change.   G.69
7-15 3rd Corps issue no Operation Orders.   G.250
7-45 3rd Corps order guns of 8th Siege Battery to proceed to
Locon via Estaires. On reaching Locon, Battery will come
under orders of 1st Corps. Battery to send an officer to
1st Corps H.Q. at Bethune for orders. Inform 1st Corps
of time of arrival at Locon, repeating to 1st Army.   G.251
  Reference above 3rd Corps to be notified when battery
will start.
7-50 3rd Corps informed that left section of 10th Brig. shelled
continuously throughout the day. Right section and 11th &
12th Brigades - quiet day.   G.9
7-58 5th Div. report fairly quiet day but sectors A & B heavily
shelled - little damage.   G.721
8-5   6th Div. wire that two guns of 8th Siege Battery await
orders from Major Webb as to move of Battery to Locon.   BM.125
  Replied that ~~two guns of 8th Siege Battery~~ section of
6th Division was to join up at Estaires at 12 noon.   BBM.30
10 pm 3rd Corps informed that section Siege Battery of 4th
Division marches from Nieppe at 8 am. Section of 6th Division
joining up at Estaires at 12 noon.   BBM.29
10-45 3rd Corps order 8th Siege Batty. to leave Nieppe tomorrow
for Locon. (copy of message to 1st Corps)   G.254

WAR DIARY
5th Jan. 1915.

NIEPPE.

Drizzling day, fine night.

4-30 am.	3/Corps informed no change.	H/60/10, BM/1/12, BM/19-G/1.
7-0 am.	5th and 6th Divs report no change.	G/725/5, G/72/6
11-15 am	3rd A.Corps say that lorries of 8th Siege Batty, should proceed via Armentieres. 3rd Corps informed lorries left 1 hour before their message arrived.	G/258, G/2.
4-30 pm.	3rd Corps say that 1 gun and caterpillar got bogged 1 mile E. of Croix du Bac.	G/262
6-0 pm.	3rd A.Corps inform us no Operation Orders.	G/263.
7-0 pm.	6th Division report no change.	G/75
8-45 pm.	3rd A.Corps informed that no shelling scarcely, on 10th Brigade Section. 11th Brigade report some shells in Ploegsteert. 12th Brigade all quiet.	GG/6
9-20 pm.	5th Division report Neuve Eglise shelled. Casualties 11 killed, 13 wounded.	G/458

W A R   D I A R Y
6th January 1915.

NIEPPE.

Wet day, fine night.

4-30 am.	3rd Corps informed no change.	BM/20/11 BM/1/12, H/66, GG/1.
7-26 am	5th and 6th Divs report no change.	G/454, G/77.
5-15 pm.	6th Div report that Saxons opposite Wez Macquart say they are going to be relieved by a Prussian Regt tonight.	IG/1 19.
7-20 pm.	6th Div report enemy having shelled Bois Grenier and Chaple D'Armentieres during the day.	G/83
7-30 pm.	5th Div report enemy having shelled some of their trenches rather heavily.	G/464
7-30 pm.	3rd Corps issue no Operation Orders.	G/275
8-34 pm.	3rd Corps informed that enemy shelled some of 10th Brig trenches, and southern slopes of Messines hill held by enemy. 11th and 12th Brigs no change.	GG/4.

War Diary, Gen. Staff, 4th Division.
7th January, 1915.

NIEPPE.

High wind and some rain during day, turning to very heavy rain in evening.

		H63/10, BM156/11
4.45 am	Brigs. reported quiet night, forwarded to 3rd A.C.	BM1/12, G 1.
6.30 am	5th Div. report all quiet.	G 755/5th
7.40 am	6th Div. report all quiet.	G 84/6th
1 pm	Instructions issued that Essex (left battn. 12th IB). will retain one platoon North of cross roads, where they connect with London Rif.Brig. (right Bn. 11th IB.)	G 2
4.40 pm	New periscope issued to 10 I.B. for trial and report.	G 4
6.45 pm	12th I.B. report situation unchanged.	BM19/12th
7.7 pm	5th Div. " " "	G 476/5th
7.15 pm	6th Div. report slight shelling.	G 93/6th
8.20 pm	3rd A.C. issue no Op.Orders.	G 280/3rd
8.20 pm	11th I.B. report situation unchanged, a few shells at Le Gheer, sniping brisk in front of E. Lancs.	BM83/11th
8.20 pm	10th I.B. report some shelling and more sniping.	H74/10th
8.34 pm	Summary of above reports of our Brigs. to 3rd A.C.	G 5
10.25 pm	12th I.B. report centre trench of right battn. flooded but they are holding high command parapet behind it and the houses.	BM24/12.

War Diary, Gen.Staff, 4th Division.
8th January, 1915.

NIEPPE.   Very heavy rain in the early morn and again at night and several cold storms during the day. The general water level of the district is sensibly rising and looks as if the local report that the whole place may be expected to be under water would prove true.

4.45 am	Quiet night reports from Brigs. forwarded to 3rd A.C.	H75/10 BM90/12 G1
6 am	Quiet night reports from 5th and 6th Divs.	G480/5th, G94/6th
9.30 am	6th Div. informed that scheme of Arty. retaliation has been drawn up, and ask them to inform us by priority wire whenever Armentieres or Houplines are shelled.	BBM57/DA
10.15 am	On our representations G.O.C. Corps wired an ultimatum to G.H.Q. re pumps.	G 4
10.25 am	Very damp situation report from 5th Div.	G 759/5th
12.28 pm	The 3 Mountain guns in Ploegsteert wood withdrawn to join H.Q. of Batty.	G 5
7.30 pm	Situation reports from 3 Brigs. summarised and forwarded to 3rd A.C. North Arty.Group shelled enemy pretty vigourously. Very little shelling or sniping of our trenches, except in front of 11th I.B.	H78/10 BM118/11 BM18/12 G 11
8 pm	5th Div. report situation normal.	G 498/5th
8.45 pm	Complaint of our aeroplane being shot at by 5th Div. forwarded to 3rd A.C.	BBM64/DA G 12
8.15 pm	3rd A.C. issue no Op.Orders.	G 288/3 AC
8.15 pm	Very damp situation report from 6th Div.	G 101/6th
10.56 pm	Inf.Brig. in Corps Reserve found by 6th Div. dispensed with for future.	G 293/3 AC

War Diary, Gen. Staff, 4th Division.
9th January, 1915.

NIEPPE.   Very heavy rain during day.

		H79/10
		BM/124/11
4.45 am	Quiet night reports from Brigs. forwarded to 3rd A.C. and exchanged with 5th and 6th Divs.	BM/1/12 G 1 G769/5 G105/6 G 2
11.30 am	In reply to G286/3 AC of 8th asking for boundaries of 3rd line prepared by Div. we replied that our sectn. was from crossing of Stilbecque to crossing of Nieppe-Bailleul road. Breastworks to hold about a platoon each varying intervals up to 200 yards are completed as trenching is unsuitable in the damp ground. No wiring has been done and very little in the way of splinter proofs for supports. Many houses required to be demolished to clear the front requiring 2 or 3 days notice. C.E. 3rd A.C. has detailed amount of work to be done.	G286/3 AC, 67, G 5.
11 am.	12th I.B. report flooding of a trench North of Warnave Road which is being reclaimed.	BM4/12
4.5 pm	12th I.B. report that Essex trench North of Warnave cross roads will be untenable tonight but position is sufficiently strong.	BM5/12
5.12 pm	Instructions received to report daily by 9 am work done in trenches from midnight to midnight.	G295/3 AC
6 pm	Forwards weekly report of tricks and inventions. See general file.	G 6
6.12 pm	3rd AC are sending an officer tomorrow to ascertain details ; amounting to a night in Bed state. Brigs. informed.	G296, G297/3AC G 6, 7, 9.
6.40 pm	Damp situation report from 6th Div.	G 117/6th
6.45 pm	12th I.B. report situation unchanged.	BM23/12
7.20 pm	3rd A.C. issue no Op.Orders.	G298/3 AC
7.50 pm	12th I.B. report that Essex have not evacuated trench referred to above.	BM24/12
7.50 pm	5th Div. report all quiet and allotment of troops, forwarded to 10th I.B.	G793-791, G 12
8.5 pm	10th I.B. report quiet day.	H82/10
8.15 pm	11th I.B. report situation unchanged but movement of trains on large scale across front about 4 am.	BM143/11
8.30 pm	Summary of above reports from Brigs. to 3rd AC.	G 11

WAR DIARY
10th January 1914.

NIEPPE.

Fine day, some sun, only slight rain in evening and during night. Level of River Lys is now 3ft 4 inches above the normal, and it has flooded the fields on its left bank from South of Erquinghem to Le Bizet for about ½ mile in width.
(H/86

4-45 am　Quiet night reports forwarded to 3/Corps and exchanged with 5th and 6th Divisions.
(BM/14
(146
BM/1/12, G/797, G/121
G/1, 2.

9-0 am　Work report to 3/Corps. Nothing beyond maintenance, wiring, construction of corduroy roads and high command breastworks. G/3

9-5 am　5th Div report enemy's snipers more active.
G/801

10-0 am.　Conference with Brig Majors shewed that 25 pc of the infantry were required for occupation of trenches, 25 p.c. in support under cover, and 50 p.c. in reserve and billets.

1-15 pm.　Air report 9-15 to 10-30 am:- Our front clear. River Lys about 100 yards broad between Frelinghien and Coutrai, bridges at Warneton, Bas Warneton and Commines, and further east.
IG/29

1-30 pm.　11/Brig report being shelled. Div Arty put retaliation scheme into effect at once.
BM/154

7-10 pm.　5th Div report all quiet.
G/817

7-10 pm.　12/Brig report increased sniping.
BM/15

7-25 pm.　6/Div report some shelling.
G/129

7-40 pm.　10/Brig report sniping of right section, only.
H/94

8-0 pm.　11/Brig report some shelling and moderate sniping.
BM/163

8-5 pm.　Summary of our Brigades report to 3/Corps.
GG/3

8-5 pm.　3/Corps issue no Operation Orders.
G/306

8-30 pm.　Evening reports to reach here by 7 pm.
GG/4.

War Diary - 11th January 1915.

NIEPPE.

Fine day - some sun - short sharp and very heavy thunderstorm in evening and some rain during night.

4-45 am	Quiet night reports from Brigades - repeated to 3rd Corps and exchanged with 5th and 6th Divisions. (H.96, BM.1/11&12, G.142 (G.825, G.130.	
8-45 am	Work report to 3rd Corps - no change to yesterdays.	G.3
11-50 am	Air report - all clear in our front.	M.30
1-15 pm	Asks for Flying to obtain photographs of enemy's defences between the Douve and Lys whenever weather is suitable.	G.1
6-45 pm	12th Brig. report no change.	BM.17
6-50 pm	10th Brig. report considerable sniping and maxim fire against right section - maxim located and artillery will shell them tomorrow.	H.103
6-58 pm	11th Brig. report situation normal but brisk sniping.	BM.10/11
7 pm	Resume of above reports to 3rd Corps.	G.3
7 pm	6th Div. report increased sniping.	G.152
7-15 pm	5th Div. report all quiet - they are shelling a gun located NW of Messines.	G.839
7-30 pm	3rd Corps report airmen are endeavouring to obtain photos.	M.32
8-15 pm	3rd Corps issue no Operation Orders.	G.318

War Diary, Gen. Staff, 4th Division.
12th January, 1915.

NIEPPE.   Fine day, slight rain in evening and during night.

4.45 am	Quiet night reports from Brigs. forwarded to 3rd A.C. and exchanged with 5th and 6th Divs.	H116/10, BM19/11, BM1/12, G 1, G715/5th, G115/6th, G2
8.10 am	Work report to 3rd A.C. - no change.	G 3.
6.35 pm	10th I.B. report no shelling and only a little sniping.	H128/10th
7.30 pm	11th I.B. report 70 shells near Ploegsteert and heavy sniping.	BM39/11th
7.42 pm	12th I.B. report slight shelling.	BM15/12th
7.50 pm	Above reports to 3rd A.C.	G 6.
7.50 pm	5th Div. report all quiet.	G851/5th
7.50 pm	6th Div. report some shelling.	G164/6th
8 pm	3rd A.C. issue no Op.Orders.	G328/3 AC
9.35 pm	12th I.B. report enemy seen carrying timber suitable for mining operations up to their front trenches opposite our railway barricade. Suitable precautions are being taken.	BM21/12th
10.15 pm	Germans in front of 1st Corps reported to be wearing British uniforms.	IG36/3 AC

War Diary, Gen. Staff, 4th Division.
13th January, 1915.

NIEPPE.   Fine night but heavy rain from 10.30 am to 3.30 pm.

4.45 am	Quiet night reports received from Brigs. forwarded to 3rd A.C. and exchanged with 5th and 6th Divs.	H134/10th BM41/11th BM1/12th G1 G561/5th G169/6th G2
7.35 am	Work report to 3rd A.C. - no change.	GG 1
1 pm	Instructions for B.G.C. R.A. to attend conference at G.H.Q. tomorrow. Subject of conference was asked - not received.	G334/3 AC G5
1.42 pm	Instructions to 11th I.B. and Div.Arty. for Mtn.Batty. to maintain its emplacements in good order.	GG4
6.42 pm	12th I.B. report some shelling.	BM13/12th
7 pm	10th I.B. report some shelling, very little sniping.	H4/10th
7.10 pm	11th I.B. report some shelling, and sniping brisk.	BM53/12th
7.20 pm	Above reports to 3rd A.C.	G6
7.20 pm	6th Div. report no change in situation.	G175/6th
7.20 pm	5th Div. report all quiet.	G881/5th
8.12 pm	3rd A.C. issue no Op.Orders.	G342/3 AC
8.55 pm	Instructions to Brigs. to forward all captured maps, Germans reported short of these.	G7
9.20 pm	Acknowledges receipt to 3rd A.C. of their G336, G340, G343, G344. (Secret documents which will be attached later).	G6
7 pm	Asks if 9.2 (How.) may be taken down in order to improve her platform, required 3 days work. Approved by 3rd A.C.	G9 G348/3AC

War Diary, Gen. Staff, 4th Division.
14th January, 1915.

NIEPPE.   Fine day - some rain during night.

4.45 am	Quiet night reports forwarded to 3rd A.C. and exchanged with 5th and 6th Divs.	H12/10th BM59/11th BM1/12th GG1 G182/5th GG2 G883/6th
8.10 am	Work report to 3rd A.C. - no change.	G1
10.15 am	Secret letter G341/3 AC received and passed to D.A.	
10.40 am	Enemy shelling East Lancs.	BM65/11th
11.28 am	Enemy shelling Rif.Brig. In both of above cases our Arty. retaliated.	BM67/11th
1.42 pm	G.H.Q. sending an officer tomorrow to explain hyposcope attachment for Machine Gun.	G352/3 AC
3.40 pm	Enemy again shelling Rif.Brig.	BM75/11th
5 pm	"Tactical Notes" received and circulated.	G6
6.45 pm	New issue of VERY pistol ammunition reported better than former issue but still inferior to German flares.	G7 BM58/11th H1/10th
7.5 pm	Asks 3rd A.C. with reference to our G10 of 9th as to replacement of long detonators by short detonators for rifle and hand grenades.	G8 (a)
7.10 pm	10th I.B. report more sniping last night and both sectns. shelled intermittently today.	H75/10th
7.15 pm	11th I.B. report increased shelling.	BM77/11th
7.20 pm	12th I.B. report same.	BM18/12th
7.35 pm	Above reports summarised to 3rd A.C.	G9
7.25 pm	5th Div. report all quiet.	G911/5th
7.25 pm	6th Div. report that our Arty. demolished Frelinghien Brewery and neighbouring houses.	G190/6th
7.30 pm	3rd A.C. issue no Op.Orders.	G384/3 AC

WAR DIARY

NIEPPE. **15th January 1915**

One or two slight showers, some wind increasing to a gale during the night.

4-45 am	Quiet night reports fowarded to 3rd A.Corps and exchanged with 5th and 6th Divs.	H/36, BM 1 GG/1, BM/81 G/1, G/915, G/192
7-49 am	Work report to 3rd A.Corps, no change.	GG/2.
6-45 pm	11/Brig report some shelling and heavy sniping during afternoon.	BM/67/11
6-45 pm.	12/Brig report no shelling except in reply to our Heavies.	BM/16/12
7-3 pm.	10/Brig report usual shelling and sniping. Consider enemy's artillery more accurate than usual.	H/54/10
7-13 pm.	Above reports to 3/Corps.	G/2
7-22 pm.	5th Div report all quiet.	G/933/5
	6th Div report a certain amount of hostile shelling, but destruction of Frelinghien Brewery had practically caused sniping to cease in that part.	G/199/6
7-50 pm.	3rd A.Corps issue no Operation Orders. This evening wire will be discontinued as long as there is no change.	G/367

War Diary - 16th January 1915.

NIEPPE.

                Cold windy day - slight rain during night. River Lys level falling.

Time	Entry	Ref
4-45 am	Quiet night report forwarded to 3rd Corps and exchanged with 5th and 6th Divisions.	(G.57, BM.88, BM.1 (GG.1, G.941, G.205, G.2
7-50 am	Work report to 3rd Corps - no change.	G.3
2-24 pm	10th Brig. report about a battalion of enemy marching from East to West in close order into patch of trees in Square V.22. Artillery of Northern Group fired on these. 3rd Corps informed.	H.72 H.77 G.5 G.6
4-26 pm	Mountain Gun emplacement in Ploegsteert Wood destroyed by hostile shells. Div.Arty. informed.	BM.111
5-55 pm	3rd Corps enquire about a revolving searchlight in direction of Lille. Circulated. Replies received and forwarded to 3rd Corps that there has been one in neighbourhood of Lille for 2 months.	IG.46 GG.4 & 6 BM.20 BM.107 H.85
6-35 pm	3rd Corps report suspicious men dressed as British soldiers making enquiries near Mont Noir - circulated.	IG.47 GG.5
6-35 pm	10th Brig. report some shelling of their left and right sections and sniping of their right section. 11th Brig. report considerable sniping. 12th Brig. report no change.	H.84 BM.106 BM.19
7-58 pm	Summary of above reports to 3rd Corps.	G.8
7-25 pm	5th and 6th Divisions report all quiet.	G.956 & G.214
9-15 pm	Hamps.R. report Germans have established a strong searchlight to left front of them and some way back. Does not traverse as far South as Le Gheer - 3rd Corps informed.	BM.109 G.10
11-58 pm	5th Div. report reliefs completed.	G.967

War Diary - 17th January 1915.

NIEPPE.

	Cold windy day - showers in morning - sharp blizzard at night. River Lys fell another 8 inches.	H.91
4-45 am	Quiet night reports forwarded to 3rd Corps and exchanged with 5th and 6th Divisions. Enemy used a trench mortar in front of left of right section of 10th Brigade. G.215 &	BM.113 BM.1 G.1 & 2 G.528
7-35 am	Work & report to 3rd Corps - no change.	G.3
6-40 pm	12th Brig. report situation ± unchanged, slight shelling.	BM.25
6-45 pm	6th Div. report heavy shelling at Chapelle D'Armentieres.	G.220
7-10 pm	5th Div. report all quiet.	G.977
7-15 pm	10th Brig. report considerable shelling of right section and sniping as usual.	H.10
7-15 pm	11th Brig. report sniping fierce and some shelling, mostly of small size.	BM.127 BM.128
7-30 pm	Summary of above reports from our Brigades to 3rd Corps.	G.8

War Diary - 18th January 1915.

NIEPPE.

Slight front during night. Heavy falls of snow at intervals during the day but turned to hail and rain later on. R.Lys has fallen 18 inches in the last few days, its level being now 1ft 10 ins above normal. Trenches on the whole are certainly drier.

Time	Entry	Ref
4-45 am	Quiet night reports forwarded to 3rd Corps and exchanged with 5th and 6th Divisions. (H.15, BM.1/11&12, G.924	G.1 & 2 G.981
7-40 am	Work report to 3rd Corps - no change.	GG.1
4-30 pm	Notes on communication in battalions while in the trenches issued. No copy available for H.Q.	GG.3
6-45 pm	11th Brig. report exceptional noise of transport, possibly heavy guns, heard moving N. to S. on main road Warneton - Pont Rouge at 6-15 pm. Forwarded to 3rd Corps.	BM.20 G.5
6-46 pm	6th Div. nothing to report.	G.226/6th
6-58 pm	12th Brig. report increased sniping and enemy's transport heard moving N. from Frelinghien.	BM.14
7-15 pm	10th Brig. report less shelling but some maxim fire at dusk. No more heard of enemy's mining.	H.24
7-21 pm	Summary of above Brigade reports to 3rd Corps.	GG.5
7-42 pm	5th Div. report a good of shelling and a trench mortar in use against them.	G.995/5th
8-30 pm	11th Brig. again report movement of transport continuing at 6-50 pm, apparently both motor and horse and in direction of Deulemont. Repeated to 3rd Corps.	BM.21 G.6
10-50 pm	12th Brig. report receiving many reports of enemy's transport being heard. They were asked to give general direction and replied N or N.E. wards. 3rd Corps informed and it was suggested that it was due to direction of wind.	BM.23 GG.6 BM.24 GG.7

War Diary - 19th January 1915.

NIEPPE.

	Dull misty day - slight showers in morning only.	H.33
4-45 am	Quiet night reports, except that St Yves battalion heard enemy's transport moving from N. to S. during early part of night. Repeated to 3rd Corps. Reports exchanged with 5th and 6th Divisions.	BM.27 BM.1 GG.1/4th G.1/4th
	G.735 &	G.1/6th
7-40 am	Work report to 3rd Corps - no change.	GG.2
9-0 am	Circular to Brigades asking for explicit reports of objectives which they recommend to be shelled by Arty.	GG.3
10-30 am	11th Brig. report Le Gheer battalion heard heavy motor and horse vehicles moving N. to S. during night, also cavalry. Repeated to 3rd Corps.	BM.35 GG.4
	6th Div. have nothing to report.	G.245
6-40 pm	11th Brig. report no shelling and less sniping.	BM.29
6-40 pm	12th Brig. report very quiet day - usual sniping.	BM.14
6-52 pm		
7-20 pm	10th Brig. report no shelling and no sniping. Sandbag parapet in rear of wire entanglement in left section completed.	H.45
7-35 pm	Summary of above reports to 3rd Corps.	G.5
7-5 pm	5th Div. report all quiet.	G.17

G.O.C. with a party of officers visited ground of French success at Vermelles.

War Diary - 20th January 1915.

NIEPPE.

	Dull foggy day - heavy rain at night. River Lys again rising.	H.58
		BM.40
4-45 am	Quiet night reports from Brigades forwarded to 3rd Corps and exchanged with 5th and 6th Divisions.	BM.1
		GG.1,2&
		G.250
		G.538
7-50 am	Work report to 3rd Corps - no change.	GG.3
9 am	G.373 from 3rd Corps received.	GG.5
2 pm	11th Brig. report 4 H.E. shells near Rif. Brig. trenches. Div. Arty. informed.	BM.45
4-55 pm	Air report that area 2 miles in rear of enemy's trenches is clear of all hostile movement this afternoon.	IG.61
5-45 pm	Div. Arty. ask for additional ammunition on 27th to mark Kaiser's birthday.	BBM.159
6-30 pm	12th Brig. report situation unchanged.	BM.13
6-40 pm	11th Brig. report some H.E. shells near left trenches. Sniping in front of Le Gheer increased. Volume of fire at our aeroplanes much heavier than usual.	BM.48
7-10 pm	10th Brig. report burst of M.G. fire for ½ hour at 5 pm and some shelling at 1 pm against right section. More sniping than usual against left section.	H.75
7-30 pm	Above reports to 3rd Corps.	GG.8
7-10 pm	5th Div. report all quiet.	G.34
15 pm	6th Div. report all quiet.	G.258

WAR DIARY
21st Jan 1915.

NIEPPE.

Wet, foggy, day. River Lys again rose.

Time	Entry	Ref
12 midn.	Report received from 12th Brig that troops opposite Le Touquet, in square C/10/C think they hear enemy mining. Trained miners from Monmouths (T.F) were put to listen, no definite report could be made, but preparations have been made to counter mine.	GG/1
4-45 am	Quiet night reports from Brigs, forwarded to 3/Corps and exchanged with 5th and 6th Divs.	H/80 BM/53 G/41. BM/1 G/261. GG/2 G/1.
7-41 am.	Work report to 3rd A.Corps--no change.	GG/3.
5-10 pm.	12/Brig ask for timbering for mining for branch galleries. C.R.E. taking necessary steps.	BM/17 GG/16
5-37 pm.	Asks 3/Corps for 2 more portable 14" searchlights.	GG/11
6-23 pm.	12/Brig report situation unchanged.	BM/22/22
6-43 pm.	11/Brig " " normal.	BM/66/11
7-40 pm.	10/Brig report very little sniping, & only few shells against right section and slow howitzer fire during afternoon against left section.	H/97/00
8-0 pm.	Summary of above reports to 3/Corps.	GG/15.
7-25 pm.	6/Div have nothing to report.	G/269/6
7-35 pm.	5/Div report all quiet and that E.Surreys go into trenches next to our 10/Brig tonight.--10/Brig informed.	G/546 GG/14

Another party of officers visited Vermelles today.

War Diary - 22nd January 1915.

NIEPPE.

	Slight frost - cold clear day - some sun. River Lys still rising.	H.101 BM.68
4-45 am	Quiet night reports received from Brigades and forwarded to 3rd Corps and exchanged with 5th and 6th Divisions.	BM.1 GG.1 G.1 G.61 G.271
7-35 am	Work report to 3rd Corps - no change.	GG.2
9-10 am	10th Brig. report two bursts of rifle and machine gun fire about 6 am against left of left section.	H.103
10-41 am	In accordance with 3rd Corps IG.63, 5th Sqdn. R.F.C. were asked to obtain when possible, photographs of enemy's defences opposite our line.	IG.63 G.6
11-50 am	Considerable concentration of enemy reported at Lille and Menin.	IG.66
12-15 pm	Area opposite our line reported clear by aircraft between 10-30 and 11-10 am. Enemy's anti-aircraft guns very active.	IG.68 IG.69
3-5 pm	Aircraft report 1-45 pm; motor transport all round Perenchies. Frelinghien clear.	IG.71
3-35 pm	10th Brig. report right section more shelled than usual today and wire in front of centre of right section reported cut by hand last night.	H.117
7-45 pm	10th Brig. report very little sniping but slight increase of shelling. A German battery seen to retire from a wood in which one of our shells had burst.	H.121
6-40 pm	11th Brig. report heavy sniping in front of left battn.	BM.63
"	12th Brig. report certain amount of shelling.	BM.23
8-5 pm	Above reports and addition of shelling near La Creche to 3rd Corps.	GG.7
7-10 pm	6th Div. report some shelling.	G.282
8-30 pm	5th Div. report all quiet.	G.91
9-10 pm	10th Brig. report heavy firing North of Messines.	H.122
10-35 pm	Informs 12th Brig. that portable searchlight will be sent out to Snipers House. They are to send 2 men to 9th Fd. Co. R.E. for training.	G.14

WAR DIARY
23rd Jan 1915.

NIEPPE.

              Hard frost, some mist.

Time	Entry	Ref
4-45 am.	Quiet night reports forwarded to 3rd Corps and exchanged with 5th and 6th Divisions.	H/125. BM/80 BM/1, GG/1,2, G/554, G/285.
7-40 am.	Work report to 3rd Corps - no change.	GG/3.
10-40 am	6th Div report movement of transport heard between 4 & 5 am. opposite Chaple D'Armentieres.	IG/71
4-20 pm.	R.F.C. report huts in Ploegsteert wood very visible and recommend painting black or green.	8/23
4-50 pm.	Director of Railway Transport asks if there is any objection to their commencing repair work on the Houplines bridge.--Replied--no objection.	G/459 3.A.C. GG/5.
6-0 pm.	11/Brig report considerable movement of transport at 5-23pm near Deulemont, believed S. to N.-- Repeated to 3/Corps.	BM45 GG/11
7-15 pm.	5th Div report all quiet.	G/558
7-15 pm.	6th Div report an unusual amount of transport.	G/297
7-30 pm.	10/Brig report some shelling, active sniping, right section only.	H/135
"	11/Brig report situation normal.	BM/91
"	12/Brig report sniping rather active, little shelling.	BM/30
7-50 pm.	Above reports to 3/Corps.	GG/13
9-20 pm.	10/Brig report our guns shelled successfully triangular breastwork in U/15/D, and at 8-20 pm. enemy's transport on roads East and South-east of Messines.	H/3.
10-52 pm.	5th Div report Devons in Sector A.	G/115.

WAR DIARY
24th January, 1915.

NIEPPE.

Cold dull day, no frost or rain. River Lys after being 3ft 9in above normal level fell 4 inches.

4-45 am	Quiet night reports from Brigades forwarded to 3rd Corps and exchanged with 5th and 6th Divs.	H/6, BM BM/94. G/117. GG/1. G/301. GG/2.
7-30 am	Work report to 3/Corps. No change.	G/1.
	Considerable correspondence passed today as regards unexploded anti-aircraft (13 pr) shells, falling near troops. It was found that the cases of the shells which must necessarily fall somewhere, were the cause of the reports.	G/304 GG/3 IG/72 G/2, BBM25
11-20 am	6/Div think a new Regt is opposing them, and their left section reports hearing considerable motor transport from 5 to 7-30 pm in Frelinghien.	G/306 6
12-30 pm.	Asks R.F.C. for report as to visibility for splinter proofs at back of 63.	G/3.
1-35 pm.	1 gun of our anti-aircraft section to be sent over to 6th Division.	G/466.
7-5 pm.	5th Div report-all quiet.	G/131/
7-15 pm.	6th Div report-all quiet.	G/312/
7-45 pm.	Evening report to 3/Corps on receipt from Brigs.--Some shelling of Left Section, but our howitzers retaliated with effect against enemy's trenches W. of Avenue U/9/C. Last night a patrol got close to La Douve Fe, and report enemy repairing trenches. 11/Brig report some shelling and heavy sniping. 12/Brig report quiet day and less sniping.	

War Diary - 25th January 1915.

NIEPPE.

Cold misty day - no rain.

4-45 am	Quiet night reports received from Brigades and forwarded to 3rd Corps and exchanged with 5th and 6th Divisions. (H.70, BM.1, BM.1, G.1, G.141, G.313, GG.1)	
7-35 am	Work report to 3rd Corps - no change.	G.2
11-50 am	Attack made against 2nd Army North and South of La Bassee Canal at 8 am.	IG.75 G.G.8
2-36 pm	Forwards report of a supposed incendiary shell to 3rd A.C.	G.G.9
2-38 pm	Informs 11th I.B. that they need not use trench mortar unless they think it advantageous.	G482
3-41 pm	Trench mortar returned to 3rd A.C.	G.G.10 G485
3.30 pm	Attack on 1st Corps - resulted in their centre being pierced, but counter-attack would be made at 1 pm	G487 G.G.12
5.10 pm	1st Corps regained all trenches capturing 2 officers and 51 other ranks of 56th and 27th Regts. Circulated.	G157/5th G328/6th
7 pm	5th and 6th Divs. report all quiet.	G 4 H20/10th BM11/11th BM29/12th
7.25 pm	Report to 3rd A.C. - very little shelling of 10th I.B. about St Yves and 11th I.B. all quiet. 12th I.B. Rly. barricade shelled. Our guns shelled enemy's trenches - reported effective.	

Report of Naval victory in North Sea in which German Cruiser 'BLUCHER' was sunk. Circulated.

WAR DIARY
26th January, 1915.

NIEPPE.

Cold misty day, no rain. River Lys falling.

4-45 am	Quiet night reports forwarded to 3/Corps and exchanged with 5th and 6th Divisions. (H/22,BM/14,BM/1,G/1,G/57,G/330,G/2)	
6-10 am	Reported that the attack on 1st Corps yesterday was made by the 56th and 70th Prussian Regt.--Circulated.	G/491 G/3.
8-0 am.	Work report to 3/Corps---No change.	G/4
8-50 am	Reported from Le Gheer that a continuous stream of transport was heard going south about 4 am--Repeated to 3/Corps	BM/15 G/6.
7-20 am.	11th Brig do not wish to use trench mortar until further tests have been carried out.	BM18
12.15 pm	Reported that 2nd Corps heard an unusual amount of transport from direction of Messines last night. This could not be confirmed by 10th I.B.	GG3 & IG91 H46/10
7.25 pm	Evening report to 3rd A.C. 10th I.B. shelled and also 11th I.B. very few against 12th I.B. Our guns retaliated on each occasion, particularly against the red estaminet North of St Yves.	GG6 H49/50 BM29 BM17
7.20 pm	Div.Arty.asks permission to use 100 rounds for 4th Siege Bty. on 28th for destroying houses east of Ploegsteert wood from which 11th I.B. are harrassed. Repeated to 3rd A.C.	BBM220 GG7
7.30 pm	6th Div. report some shelling and hearing transport move.	G341
7.45 pm	5th Div. report Devons reliaving Manchesters in Sector 'A'. All quiet on their front.	G172 G175
8.45 pm	Rumour of guns mounted on boats on River Lys.	BM32
?.35 pm	G.H.Q. Intelligence (Secret) received. Will be attached later.	
10.52 pm	Places LaCreche battn.(Div.Reserve) at disposal of 10th I.B. if attacked tomorrow and orders all Brigs. to report at once any increase of shelling during next few days.	GG8 GG9
11.46 pm	12th I.B. report increased rifle fire since 11 pm.	BM22

WAR DIARY

27th January 1915.

NIEPPE.

Cold, dull, day. River Lys fell 7". No rain.

Time	Entry	Ref
4-45 am	Quiet night reports forwarded to 3/Corps and exchanged with 5th and 6th Divs.	(H/57,BM/34,BM/1,G/1,G/580,G/350,GG1
7-45 am.	Work report to 3/Corps.--No change.	G/2
9-2 am	Aeroplane report refers to bridge at Frelinghien which appears to be either the old bridge repaired or another constructed on the same site.	G/3,4. G/84 IG/85 G/9.
9-50 am.	Approval received for expenditure of ammunition for Siege Battery tomorrow.	G/507
3-50. pm.	Unusual shelling of 10th and 11th Brigs reported.	H/69, BM/44
5-45 pm.	5th Corps informed of R.F.A. wagon removing timber from G.Hq. and asked to have it stopped.	G/12
6-0-pm.	11th Brig asked for postponement of tomorrow's bombardment till 10 am.--Approved.	K/231, GG/8.
7-47 pm.	Evening report to 3/Corps--10th Brig more sniping than usual and some shelling of right section. Our guns made good practice on trenches and Douve Farm, near the Ave. 11th Brig sniping active, some shelling, considerable transport movement heard during the day. 12th Brig quiet day.	BM/48 (H/80 (BM/46 (BM/54 (BM/17 (G/13 (
7-10 pm.	5th Div report all quiet.	G/205
7-40 pm.	6th Div report considerable shelling, but enemy's snipers less active.	G/359

Brig.Gen G.F. Milne, CB, DSO, who has commanded 4th Div Arty throughout the campaign, up till now, left to take up the appointment of Brigadier-General, Gen Staff, 3rd Corps.

WAR DIARY.
28th January 1915.

NIEPPE.

Cold frosty clear day.

4-45 am.	Quiet nights reports forwarded to 3/Corps and exchanged with 5th and 6th Divs. (H/90, BM/1 & 59, GG/1, G/211, G/363, GG/2)	
7-35 am	Work report to 3/Corps--No change.	G/1
8-53 am	E.Lancs at Le Gheer report Germans singing loudly all night.	BM/60
10-35 am	10/Brig report that U/14/D being shelled.	H/3.
11-30 am.	11/Brigade report result of bombardment by Siege Battery --3 direct hits on the White Estaminet, east of Ploegsteert wood.	BM/63
11-35 am	Air report-no movement of enemy's troops near trenches between Messines and Hollebeke. Motor lorries in two's and threes moving both ways between Hoolebeke and Commines. Lorries and trucks at Menin, Wulghem. Small bodies transport on Warneton - Messines road. Considerable amount of transport and small bodies of infantry moving both ways between Ypres and Menin.	1986.
11-40 am.	3 Officers of 13th Division to visit Ploegsteert Wd.	G/368 GG/4.
12-0 noon	11th Brigade report White Estaminet and Bennett House have ceased to exist.	BM/64
1-10 pm.	Trenches North of Le Gheer and at St Yves being shelled.	BM/65 H/9
2-45 pm.	Shells falling beyond Point 63.	H/12
6-35 pm.	Air report at 4 pm. roads between Messines and Commines via Warneton and Messines to Wyschaete, clear.	I.G/87
7-45 pm.	Evening report to 3/Corps-- very little shelling except against St Yves which was probably intended to knock out 4th Siege Batty observation station, whilst it was knocking out houses referred to above. 6th Siege Battery also made good practice on farms on River Douve.	G/6 H/14 BM/73 BM/28
7-5 pm.	5th Div report all quiet.	G/227

Enquiries as to whether opposing forces opposite us have changed. Elicited replies that no change was suspected.

War Diary, Gen. Staff, 4th Division.
29th January, 1915.

NIEPPE.   Cold bright frosty day.

4.45 am   Quiet night reports forwarded to 3rd A.C. and exchanged
           with 5th and 6th Divs.
                   (H22/10, BM81/11, BM1/12, G1, G582/5, G379/6, G2)

7.45 am   Work report to 3rd A.C. - no change.   G3

9.20 am   R.F.C. report huts at 63 visible. We asked them to   I29
           report again on those in Ploegsteert wood.   GG1

12 noon   Air report - large number of trains in Commines,   IG89
           Bisseghem and Courtrai. No movement of troops behind
           battle line 8 to 9 am.

1.5 pm   11 I.B. report motors and half battalion infantry seen BM87/11
           at 10 am moving North West through Deulemont. 3rd A.C. GG2
           and 5th Div. informed.

3 pm   Air report 11 - 11.50 am - nothing concerning our   IG90
           front.

4.40 pm   Air report - 2.50 _ 3.15 pm - our front all clear.   IG91

6.5 pm   Frelinghien bridge previously referred to, now   G 3
           definitely located to be immediately North of the
           broken permanent bridge. 12 I.B. and D.A. informed.

8.10 pm   Evening report to 3rd A.C. - Pt.63 heavily shelled,   G5
           we replied against enemy's trenches South of Messines. H31/10
           11 I.B. quiet, less sniping. 12 I.B. quiet. BM97/11, BM20/12

7.30 pm   5th and 6th Divs. nothing particular to report. Cornwalls G249/5
           relieved Manchesters in 5th Div. Sector A.   G259, G392.

                          Attached.

           3rd A.C. No. G503, of 26/1/15, referring to
supposed concentration of hostile troops east of our
2nd Army, and warning us to take particular precautions
against attacks during the next few days.

WAR DIARY.

30th January 1915.

NIEPPE.

Very cold day, one or two attempts to snow. River Lys fell to normal level.

4-45 am.	Quiet night reports to 3/Corps and exchanged with 5th & 6th Divs., except that 6th Div report 2 German Regts moved from Lille to Premesques on morning 29th.--Circulated. (H/36,BM/100,BM/1,G/1,G/394/6,G/267/5, G/2/, GG/1.)	
6-10 am.	3/Corps repeats above information, re move.	IG/101
7-40 am.	Work report to 3/Corps--no change.	GG/1.
10-15 am.	R.F.C. report huts visible owing to light and shade, consider that dark green with light green stripes would be less conspicuous.	G552
10-15 am.	Aeroplane report column of 1500 moving on Perenchies from Lille. This column was shelled by 6/Div Arty, reported effective.--Report circulated.	IG/101 GG/3.
12-45 pm.	Air report 8-40 to 9-25 am. Area immediately east of us, practically clear of movement. Menin unobserved. No special activity in Rly Sta. Ru Baix,-No activity. Tourcoing, very active. Courtrai--full of transport.	IG/105
1-50 pm	3/A.Corps asks front held by L.R.Brig.--Replied from River Warnave, just N. of Point 18 to small hedge 250 yards S.E. Trench nearly parrellel and 50 yards E.of road U/28/C.	GG/4. IG/107 G/5 BM/08
4-5.pm.	3/Corps asked for recommendations (a) Value of 4 inch French Mortar (b) whether it should be handled by R.A. or R.E.. Replied (a) not considered of much value, as long as Howitzers are available. (b) Div Arty.	G/544 GG/4.
7-52 pm.	Evening report to 3/Corps.--10/Brig less shelling, some bombs. 11/Brig a few shells. 12/Brig little shelling, Germans have erected a hoarding from their barricade in Le Touquet towards Frelinghien bridge, probably a screen to movement. (G/7, H/46,47,BM/109,BM/15)	
7-25 pm.	"All quiet" reports from 5th and 6th Divs.	G/293,G/40
8-0 pm.	3/Corps issue no Operation orders. Supply Railheads changed to Strazelle, probably on account of shelling of Steen werck. Ammunition Railheads remain at Arcques.	G/405 G/557

WAR DIARY.
31st January 1915.

NIEPPE.

Very cold day, several hail & snow storms, but no snow lay on the ground.

4-45 am.	Quiet night reports repeated to 3/Corps and exchanged with 5/6th Divisions. (H/50, BM/14, BM/1, GG/1, G/589, G/410, GG/2)	
7-45 am.	Work report to 3/Corps--no change.	G/1.
8-45 am.	Morning air report--All clear ½ mile behind enemy's lines	IG/110
	A report was received from 14/Brig of Germans being behind our lines. Further inquiries were made.	G/2,3. BM/484/14
1-0.pm.	Photograph of enemy's trenches received from R.F.C.	GG/3
3-30 pm.	No.14 Anti-aircraft section to replace No.9, on arrival. --No 9, goes to 4/Corps--Merville.--	G/571.
3-30 pm.	Supply railhead returns to Steenwerck tomorrow.	G/572
7-50 pm.	Evening report to 3/Corps--10/Brig considerable shelling, less sniping. 11/Brig--Normal situation, enemy busy in ruins of White Estaminet, also in front of Hants, where they have dug 3 small pits in front of their line.-- 12/Brig--situation normal.	GG/6 H/63 BM/122 BM/12.
7-0 pm.	5/Div-all quiet--	G/329
7-35 pm.	6th Div--some shelling and sniping.	G/426
7-30 pm.	3/Corps Secret letter-~~No Germans~~ (Preparation of plan of defence) G/568, received.--	GG/5.
9-5 pm.	12/Brig report--No Germans can be seen opposite trenches, 400 yards south of Warnave, where they usually can be seen.	BM/16
11-0 pm.	12/Brig again report less sniping and fewer fires, but may be due to reliefs going on.	BM/24

WORKS REPORTS.

4/Div. No. G 62

3rd Army Corps.

In accordance with your telegram No. G125 of the 27th
th December, the following is a summary of our doings and
those of the enemy between 22nd and 31st December.

These have not been arranged by days as nothing of
special importance has occurred on any particular date.

Our Doings.

During the whole of this period arrangements have been
made to hold our front by a line of posts protected by
breastworks and wire entanglement instead of a continuous
line of trenches, in accordance with memorandum from 3rd
Corps, No. G.60 of 22nd December.

This work is nearing completion but there has not been
sufficient men available to complete it entirely, owing to
the number of men being required to rebuild the trenches and
parapets of our present line which have been knocked down by
the enemy's shells or by which have fallen in on account of
water.

During this period experiments have been made with
trench mortars and bombs. Two officers were sent in to
Bailleul to learn how these mortars should be used, but the
reports they gave on them were very unfavourable.

There are also at present classes going on in the Machine
Gun. This is now being done in each Brigade under the Brigade
Machine Gun Officer and it is proposed to have a class
continually going on.

Enemy's Doings.

The enemy has been very inactive during the period in
question and his sniping has considerably eased off. Every
day, however, he shells our left trenches on the Douve River
with two field guns which cannot be located. This shelling

causes us considerable annoyance. He also put a few shells between Le Bizet and Le Touquet.

As far as can be ascertained there has been no change in the enemy's line in front of us. At one time it was thought that the 19th Saxon Corps had been relieved, but various regiments of this Corps have now been definately located in front of us during the last few days. These regiments now the 104th, 106th, 133rd and 134th.

The enemy has often been seen baling out his trenches which probably are in as equally bad a state as ours as regards water.

On the 30th December one of the enemy's aeroplanes dropped 2 bombs near our trenches at Le Ghear but did no damage.

[signature]

1/1/15.

Maj-Gen.
Commdg. 4th Div.

Hdqrs. 23/1/15

3rd Corps

The following information required by your G/366, para.4, of the 16th inst.:-

12th Brig Section.

(a) Efforts have been made to reclaim those portions of the front line trenches which were flooded, but the continued rain of this week has prevented any tangible result being effected, difficulty being experienced in keeping the dry trenches free of water, and revetting the same. A new trench was dug just north of the Le Touquet road.

The High Command parapets have been improved, as also have the defended houses on the Le Touquet Road, and the work which is being constructed on the railway, 1000 yds N.E. of Touquet station.

(b) It is proposed to continue improving the works mentioned, and to reclaim further portions of the front line trench, if the weather admits of it.

(c) The enemy has not been noticed constructing any new trenches. The only signs of activity he has shewn have been baking his trenches and collecting planks and rather heavier timber opposite the left section of the section of the King's Own Regt.

(d) It is not considered that any change has taken place in this section. The attitude of the enemy is to snipe a little and to shell various tracts of country in this section, in answer to the fire of our guns. The guns he uses being field guns and 5.9" howitzers.

11th Brig section

11th Brig section.

(a) The work in this has been of the same nature as the 12th Brig Section. Defended houses, especially Le Gheer, being improved and a row of Breastworks in course of construction at the front edge of the wood in the Rifle Brigade Section.
Farms and Breastworks in rear of the Som.L.I. section, and works in rear of the Hampshire Section have been improved for defence.

(b) It is proposed to continue the works enumerated above.

(c) The enemy has not been noticed constructing any new works or trenches.

(d) Opposite the E.Lancashire Section, the enemy has shewn considerably greater activity in shelling and sniping, and at one time it was thought that a change might have taken place, but this is now not considered to be so

10th Brigade Section

(a) Work in this section has been of a nature similar to that in the other brigades. The defence of the village of St Yves and the farm of Le Rossignol have been improved, and work, in the nature of a sandbag breastwork has been carried out in the left company of the Irish Fusiliers, which was necessitated by the flooding of the front line trench in this position.
Triangles of wire have been put up, especially in places where the trenches in rear have had to be evacuated on account of floods and have then to be defended by means of flanking fire.

(b) It is proposed to continue the defences now in course of construction.

3rd page.

(c)   No new defensive works of the enemy have been noticed in course of construction.

(d)   The enemy has shewn less activity with his guns in this section, in shelling the front line trenches but has devoted his attention to shelling the Hdqrs of the right battalion. It is not considered that there has been any change of troops in this section.

23/1/15.

Maj Gen. Commdg.
4th Division.

WEEKLY REPORT.   29/1/15

Headquarters,

   3rd Corps

The map which is forwarded herewith does not show the general line of our defence as it is the same as that shown on the map rendered last week. The map only shews the positions of Machine Gun emplacements (marked m.g.) and any alterations in the former map.

12th Brigade Section.

(a) Efforts have been made during the week towards recovering portions of the trenches, south of Le Touquet - Le Bizet road and revetting the same. The snipers house on the Touquet road has been strengthened, so also has the work on the railway where the latter crosses the Le Touquet - Le Gheer road.
   A new trench has been constructed on the left of this work.
   Other works in this section have been improved.

(b) It is proposed to continue to improve the existing works and to reclaim further portions of the front line trenches.

(c) The enemy has not shewn great activity in the construction of his trenches, except where marked "A". Here, he has been collecting timber and planks.

(d) The enemy has been more active in shelling and sniping but this is considered to be a retaliation to our greater activity.

11th Brigade Section.

(a) The breastwork at "B" has been completed and work on the farm and breastworks at "C" has been continued.
   A large amount of wiring in front of the London Rifle Brigade has been put up.
   Three houses along the road marked "D" from which the Germans were annoying us have been demolished by shell fire.

(b) It is proposed to continue to improve existing works and to dig a second line trench where marked "E".

(c) No new defensive works have been noticed in course of construction by the enemy.

(d) The enemy has been slightly more active in shelling and sniping in front of Le Gheer, but it is not believed that any change, except reliefs, has taken place.

10th Brigade Section.

(a) The existing works have been improved by means of further revetting. St Yves village has been further strengthened, and the defences of Le Rossignol Farm are now complete. A breastwork has been constructed on the left of this section at "F" to cover a portion of the front which had to be abandoned on account of floods. A breastwork has also been constructed at "G".
   A house from which the enemy sniped at "H" has been demolished by our engineers.
   Cinder tracks and corduroy roads have been constructed so as to improve the communication.

(b)

2nd page

(b)   It is proposed to strengthen further the existing line and strengthen considerably the defence of the farm "J".

(c)   The enemy was noticed constructing a breastwork at "K". This was knocked down by gun-fire after which it was reconstructed by him, but again knocked down by our fire. He also constructed another work on the left bank of the Douve, East of the Messines road. This has also been knocked out.

(d)   Except for a little shelling and sniping on the right of this section the enemy has shown little activity, and no change is believed to have taken place.

    A map scale 1/100,000 is attached shewing the limits of billetting areas of brigades.

29/1/15.

Major General,
Commanding 4th Division.

ARTILLERY REPORTS.

G.S.

28
6.57 am

1) C Art, Group. Enemy shelled our trenches about 9.15 am with Heavy How. 18 pr Bty retaliated against the guns near Les Ecluses + Enemy's fire stopped. Later, a light howitzer reopened fire, and the 6" Howitzer (Amelia) retaliated against the German Trenches, with satisfactory effect.

2) N A Group - Fourth Siege battery shelled a Communication Trench E. of Ploegsteert Wood + knocked 6 holes in it. It appears to consist of two earth walls, with bullet proof roof. An 18 pr battery also fired at a Commu: Trench, East of St Yvon, where activity was seen.

Very foggy.

25-1-15ᵃ

Ptt Bn.

G.S.

North Arty Group.

(a) Early this morning, 31 Howitzers put 2 shell into a German trench just S.W. of Messines, where fires & movement were seen. At 9 a.m. the 5th Div. trenches S.W. of Messines were shelled, & 31 Howitzers responded by putting a few shell into the German trenches opposite the part shelled -

(b) Later, a few Pufflehenirers were fired against Hill 63, so an 18 pr Bty shelled the farm (observing Stn) at North end of the Avenue.

(c) Another 18 pr Bty shelled the Red Estaminet N. of St Yves, where snipers do reside. This haunt of vipers + machine guns was further effectively dealt with by a Siege battery, and is now unhealthy.

d) Later the Warwicks H.Q. was shelled, and we retaliated at the Zareba and trench running East from the S. end of the avenue.

e) This afternoon, La Sheer was shelled, & 134th battery retaliated against the German trenches there and searched for two guns which were thought to have been on motor cars.

PHSL
Bn.

26-1-15.

G.S. 27-1-15

a) There has been a certain amount of indiscriminate shelling by the enemy today, against our centre and left, necessitating Retaliation Schemes B & C being put into effect. La Douve Farm has been dealt with by 18 prs. and 6" howitzers, some direct hits being recorded by the latter. In addition the Red Estaminet, N. of St. Yves, has again been pounded, as snipers were worrying the Warwicks; and 4" Siege Bty dealt with the triangular work East of St. Yves.

b) Centre Arty Group only fired 5 rounds.

c) No attack having been made, the 3 extra batteries which were sent into action today, to reinforce the normal

batteries, have been ordered to withdraw into reserve again.

E.H.G. Leggett Maj,
Bde. 4 D.A.

7 pm.

INTELLIGENCE.

Noon, 25th January, 1915.

LATE INFORMATION.

There has been a naval engagement in the North Sea. Admiralty wire the following announcement :-

"British patrolling squadron of battle cruisers, light cruisers and destroyers sighted four German battle cruisers and a number of destroyers making for the English coast. The enemy at once made for home. They were pursued and at 9.30 a.m. was joined between British LION, TIGER, PRINCESS ROYAL, NEW ZEALAND and INDOMITABLE, and the German DERFFLINGER, SEYDLITZ, MOLTKE and BLÜCHER.

Soon after 1 o'clock BLÜCHER capsized and sank; two other cruisers seriously damaged, but escaped. No British ships lost and casualties slight."

The BLÜCHER (cruiser) had a speed of 26 knots and carried 12 8.2-inch guns, besides smaller armament.

W.W.PITT-TAYLOR, Captain,
General Staff,
IIIrd Corps.

URGENT & SECRET.

4th Division.
~~6th Division.~~

2nd Army notify that there is a considerable amount of information pointing to a concentration of hostile troops east of the line occupied by the 2nd Army. There is, however, no evidence as yet as to whether these troops are to be used for an attack against a portion of our line, or merely to replace troops which have hitherto been holding the trenches. It is, however, conceivable that the recent attack on the 1st Corps was made with the intention of drawing our troops down to that area, prior to an attack further north.

The G.O.C., 3rd Corps, therefore directs that particular precautions be taken against a sudden attack during the next few days.

Intelligence report from G.H.Q. is forwarded herewith.

C.H. Harington
Major,
General Staff.

HEADQUARTERS
G.503
Date 26/1/15.
CORPS

CORRESPONDENCE & MISCELLANEOUS PAPERS.

CORRESPONDENCE ON THE FOLLOWING SUBJECTS WILL BE FOUND IN BOX MARKED "4th DIVISION - CORRESPONDENCE."

CANADIAN DIVISION

NORTH MIDLAND DIVISION

ANTI-AIRCRAFT

ARTILLERY

SUPPORTING LINES

OFFENSIVE ACTION

MINES

SAPPING AND MINING

PRESS CORRESPONDENTS

TRICKING ENEMY - Devices for

TRENCH MORTARS

VERMELLES - Trip to

TRENCHES - Strengthening of

ARMISTICE - Informal

MACHINE GUNS

BRIGADE ENGINEER

WEEKLY REPORTS ON WORK CARRIED OUT

GRENADES

PERISCOPES

DEFENCE SCHEME

RANGE FINDERS

PRISONERS

COUNTER ATTACKS

RELIEF OF 5th & 6th DIVISIONS

EMPLOYMENT OF R.E.

ARMOURED MOTOR CARS

LEAKAGE OF INFORMATION

ST. ELOI - Increase of Troops.

11th Brig.

Herewith 30 copies of Provisional Instructions for the Training of Grenadiers.

The G.O.C. would be glad of any suggestions you may wish to make for improving them when you have gained more experience.

He wishes to have these Grenadier Platoons ready for employment within the next month or six weeks when more active operations may be expected to begin. He considers they will have a very important say in the success of any operations we may be called upon to undertake and is convinced that everything will depend in the thoroughness of their training on definite lines and on how they are handled by Company and Platoon Commanders.

24/1/15.

Colonel,
General Staff, 4th Division.

4th DIVISION.

PROVISIONAL INSTRUCTIONS FOR THE ORGANIZATION AND EMPLOYMENT OF GRENADIERS.

1. **PROBABLE CONDITIONS UNDER WHICH GRENADES WILL BE USED.**

(a) In the event of an attack on a length of the enemy's trenches by our infantry succeeding, either after an artillery bombardment or by surprise, it will be necessary at once to bring up a party of grenadiers to clear neighbouring lengths by working down them from traverse to traverse, or down communication trenches to the next line of trenches.

(b) Under the same conditions the party of grenadiers must be prepared to meet a counter attack coming from the support trenches, or up the communication trenches, or from trenches on either flank, this counter attack being probably made by men armed with grenades.

(c) Should the enemy be successful in capturing any part of our front line of trenches, a party of grenadiers, sent up at once might be required to counter attack and drive the enemy out, this counter attack being made for choice up communication trenches, or from neighbouring lengths of trenches still in our possession.

(d) When, by means of a sap, our infantry have approached within 20 to 30 yards of the enemy's trenches, grenadiers may be required to move up a party to turn the enemy out of their trenches by means of grenades.

(e) When the enemy has sapped up near our trenches it may be necessary to drive him out by means of grenades.

2. **GENERAL ORGANIZATION WITHIN THE DIVISION.**

Each battalion in the Division will train 1 officer, and each company and the Div. Cyclist Co. 1 N.C.O. and 24 men who will form a Grenadier Platoon.

A Grenadier Company will be composed of 2 or more platoons.

For tactical purposes two or more platoons will be drawn from battalions for a particular task and will work as a company, either under the officer in charge of the Grenadiers of one of the battalions, or under an officer of the Div. Cyclist Co.

Each Brigade should always have 2 platoons from battalions in Reserve on duty ready to turn out at short notice with carriers and ammunition complete.

The Grenadier platoons perform their ordinary duty in the trenches when not required to act as Grenadiers only.

The duties

The duties of the Grenadier Company Commander (when formed) will be to determine the best method of dealing with the tactical situation, in accordance with his orders, and issue such orders as are necessary to the platoon commanders. He will keep in reserve such part of his company as he deems necessary to meet the situation, and will arrange for the supply of grenades to platoons.

3. ORGANIZATION OF A PLATOON.

A Platoon will be divided into 6 Sections. Each Section will consist of 4 men 3 for throwing grenades and 1 who will act as Section Commander.

The Platoon Commander will be responsible for selecting suitable positions to carry out the orders of the Company Commander and for posting his Sections. He will indicate the target generally and give Section Commanders all necessary instructions. He will arrange for the supply of grenades for his platoon. He will select a refilling point for grenades.

A platoon might, for instance, be employed as follows :-
    4 Sections for throwing grenades.
    1 Section in Reserve.
    1 Section for refilling carriers and attending to the supply of grenades.
At least one Section should be kept in Reserve.

The Section Commander acts as 'Observer' and arranges for extra grenades to be brought up from the refilling point when required.

He should not throw grenades himself except under special circumstances, such as when one of his Section is away fetching grenades.

He must see that safety pins are replaced before grenades are put back into the carriers.

4. DRILL.

For safety's sake it is better to carry out the drill with dummy grenades, and, when it is desired to practice the men in throwing live grenades, to work the men separately and not in groups.

So that the Section Commander may keep thorough control of his Section and that the men may be taught from the beginning to work systematically and without flurry, the following words of command should be given.
    "Prepare Grenades". On this word of command the men take a grenade from the carrier, insert detonators (if not already there), unwind the tape and arrange it for throwing.
    "Remove Pin". The safety pin will be removed.
    "Throw". One or more of the Section as stated throw the grenades in their own time, taking care to follow the backward path of the grenade with their eyes so as to ensure that they do not strike the back of the trench with the grenade.

5. OBSERVATION

5. OBSERVATION.

After the command "Throw" is given, the Section Commander will, when possible, observe the fall of the grenade. By day a periscope would be useful for this purpose.

6. METHODS OF THROWING.

When throwing grenades from a trench they will either be thrown to the front, or to a flank down the trench the men are standing in.

In the first case they will have to be thrown round arm in order to get the necessary distance, the back of the trench preventing their being thrown overarm.

In throwing to the front, direction is not so important as range, as presumably the target will have considerable width.

In throwing to a flank direction is of the utmost importance and it will therefore be necessary to throw overhand. This will be possible as there will be no back wall, and by throwing overhand direction is better obtained.

When throwing to a flank not more than one man can throw at a time. When throwing to the front all the Section can throw if required.

7. GENERAL.

Men should invariably work in Sections and by "word of command" (see para. 4).

Men should not be allowed to throw a live grenade until they can throw a dummy at least 30 yards from inside a trench.

All practice with live grenades must be done from inside a trench whether to the front or to a flank. If the latter the trench must be traversed and the grenade thrown from behind a traverse.

When practising with dummy grenades men should always go through the motions of "preparing grenades" & "removing pins".

8. SUPPLY OF GRENADES.

Each man will normally carry 2 carriers, each with 5 grenades. He should carry 3 or 4 spare detonators.

Each Section will therefore have with it 40 grenades. + 4 m---

The Refilling Section (see para. 3) will in addition to its 40 rounds in carriers, normally carry 2 boxes (25 grenades each), one box to two men.

This will give a platoon a total of 210 grenades which ✓✓ should be sufficient for any situation likely to occur.

Any further supplies must be arranged for by the Grenadier Company Commander.

9. TACTICS.

3. TACTICS.

As soon as the men have been taught to throw and have learnt to work in groups, they should be practised in platoons. A simple tactical scheme should be given to the Platoon Commander to carry out in the field on the lines stated in para. 1.

The "Torres Vedras" lines or any other back line in our defences will give ample opportunity for this without the necessity for digging any new trenches.

Schemes for two or more platoons working as a company can then be set.

The question of the supply of grenades should never be lost sight of in these exercises.

For these schemes the O.C. Div. Cyclist Co. is available for assisting Brigades and Battalions, and the General Staff of the Division will always be glad to help whenever required.

A.A. Montgomery
Colonel
Gen. Staff, 4th Divn.

24/1/15.

Index

5th Copy.

SUBJECT.

Volume II.

Introduction.

No.	Contents.	Date.

III. Corps
Second Army.

GENERAL STAFF

4th DIVISION

FEBRUARY

1915

Note: The messages mentioned in the Diary will be found in a separate box marked "Messages."

Attached:

    Work Reports.
    Artillery Reports.
    Distribution of
      Infantry.
    Casualties.
    Correspondence.

War Diary, Gen. Staff, 4th Division.
1st February, 1915.

NIEPPE. Cold dull day, no frost.

4.45 am	Quiet night reports forwarded to 3 A.C. and exchanged with 5th and 6th Divs. (H69/10, BM1/11, BM1/12, G1, G431/5, G33/5, G2). The system of beginning fresh numbers for telegrams daily, was abandoned from this date.	
7.45 am	Work report to 3rd A.C. - no change.	G3
11 am	3rd A.C. asks for composition and position of Div. Res. Replied a battn. at La Creche and another at Le Bizet. Sqdn., Cyclist Co., How. Bty. and Mountain Bty. at Nieppe, 3 18 pr. batteries about La Meneenagate.	G580/3 AC G4
1 pm	Notified that photographs and information obtained by R.F.C. will be co-ordinated by 3 A.C. and passed to Divs. Some objections to this arrangement were pointed out, notably that the intimate knowledge of the ground required.	G584 GG1
1.14 pm	3 A.C. ask if Arty. of enemy had been registering on trenches lately. Reply H.Q. right Sectn. of 10 I.B. registered, also edge of Ploegsteert Wood and Hants trenches. G565 (3 AC Secret Letter) special precautions against attack shown to Brigadiers and returned to 3 AC.	BM17 BM8, GG6 G589, GG2.
2.10 pm	A third Fd.Co. R.E. may be expected by the Div. at an early date.	G590
2.10 pm	Air report - 12.20 to 2.40 pm. No movement of enemy, one mile in rear of enemy's trenches.	IG116
2.35 pm	Air report, towns east of us clear of enemy at 1.20 pm.	IG117
3.35 pm	Asks position of anti-aircraft detachment. Replied one sectn. of No.14 in B 11 C South Centre, and one with 6th Div.	G594 BBM6/DA GG4
5.25 pm	Informs 3 AC that 9.2 How. (Mother) will leave to join 1st Corps at 6.30 am tomorrow.	GG3 BBM9
5.40 pm	Enemy's attack on 1st Corps this morning beaten off - circulated.	IG118 G5
7 pm	5th Div. report all quiet, Surreys relieved Cornwalls in Sector A.	G355 G357
7.35 pm	Evening report to 3 AC. 10 I.B. right sectn. heavily shelled, usual sniping. 11 I.B. normal, aeroplane dropped 4 bombs. 12 I.B. normal, enemy shelled Le Touquet and barricade. Our guns shelled breastwork south of Avenue in U 15 A.	GG5 H85/10 BM11/11 BM22/12
7.15 pm	Air report of 12 noon (delayed) all clear east of Messines.	IG120
7.40 pm	6th Div. report situation normal, severe sniping at Rue Du Bois. More sniping than usual at Houplines; some shelling.	G448/6

War Diary - 2nd February 1915.

NIEPPE.	Cold damp day but very little actual rain.	
4-45 am	Quiet night reports forwarded to 3rd Corps and exchanged with 5th and 6th Divisions. (H.57, BM.15, BM.1, G.6, G.504, G.452, G.7)	
7-45 am	Work report to 3rd Corps - no change.	GG.7
9-40 am	On enquiry from 3rd Corps, 1st Corps was informed of route taken by 9.2 howitzer.	G.605 BBM.17 G.8
12 noon	Requests 5th Div. to arrange with 10th Brig. before constructing Artillery observation stations on Hill 63.	H.89 GG.8 G.9
1-45 pm	Informs 10th Brig. of trial of star shell at 7 pm tomorrow.	GG.8
7-46 pm	Evening reports to 3rd Corps - 10th Brig. increased sniping in left section, slight shelling, one of which damaged a hut at 63 but did no harm to occupants. Our guns shelled Red Estaminet in U.15.B S.W. 11th Brig. very little shelling. Enemy still trying to establish themselves in White Estaminet. 12th Brig. situation unchanged except that without any definite reason they think the battalions in front of te them have been relieved.	GG.11 H.12 BM.22 BM.18
7 pm	All battalions have got sufficient trained detachments for 4 machine Guns.	GG.12 SC.18 BM.26 BM.19
	5th and 6th Divisions report situation unchanged.	G.379 G.460
10-20 pm	Message to Div. Arty. re shelling of a triangle of ground in C.10.B.	GG.14
	Received from 3rd Corps - No. G.608	

War Diary -   3rd February 1915.

NIEPPE.

          Clear fine day - temperature warmer.
4-45 am   Quiet night report to 3rd Corps and exchanged with 5th
          and 6th Divisions.
              (H14/10, BM28/11, BM1/12, GG15, G387/t, G461/6, GG16)

7.50 am   Work report to 3rd Corps. No change except that 10 IB   GG12
          making progress with breastwork in U 14 D N.E. and farm
          in U 8 D.

2.17 pm   Air report - no movement of enemy to your front - 9.20   I.G.123
          to 10,5 am.

3.12 pm   Air report 8.30 to 8.50 am contents of Railway stations. I.G.124
          Small column of Infantry and Horse transport marching
          from Courtrai on Menin and another on Courtrai - Tour-
          going road. Another on Halluin - Lille road moving
          towards Lille. 6 guns in U 30 C central.

4.7 pm   Air report shows that there is a pontoon bridge just east of site
          of destroyed permanent bridge at Frelinghien and 2   IG125
          others 200 and 300 yards further down stream. A small   GG17
          redoubt in curl of river in Q 35 B N.centre. Circular
          ring of trenches around Wervicq. Information re bridges
          passed to D.A. and 12 I.B.

  pm   Air report - our front clear of movement 3 to 4 pm.   IG126

7 pm   O.C. No. 14 Anti-aircraft guns to report to O.C. No.5   G636
          R.F.C. to discuss action of guns tomorrow.

7.10 pm   5th Div. report all quiet.   G411/5

7.50 pm   Evening report to 3rd A.C. 10 I.B. less shelling but   GG18
          heavier sniping in morning. II I.B. enemy shelled   H27/10
          convent morning and afternoon. Sniping active immedi-   BM52/11
          ately North of Le Gheer. and Armentieries. 12 I.B. some BM17/12
          shells along Warnave and in Armentieries.

8.10 pm   6th Div. report considerable movement on Quesnoy road   G473
          moving east to west and also north of Frelinghien by   G12
          column of horse vehicles and infantry. Movement   16
          continuing after dark. D.A. and Brigs. informed.
          12 I.B. also informed by 18 I.B.

8.15 pm   6th Div. report enemy's arty. and snipers very active. G474

10.20 pm 6th Div. in continuation of their G473 - nothing new.   G477

WAR DIARY
4th Feb 1915.

NIEPPE

Fine day.

4-35 am.   Quiet night reports forwarded to 3/Corps and exchanged   G/14.
with 5th and 6th Divs. (H/32, BM/52, BM/1, G/13, G/602, G/479,
                                                                         GG/14

7-45 am.   Work report to 3/Corps---no change.

9.30 am   Batty selected to go to 27th Div is 39th of 14th FAB.   BBM/41
Ready to move at 24 hours notice. SAA section of   GG/16
Brig Amm Col not to accompany.   SC/32, G/15

11-45 am   G/639 (Preparation of supporting point) from 3/Corps.   G/16

12 noon.   Air report 4 pm. last night, noticeable movement of
transport at Lille, Tourcoing, and Roubaix.   IG/132

12-30 pm. Air report 9-45 to 10-30 am no movements east of our
line. Zeppelins seen 30 miles SE of Armentieres.   IG/133

1-32 pm.   Asks for report of use and efficacy of 4.7 trench   G/650
mortar.--11th Brig have not used it.   GG/18
                                                                   BM/56

1-58 pm.   Air report 7-45 am Long details of railway trains
and motor transport. Small column of 1000 men, moving
on Roubaix from Lille. --4 new hangars.   I.G/134

4-25 pm.   As result of A.A. guns being moved to Bailleul, enemy's BBM/45
aeroplanes observed for their artillery with impunity   GG/19
over our lines.--3/Corps informed.

7-50 pm.   Air report delayed by chasing enemy.--No movement observed.   IG/140

7-40 am   Evening report to 3/Corps and 6/Div. Quieter day all   GG/20
round, except snipers active in front of Le Gheer.   H/44
Enemy observed on Messines - Lille road in dark blue   BM/58
coats.   J/11

7-10 pm.   5th Division report all quiet.   G/439

7-40 pm.   6th Div nothing particular to report.   G/490

7-30 pm.   Heavy firing was heard from 6/ Div direction. At 8 pm   G/493
6/Div informed us that enemy were shelling civilian   G/495
labour working on new second line, and later that   GG/21
Leicesters had repulsed a small attack.--Circulated   GG/22
to Brigades.

10-4 pm.   3/Corps ask if we have anything later to report--We replied
--Nothing---   (G/652, GG/23)

War Diary, Gen.Staff, 4th Division.
5th February, 1915.

NIEPPE.   Fine bright day after slight frost.

Time	Entry	Ref

4.45 am   Quiet night reports forwarded to 3 AC and exchanged with
           5th and 6th Divs.
                (H53/10, BM60/11, J1/12, G1, GG25, G608/5th, G499/6th, GG26).

4.47 am   Work report to 3 AC - no change.   G 18

8.50 am   Anti-aircraft sectn. returns to us today and reoccupys G656.
           position near Ploegsteert Windmill.   BBM54.

10.30 am   Air report - 7.55 to 10.15 am. Our front all clear.   IG 141.

11.25 am   12 IB asks if Div.Reserve Bn. may be composed of 3   J4/12
           Coys. and 1 Coy. of another Bn. Approved.   GG29

11-45 am   Air report 7-55 to 8-25 am. Frelinghien bridge possibly
           repaired. Various trains and barges detailed.   IG.142

   "   Air report 9-20 to 10am - all clear 2 miles behind
           enemy's line.   IG.143

12-55 pm   O.C. 4·7 trench mortar to report to 11th Brig. who
           will report on the weapon.   GG.28

3=40 pm   Further report on Germans seen on Messines wearing
           dark blue greatcoats and some with greenish tunics.   H.69

3-40 pm   Air report 11-45 to 12 noon - all clear 2½ miles in rear
           of enemy's trenches.   IG.144

4-10 pm   Instructions for working parties for reconstruction of GG.33
           supporting line and supporting points.   GG.34

6-59 pm   5th Div. report all quiet.   b   G.463

7-18 pm   Air report - south of us.   IG.145

7-36 pm   Evening report to 3rd Corps and 6th Div. 10th Brig.
           intermittent shelling of St Yves which set on fire
           artillery observing station there, 19 out 39 shells   G.20
           blind - sniping more active in morning. 11th Brig.   H.71
           snipers very active in front of right section troops   BM.67
           apparently relieved. 12th Brig. no change.   BM.10

8 pm   6th Div. report situation unchanged.   G.518

10-10 pm   Calls for weekly report which was sent in. This is   G.671
           now due on Fridays.   G.22

           Received from 3rd Corps - G.664 training of
           Territorials. G.666 use of Siege Howitzer with 6th Div.
           G.665 Ammunition expenditure. G.667 nomenclature of
           sections and sectors.

WAR DIARY.
6th Feb 1915.

NIEPPE.   Fine day after slight rain, in early morning.

4-45 am.   Quiet night reports to 3rd Corps, and exchanged with
5th and 6th Divs. (G/23,H/75,BM/74,BM/1,GG/35,G/271,G/523)

7-40 am   Work report to 3rd Corps--No change.   GG/37

7-40 am   Instructions to destroy Pont Rouge Bridge received.   3rd Corps
Secret G669.

9-30 am   Informs 12th Brig of another pontoon bridge over River
Lys in C/5/A/S.W having been verified.   G/24.

2-15 pm.   Further instructions re working parties, on supporting
lines.   (H/81,GG/41,GG/87,G/42)

3-35 pm)   Small successes by 1st Army circulated.--(G/680,685,GG/46,G/26)
6-45 pm)
G/655
G/678
4-13 pm.   Messages reached here of No.14 Anti Aircraft section, which   G/682
now has to protect area River Lys - Neuve Eglise -Bailleul.   G/43.
G/25
5-20 pm   Notifies experiment with rocket at night firing.

6-15 pm.   Air report 3-10 to 3-35 pm. All clear ½ mile in rear of   IG/14
enemy's trenches.   148

7-40 pm.   Evening report to 3/Corps. Right Sector (12/Brig) situation
unchanged. Centre Sector (11/Brig) some shelling. Left Sector (10/Brig) reserve trenches of right section shelled.   G/27
Quiet day Left section--Our Artillery shelled enemy's   H/91
trenches east of St yves.   BM/80
G/7.
G/491
7-40 pm.   5th Div--report all quiet

6th Div report factory set on fire in Armentieres, by   G/635.
enemy's shells. Snipers active .

WAR DIARY
7th February 15.

NIEPPE.	Fine day, somewhat misty.
4-45 am.	Quiet night reports to 3rd Corps and exchanged with 5th and 6th Divs. (H.2, BM/86, BM/1, G/28, G/616, G639, G/29)
7-50 am	Work report to 3rd Corps--No change except that work on reconstructing the new supporting line was commenced. This line with its supporting points runs from Le Touquet. Northwards about 800 yards east of, and parallel to, Le Bizet - Ploegsteert road through the wood - East of La Hutte- then westward through La Rossignol- then La Plus Douce Farme, where it connects with 5th Division. Supporting points are about 200 yards in rear of the line and about 500 yards apart. G/60
4-5 pm.	Asks 3rd Corps if N.C.O'S can go to Vermelles--reply-- referred to G.H.Q.. G/33 G/699
5-0 pm.	29th Batty R.F.A. to join 5th Corps. Will reach Westoutre at 1.pm. tomorrow. G/676 BBM/89
7-55 pm.	Evening report to 3/Corps and 6th Division--Quieter day all round. Right Sector have secured 4 houses in advance of sniper's house. (BM/102, H/13) G/36 BM/12
7-0 pm.	5th Division report all quiet. G/509
7-55 pm.	Warning from 3/Corps with reference to enemy's habit of loosening or removing his wire before attack. Anything noticed to be reported--Circulated.-- G/700, G/37.
9-0 pm.	6th Div report situation unchanged but considerable shelling of Rue De Bois, where many houses were destroyed. G/662

WAR DIARY
8th Feb. 1915.

Fine day, particularly clear.

4-30 am.   Quiet night reports to 3/Corps and exchanged with 5th and 6th Divisions. (GG/52,H/21,BM/1,BM/11,G/624,G/666,G/41)

7-40 am   Work report to 3/Corps--no change-- strengthening of houses captured on Le Touquet road and general continuation of work of reclaiming and strengthening trenches.   GG/53

9-25 am   Message received from 5th Division says--Cornwalls in Sector A, Manchesters Sector B, 9th London, Sector C, West Kents, Sector D, KOSB, Sector E.   G/519

10-20 am   12/Brig forwards report of Essex that Germans have pushed a new trench forward to within 30 yards of barricade at Central   BM/6
Farm. Subsequent message says other units do not confirm.   J/4

12-40 pm. Receipt for Secret letters G/703,G/706, forwarded to 3/Corps.

(Re arrival of 5/S.L.R. to 12/Brig(G/703) and reinforcemts.
(R.A. & Cavalry (G/706))   GG/54

12-45 pm. Air report 9-15-9-45--all clear area Armentieres -Perenchies
--Lille--Quesnoy--Frelinghien.   IG/155

2-30 pm.   Div R.A. report 126th Batty has one gun's night line, laid on road U/29/a.--N.W. corner, and 11/Brig have been informed.   BBM/94

====   11/Brig report 3 pits reported by Hants on 5th inst. turned out to be manure heaps.   BM/7

5-0. pm.   Instructions issued to Capt Shelley to provide 150 grenade carriers for Brigade.   GG/56.

6-30 pm.   6/Div report red rockets seen near Steenwerck--train communicated with. (G/675,G/44,GG/57, C/174)

7-45 pm.   Evening report to 3/Corps and 6th Div--normal day. Ploegsteert shelled with incendiary shrapnel-- hotel next church and another house burnt out--otherwise little shelling or sniping-- our Arty failed to down bridge at Pont Rouge. (G/45,H/33,BM/20, BM/18)

7-00 pm.   5th Div report all quiet.   G/533

8-52 pm.   6/Div report more movement than usual just before dark on   G/46.
roads from Quesnoy-N. of Frelinghien.--12/Bde informed.   G/679.

10-5 pm.   3/Corps approves one section 4/Siege being sent to us tomorrow evening, for purpose required.   G/717

Captain E.T. Humphreys who has been G.S.O. 3rd Grade, since beginning of the war, left the Division to take up an appointment in England.

War Diary - 9th February 1915.

NIEPPE.

4-40 am	Fine day - turned to rain at 12 noon and rained hard until 6 pm. Quiet night reported to 3rd Corps and exchanged with 5th and 6th Divisions. (GG.60, H.58, BM.30, J.1, G.539, G.681, G.43)	
7-40 am	Work report to 3rd Corps - normal, nothing new.	GG.61
6-40 am	6th Div. informed that explanation of rockets near Steenwerck is probably R.F.C. signalling to a late returning aeroplane. (C.185, C.175, GG.59, G.49 and ..	GG.68 G.719
9-4 am	3rd Corps ask for explanation of overexpenditure of ammunition in attempted destruction of Pont Rouge.	G.51
1-58 pm	Div. Arty., 10th and 11th Brigs. informed that sanction given for a section of Mountain Battery to be placed in position near the moated farm Ploegsteert Wood.	GG.62
4-25 pm	Receipt sent for 3rd Corps G.608 - remarks on defensive scheme.	G.57
7-40 pm	Evening report to 3rd Corps and 6th Div. Normal - only exception 84 shells fell in vicinity of Ploegsteert during the day. (GG.69, H.51, BM.47, PSM.15)	
7-50 pm	5th and 6th Div. evening reports received - all quiet and normal.	G.693 G.563
8-45 pm	3rd enquire re stove pipe attachment for machine guns trial.	Q.936 G.58

WAR DIARY.
10th February 1915.

NIEPPE.   Fine day, but hazy, sunny during morning.

4-30 am.   Quiet night report to 3/Corps and exchanged with 5/6th Division. (GG/70,H/59,BM/50,BM/1,G/630,G/700,GG/71)

7-45 am   Work report to 3/Corps--nothing fresh except right sector secured and made good 5th house in Snipers Row, at Le Touquet.   GG/72.

9-20 am   12/Brig ask for 100 Rifle Grenades--Div Amm Col unable to supply--possibly tomorrow.   SC/34 GG/73

10-15 am   11/Brig ask for permission to use Armentieres range for M.G. daily for 4 hours--from 12th to 15th Feb.-- Sanction given.   BM/59,G/59 BM/72,Q/64

10-15 am.   Receipt given to 3/Corps for their G/372.   G/60

12 noon.   3/Corps wire sanction cannot be given yet for parties to visit Vermelles--Brigs informed.---   G/735 G/61.

1-26 pm.   10/Brig report that shells used against War Regt this morning, were, they think incendiary.--Piece of one handed to Arty.   H/70

1-50 pm.   Air reconnaissance 10-50 to 11-30 am Klein Zillebeke - Commines - Warneton - Frelinghien clear of all movement.   IG/162

5-0 pm.   Minute to Brigs and Div Engineers--Secret GGG/53/2. construction of communications to supporting points.

7-25 pm.   Air reconnaissance 3-30 to 4-30 pm. area Frelinghien - Premsques - Touquet clear of all movement   IG/168

7-25 pm.   5/6th Div report all quiet   G/587, G/714.

8-0 pm.   Evening report to 3/Corps. -Arty actively employed Amelia completely destroyed wall of White House, near railway line, and Heavies shelled a batty in U/29/ab. Pont Rouge bridge also shelled. White House hit seven times by Amelia. Sectors report all quiet, less sniping than usual. (GG/78, H/81, BM/77, BM/18) B.M.19)

12 pm.   11th Brig. report that E.Lancs report at 8 pm. airship flying low over Ploegsteert wood going west. No confirmation from other units. Thought possibly it might be a search light in clouds.   BM/78 G/65 G/171 G/66 BM/86

    Circular issued to all concerned that infantry may fire at hostile aeroplanes by order of an officer only.

W A R   D I A R Y
11th February 1915.

HIEPPE.

Fine sunny day, not very clear.

4-45 am.   Quiet night reports to 3/Corps, and exchanged with 5th and 6th Divs. (G/68, H/86, BM/38, J/1, G/593, G/718, G/68)

7-52 am.   Work report to 3/Corps--considerable baling and building up after rain, revetting and making new trenches and new dugouts. Work on supporting line continuing without interuptions.   GG/79

11-0 am.   Continuation of last night's evening report -12/Brig report--officers have been forward from snipers house to 9th German house, where they can see German trench about 40 yards away.   GG/81.

12-25 pm.   Air reconnaissance 10-15 to 10-45 am--Area Frelinghien-Les Ecluses- Verlinghem - Perenchies -Erquinghem - La Bontillerie clear of all movement of troops and transpt.I.G/173

4-32 pm.   Receipt to 3/Corps for their G/473.   G/72

7-35 pm.   Evening report to 3/Corps and 6/Div--all quiet, less shelling and sniping.   (H/6, BM/103, BM/15.)   GG/85.

7-10 pm.   5/6th Divisions report all quiet.   G/613
                                                                                              G/734.

War Diary - 12th February 1915.

NIEPPE.

Dull day - rain in evening.

Time	Entry	Ref
4-20 am	Quiet night reports to 3rd Corps and exchanged with 5th and 6th Division. (G.74, H.14, BM.107, J.1, G.521, G.735,	GG.88
7-45 am	Work report to 3rd Corps - normal - improving traverses, etc. Work in supporting line continued.	G.75 ~~GG.39~~
11-7 am	Receipt to 3rd Corps for their G.750 (second and third line of defence).	GG.89
12-30 pm	Message to Chief Engineer, 3rd Corps in answer to question by C.E. re point of junction between 4th and 5th Divisions in G.H.Q. line.	E.609 G.77
4-40 pm	Receipt to 3rd Corps for their G.765 (Sapping and Mining Organization) and G.UPY (Arty. reinforcements).	GG.90
7-10 pm	3rd Corps ask if we have moved two Mountain Guns into Ploegsteert Wood. Replied - Yes.	G.768 GG.94
7-24 pm	12th Brig. asked for plan of houses in Le Touquet road.	GG.92
7-33 pm	5th and 6th Divisions report all quiet along their front.	G.747 G.631
7-52 pm	Evening report to 3rd Corps - Right Sector, first five houses beyond Snipers House now defended and communication complete. ninth and tenth houses being held. Remainder of line no change and all quiet. Very little artillery shooting on our part - Div. Arty. report weather too thick for decent shooting.	GG.93 H.31 BM.123 BM.18
9-55 pm	11th Brig. informed that artillery will fire 6 rounds at trenches opposite E.Lancs. at about 10-30 pm to endeavour to stop the extra sniping going on (This artillery shooting had no effect).	GG.95

W A R   D I A R Y
13th Feb. 1915.

NIEPPE.

          Raining hard all morning, cleared up in afternoon, & then rained again during night.

4-30 am.	Quiet night report to 3/Corps, and exchanged with 5th and 6th Divisions. (GG/96,H/38,BM/129,BM/1,G/642,G/750,GG/97)	
8-10 am	Work report to 3/Corps---Right sector--strengthening of Snipers Row. Work commenced on 9th and 10th House, wire in front of this sector now considerably strengthened. Other sectors reconstruction work on main supporting line continued.	GG/98
9-30 am	11/Brig report Germans appear to have received good news last night--much cheering and singing.	BM/132
10-45 am	Receipt to 3/Corps for G/679 (Demarcation of GHQ line(	G/84
3-20 pm.	Your G/769 received to 3/Corps (Amendment to GG/83)	GG/106
7-25 pm.	Evening report--Right sector quiet day, Centre sector normal, Left Sector 36 shells from German light gun, and enemy's snipers more active than for some days, but with no result. (GG/88, BM/15, BM/143, H/57)	
7-25 pm.	5th Div report all quiet.	G651
7-30 pm.	6th Div report all quiet--Enemy shelled Bois Grenier, and road junction at L'Armee. Only one casualty.	G/753,4.

WAR DIARY
14th Feb 1915.

NIEPPE.   Rained all day, and off and on during the night.

4-30 am.   Quiet night report to 3/Corps and exchanged with 5th and 6th Divisions (H/62,BM/154, G/1, G/90,G/648,G/759,G/91)

7-50 am   Work report to 3/Corps--considerable pumping and baling continuation of work on parapets of trenches. Work on supporting line continued.   GG/108

3-37 pm.   Receipt to 3/Corps for their G/789 (Arty reinforcements --GGG/54/3)   GG/111

7-47 pm.   Evening report to 3/Corps-- Normal day, rather more sniping than usual, a certain amount of shelling, but very little by our own guns.(G/92, H/72, BM/172, BM/19)

7-37 pm.   5th and 6th Divs report no change.   G/766 G/675.

9-45 pm.   3/Corps wire message received from 2/Army--Informed by 4/Corps information received from 9/French Corps that two Alsatians who surrendered today, when cross examined separately, both stated that Germans intended to deliver a general attack on the 15th or 16th--All concerned informed.   IG/181 GG/113

War Diary - 15th February 1915.

NIEPPE.

Rained early in morning and again in afternoon - very dull day.

4-45 am   Quiet night reports forwarded to 3rd Corps and exchanged with 5th and 6th Division.
(GG.114, H.74, BM.1, G.685, G.711, GG.115)

7-40 am   Work report to 3rd Corps - Considerable progress on supporting line. Defence of houses in Le Touquet continued right up to last house outside German lines.   G.93

8 am   Acknowledges receipt of G.769 to from 3rd Corps - (Demarkation of G.H.Q. second line)   GG.116

5-25 pm   3rd Corps intimate 37th F.A.Brig. may be ordered to leave for 4th Corps 4th Division tomorrow (16th), but informed us later that this brigade would leave for 4th Corps on 17th, being at Sailly cross roads by midday. 3rd Corps were thereupon asked that the Section of our Siege Howitzers now with the 6th Division be returned as we should be left without howitzers on our right. They replied that this section would be returned on the 17th. Div. Arty. informed.
(G.814, GG.122, G.815, G.817, G.825)

7-35 pm   Evening report to 3rd Corps. Right Section - situation unchanged. Some incendiary shells were fired into Le Bizet but caused very little damage. Centre Sector - situation normal very little shelling. Left Sector - quiet day, little shelling, especially against left section. Increase of sniping from Messines which may indicate presence of new troops there. Fairly quiet day with our Arty. (G.96, H.1, BM.17, BM.14)

7-20 pm   5th and 6th Divisions report all quiet. (G.701, G.780)

9-40 pm   Message from 2nd Army states that prisoners taken yesterday confirm previous intelligence that general attack by enemy is expected on 15th or 16th inst. Circulated.   IG.187   G.97

(Lt-Gen. Sir B.T.Mahon, C.B. D.S.O., his chief S.O. and A.D.C. and some officers of his Division (10) arrived for 3 days attachment).

WAR DIARY
16th February 1915.---

NIEPPE.

Fine, sunny day.

4-40 am. Quiet night reports received from Brigs and forwarded J/1,BM/21, to 3/Corps. Also exchanged with 5/6th Divisions. H/6,G/98,G/654.
(G/786,G/99.
G/133

7-50 am Work report to 3/Corps--normal.

12-19 pm. Aircraft report 9 to 10 am--All roads in front of our area clear of movement. IG/191

12-30 pm 4/Div Arty ask to be informed of the name of the infantry officer under whose orders the section of No/2 Mountain Battery at the moated farm at Ploegsteert Wood will be placed for the close defence of that locality. They were informed that for close defence only, the Section would come under the orders of the O.C. Som L.I.--11/Brig also informed.-- BBM/16 167 GG/126

12-50 pm. Aircraft report 10-20 to 10-45 am--most of roads behind enemy in front of 3/Corps, clear of movement. A large square earthwork being constructed in F/25 D, sheet 36. I.G/192

2-15 pm. Aircraft report Warneton--Pont Rouge and Messines, clear of movement. IG/193.

2-45 pm. Message from 10/Brig that Dublins report German balloon observing from Warneton--D.Arty informed. H/18

4-25 pm. Receipt to 3/Corps for Secret message G/789 G/103.

4-55 pm. Aircraft report from 1st Corps--Trenches in front of Lille increased in number and many detached trenches joined up, during last few days. Lille-Lomme road barricaded in two places. Messines-Warneton-Pont Rouge -Frelinghien clear of all movement. IG/195

7-0 pm. 5/Div report all quiet. G/825

7-0 pm. Div Arty claim that Archibald bagged an aeroplane which fell in German lines. 10/Brig report some sniping and a few shells in right section. Enemy did not fire on our aeroplanes with rifles and machine guns, as is usual. Left section received about 40 shells. 11/Brig report situation normal. German aeroplane dropped 3 bombs near Hants. Enemy's wire strengthened. 12/Brig report more shelling than usual and that Germans have removed their wire for space of 12 yds in front of trench opposite right of railway. Germans sent some grenades into railway barricade this afternoon. H/24 BM/37 G/107

7-10 pm. 12/Brig informed that G.O.C. considers that garrison of railway barricade should be increased and that they could use their reserve of hand grenades if necessary.

7-15 pm. 3/Corps informed that Germans have cut their wire for a space of 12 yards in front of trenches in C/4/D. G/108.

7-35 pm. Resume of Brig reports to 3/Corps. G/109.

7-30 pm. Asks 11/Brig whether they can confirm Archibalds report of having bagged an aeroplane.--They replied that German machine turned and planed quickly to earth in German lines, apparently hit, after having been fired on by Archibald. G/106 BM/41

7-40 pm. 6/Div report quiet day. G/804

8-47 pm. 10/Brig report large movement of German infantry into trenches opposite Dublins right. Transport also heard. Movement lasted for half-an-hour. H/27

9-21 pm. Asks 3/Corps if 2/Army HQ are still at Bailleul. Reply Yes. G/110

9-50 pm. 12/Brig consider garrison at railway barricade ample. Officer at Barricade thinks that wire reported cut is probably only covered with earth thrown from German trench. G/845

9-50 pm. 10/Brig report all quiet with Dubs now.

10-37 pm. Dubs say one of our shells caused large columns of smoke in front of their right trench. H/31. H/32

W A R   D I A R Y
17th February 1915.

NIEPPE.

Cold day and considerable rain.

4-45 am	Quiet night reports as usual (H/24, BM/37,BM/1,GG/128,G/658, (G/808,G/111.)	
7-50 am	Work report to 3/Corps, no change.	GG/129
7-53 am	Instructions re light howitzer. Ammunition received----Secret.--	G/842
12-10 pm.	37th Howitzer Brigade left to join 4/Corps.	BBM/193
7-10 pm.	Evening report--Right sector slight shelling of working party. Centre sector slight shelling only and sniping in right section. Enemy reported to have put up more wire on Messines, near culvert, over river Douve.	GG/135 BM/6 BM/54 H/53
7-12 pm	5th Div report all quiet.	G/745
8-40 pm.	6th Div report shelling of railway barrier at Rue de Bois.	G/818

War Diary, Gen.Staff, 4th Divn.
18th Feb.1915.

NIEPPE.   Cold windy day, no rain. R.LYS after being in heavy
           flood again began to fall.
           16 officers of 10th Div. New Armies, completed attachment.
           G.S.O.I returned from leave and took over again from GSO II.

4.45 am   Quiet night reports as usual to 3rd A.C. and exchanged
           with 5th and 6th Divs.
                    (H.61, BM61, J1, GG137, G747, G821, G115).

10.10 am   Air report 8 am to 8.20 am. All clear to our front. A   I.G.199.
           new pontoon bridge being built over R.LYS and floods 15   G116.
           yards down stream of Frelinghien permanent bridge. D.A.
           and 12th I.B. informed.

12.15 pm   3rd A.C. G715 and G831 (secret) - attachment of Canadians -
           received.

4.37 pm   Daily work report to be discontinued.   G878.

7.35 pm   Evening report. Increased shelling all round and more
           sniping against Left Sector.
                    (GG141, H576, BM75, BM16).

6.55 pm   5th Div. report all quiet.   G771.

9 pm   6th Div. report some shelling.   G387.

War Diary, Gen.Staff, 4th Divn.
19th February, 15.

NIEPPE.   Cold windy day. Some rain in afternoon.
           River LYS falling.

4.45 am   Quiet night reports as usual. (H84, BM82, BM19, G120, G770,
                                                        G842, G121).

10.40 am Air report 7.15 am to 8.45 am - neighbourhood of Messines IG201
          and Warneton clear of movement of troops.

4.8 pm   Attachment of Arty.Officers for a week from Feb.22nd.   G899.
          6 from South Midland Div. and 3 from 9th Div.

          Arrangements were made with 6th Div. that they should
          have the Southern and ourselves the Northern range at the
          Blue Factory and that the 7th A.and S.Highrs. should
          keep both in repair.

7.25 pm   Evening report. Less shelling than yesterday and less
          sniping.   (J20, BM99, H95, G128).

7 pm   5th Div.report all quiet.   G809

8.30 pm   6th Div. report a good deal of shelling and active
          sniping.

          The following attachments are to take place from the
          Canadian Div. from 21st to 28th for purposes of
          instruction :-

          H.Q. and Sig.Sectn. 2nd Inf.Brig.)
          2nd Inf. Brig.   )
          Staff, Officers and N.C.Os. of a Brig. R.F.A.
            "   "   "   "   "   of a Heavy Batty.
          A Fd.Co. complete also other R.E. officers.
          O.C. Div.Sqdn.
          Two officers and 30 men Cyclist Co.
          Portions of 2 Fd. Ambces.
          Train Co.
          Also Staff Officers from time to time.

War Diary - 20th February 1915.

NIEPPE.

Cold day - very wet afternoon.

4-45 am	Quiet night reports as usual. (H.3, BM.104, J.1, GG.148, G.821, G.857, G.149)	
10-15 am	C-in-C holds conference with Div. Commdrs. and Corps Commander at Bailleul at 2-30 pm.	G.908
12 noon	Som.L.I. report upper strands of German wire removed along a portion of their front. Repeated to 3/Corps.	BM.113 G.131
12-15 pm	12th Brig. report some activity by the enemy last night.	BM.5
12-50 pm	Major Griffin, Lan.Fus. to command 12th Inf. Brig. during absence on leave of General Anley.	BM.6 G.133
4-35 pm	Small parties of Germans reported moving in a Southerly direction in U.10.a at 3-20 pm. 11th Brig. informed.	G.135 H.21
7 pm	5th Div. report all quiet.	G.849
7-35 pm	Evening report - Less shelling generally. Considerable movement of transport heard in BASSE VILLE moving from North to South at 6-27 pm.	G.138 J.25 BM.122 BM.123 H.28
8-45 pm	6th Div. report quiet day.	G.885
9-40 pm	Asks R.F.C. for photo of enemy's trenches on our right front.	

War Diary - 21st February 1915.

NIEPPE.

    Fine sunny day.

4-40 am	Quiet night reports as usual. (H.36, BM.125, BM.1, G.150, G.857, G.888, GG.152)	
4-20 pm	Aircraft report, 2 to 2-30 pm - all roads clear. Road bridge just below Frelinghien & permanent bridge appears to be complete.	IG.211
6-50 pm	Quiet day reported by 5th Div.	G.883
7-5 pm	Evening report - Very little shelling. Unusual activity on the part of enemy's snipers opposite Left Sector but less sniping than usual in Centre Sector, the right section of which thinks unit in front of it has been relieved. Right Sector made good practice with rifle grenades.	G.159 BM.145 H.50 BM.13
8-20 pm	6th Div. report quiet day.	G.903

WAR DIARY
February 22nd 1915.

NIEPPE.   Misty till 10 am, then fine day--turned misty again late in afternoon.

4-30 am.   Quiet night reports as usual.(H/55,BM/1,J/1,G/163,G/884,G/906, (G/164.)

7-0 pm.   5/Div report all quiet along their front   G/909.

7-30 pm.   Evening report-quiet day in right sector. On night of 21/22nd part of German trenches was seen to be on fire and explosions were heard. Amelia shelled enemy's trenches with good effect. Centre sector received about 45 shells at the Convent, Le Gheer. Left sector report sniping much heavier than usual but very little shelling. (GG/156, H/77, BM/10, BM/21)

7-30 pm.   6/Div have nothing to report.   G/943

========   3/Corps report ringing of Church bells and considerable movement in direction of Lille.   IG/215
     IG/216

10-29 pm.   10/Brig report 5 Germans seen by Dub. Fus to be working in front of their trenches. At least one was killed.   H/80.

WAR DIARY
23rd February 1915.

NIEPPE.

Dull day, rather cold.

4-45 am	Quiet night reports as usual.(H/83,BM/14,BM/1,GG/158,G/688, (G/955, GG/159)	
9-35 am.	Div Engrs informed that the fatigue party for digging furnished by the Div Cav Squadron would not be available on Wed and Sats.	GG/160
12 noon.	10/Brig say they are unable to confirm statement of 32 FAB as to continuous rumbling of transport N.E of Messines. (G/178,G/179,H/96.)	
12-15 pm	Air reconnaissance 10-10 to 10-40 am--Area La Boutillerie- Capmghem-Perenchies-Frelinghien clear of all movement. Large quantities of planks seen in trenches between Verlinghem and Capmghem.	IG/217
1-0 pm.	Air report 10-15 to 10-25 am. Area Messines - Warneton Houtham - Zandvourde - Gheluwe - clear of all movement.	IG/220
5-0 pm.	Air report 2-30 pm Messines -Warneton -Houtham clear of movement.	IG/223
7-0 pm.	5/Div report all quiet.	G/947
7-40 pm.	Evening report. Little shelling and usual amount of sniping. Germans make overtures of peace with Hants by shouting and holding up shovels.	G/184 H/6 BM/36 BM/13.
8-40 pm.	Evening situation report from 6/Div.	G/968
11-28 pm.	Receipt to 3/Corps for their Secret No/976--Lines of demakation for 2nd Line.	G/165.

W A R   D I A R Y
24th February 1915.

NIEPPE. Weather fine early morning, but later turned into very wet day. Sharp frost during night.

4-40 am Quiet night reports as usual.(H/10,BM/38,J/1,G/187-G/952,G/993 (G/188.)

12-25 pm. Receipt to 3/Corps for their I.R/121/1 G/193

7-35 pm. Evening report--Machine Guns more active than usual opposite 12/Brig. Enemy shelled Ploegsteert Wood, and wood opposite Birdcage, and put 24 shells near 10th Brig H.Qrs. Our Arty retaliated against enemy's trenches and Frelinghien. (G/203, H/28, BM/52, BM/14.)

6-35 pm. 3/Corps asked to hasten posting of new Commander of ~~11th~~ 11/Brig, in place of Gen. Hunter-Weston who is now in England, and about to receive another appointment. GG/173

6-50 pm. Receipt to 3/Corps for their G/983. (Report on future plans). G/202

7-0 pm. 5/Division report all quiet G/987

8-10 pm. 6/Division report situation normal. G/994.

Message from 3/Corps states that the period of attachment of troops of Canadian Division cannot be extended, and that troops now attached will return on date originally fixed, i.e. 28th.

WAR DIARY
25th February 1915.

NIEPPE.

        Fine day, frosty night.

4-45 am Quiet night reports as usual.(BM/1,BM/55,H/36,G/208,G/694,G/1, G/177.)

11-15 am. 11/Brig report Germans shelling Ploegsteert. Div Arty told to retaliate on Warneton at once. 11/Brig informed. BM/61 GG/179

1-20 pm. Receipt to 3/Corps for their G/993. G/213

4-20 pm. Air reconnaissance 2-20--2-45 pm.--Area four miles in rear of enemy"s trenches between Boutillerie and Messines clear of movement. IG/228

7-0 pm. 5/Div report all quiet. G/21

7-50 pm. Evening report.--Considerable increase in shelling, especially of Left Sector, which received over 300 shells Enemy's howitzers opened for first time from a point due E. of centre of Avenue. (GG/183, H/54, BM/18, H/55, BM.)

8-30 pm. 6/Div report situation normal. G/15.

WAR DIARY
26th February 1915.

NIEPPE.   Fine day, slight frost during night.

4-45 am   Quiet night reports as usual.(H/56,BM/65,J/1,GG/185,G/696,G/216

8-45 am   11/Brig ask for an hour's warning of commencement of   BM/66
          shelling by our Arty. They were told that the Arty.   G/217
          would give them warning.

10-23 am 11/Brig and Div Arty informed that proposed bombard-
          ment of Birdcage would be postponed until 11 am to-
          morrow.   G/219

10-26 am. 11/Brig report enemy very talkative in front of Hants
          and say they are Saxons.   BM/71

5-44 pm. Air report 1-55 to 3-30 pm.--Usual detail of lorries etc.
          More traffic than usual on roads from Lille to Quesnoy,Com-
          mines and Wervicq.   IG/230

6-46 pm. 5/Div report all quiet.   G/55

7-26 pm. Evening report--Very little shelling and some sniping.   G/225
          Fragments of shell picked up in Ploegsteert yesterday   BM/11
          show that enemy was firing yesterday H.E. shell of new   BM/68
          inferior type made of cast iron.   H/71

9-25 pm. Evening report 6th Division.   G/33

10-0 pm. Receipt to 3/Corps for G/9/1 and G/9/2 (Move of Canadian
          Division.   GG/29

WAR DIARY
27th Feb. 1915.

NIEPPE

Dull, cold and windy day.

4-40 am.	Quiet night reports as usual.(BM/1,BM/90,H/78,GG/190,G/69,G/40)	
9-50 am.	Air reconnaissance 7-30 to 7-55 am. No movement observed. Pontoon bridge apparently new, 45 yards North of permanent bridge at Frelinhien.	IG/234
11-0 am	Receipt to 3/Corps for their G/9/4.	GG/173
11-8 am.	5/Div report extraordinary message received by 15/Brig from Germans by lamp, who said, they were going to attack and take hill at noon on Saturday. All informed in case it may be genuine.	G/77 GG/195
12-0 noon	Air report 9 am. Raod Warneton-Commines-Houthem and road behind Messines clear.	IG/236
1-10 pm.	3/Corps report that 14/Brig have heard firing South of Sector A, which is on extreme right of 2/Corps line.	G/24
2-30 pm.	10/Brig report one officer and three men wounded last night in Warwicks trenches, by snipers.	H/90
3-7 pm.	32nd Arty report English aeroplane down in T/11/D. Officer hit by German shrapnel. Repeated 3/Corps.	SC/100 G/233
5-15 pm.	11/Brig report Ploegsteert being shelled.	BM/108
7-50 pm.	Evening report--Right sector (12/Brig) situation unchanged. Considerable shelling in Centre (11/Brig) and Left (10/Brig) Sectors.--Many of the shell were blind.	H/95,GG/199 BM/109,BM/40
7-8 pm.	5/Div report quiet day.	G/97
8-20 pm.	6/Div report 19/Brig received a few shell and some rifle grenades in the trenches of their Left Section--No casualties.	G/57
8-55 pm.	10/Brig notify us that a Fd Batty will fire 12 rds at a German communication trench in U/2/D West of Messines at 11 pm.	H/1.
9-45 pm.	Night Report of Arty fire on Birdcage by 4th and 6th Siege Batteries, with good results on breastworks and buildings in U/16/D.	GG/201 BM/113.

WAR DIARY
28th Feb. 1915.

NIGHT.

Very bright day, with cold drying wind, heavy rain again at night.

4-40 am.   Quiet night reports forwarded to 3/Corps and exchanged with 5/6th Divs. (H/3, BM/1, J/1, GG/202, J/705, G/61, GG/203)

10-15 am   Air reconnaissance 8-8-30am Column 100 yards long, of hostile Infantry moving N. towards Chaple Head, otherwise no movements between La Boutillerie-Hallenes-Perenchies - Quesnoy Bas -Warneton - Messines.   IG/237

10-25 am   Secret letter G/954/1 acknowledged to 3/Corps.   G/236

7-45 pm.   Evening report - Right Sector - No change. Enemy shelled 2nd line a little this morning. Centre Sector--situation normal. 37 shell received, six being blind. Left Sector- Right section-quiet day. 12 light shell over centre section The Arty fired with effect on German howitzer which had previously bombarded St Yves. (BM/7, BM/12, H/17, G/238)

7-00 pm.   5/Div report all quiet.   G/143

7-20pm.   6th Div report fair amount of shelling.   G/76.

Attached
distribution of Infantry during February
Casualties   "

WORK REPORTS.

WEEKLY REPORT.

4/Div. No. yyy 28

5/2/15.

Hd. Qrs.
   3rd Corps.

There has been no change in the general line of our defence.

12th Inf. Brig. Section.

(a) Portion of trench South of Le Touquet - Le Gheer road which had been flooded out has been recovered and is being revetted and put in order again. More work in strengthening the Snipers House on the Le Touquet road has been carried out and preparations have been made to get forward to the houses immediately in front of it. A portion of the trench immediately to the East of our railway barricade has been recovered and is now re-occupied. Drainage and revetting of a further section is in progress. The high command parapets in rear of the trenches have been continued and the wire in front of the trenches has been considerably strengthened.

(b) It is proposed to continue reclaiming flooded trenches and to strengthen the right at the Snipers House.

(c) No marked activity on the part of the enemy in strengthening trenches has been noticed. The point where he had been collecting timber and planks, reported on last week, has been shelled by a Siege Howitzer.

(d) This section has not been much shelled this week and sniping has been about the same as usual.

11th Inf. Brig. Section.

(a) The breastwork line has been completed and the defences of the moated farm and Fort Boyd strengthened. Wiring has continued and the huts in rear of Ploegsteert Wood are almost completed.

(b) The works on hand will be continued.

(c) No new works have been noticed to be made in the enemy's line except that three pits have been dug about 30 yards in front of the enemy's line opposite Le Gheer.

(d) Until yesterday there was no increase in shelling, but then a good deal of indiscriminate shelling of the wood took place.

10th Inf. Brig. Section.

(a) Existing trenches have been considerably improved and the defences of houses selected to be held have been strengthened. The defences of La Hutte Chateau as a supporting point are nearly completed. Communications have been improved and a great deal has been done in strengthening the wire at St Yves.

(b) It is proposed to continue strengthening the existing line and wire.

(c)

(c) No new works have apparently been undertaken by the enemy.

(d) The shelling of this section has slightly decreased, especially on the left. Sniping has been rather more active opposite St Yves.

Generally.

(a) It is not thought that any change has taken place in the troops opposed to us, but yesterday troops wearing dark blue greatcoats some of which had red tabs while others were quite plain, were observed on Messines hill. Some of these were wearing greenish tunics while others had tunics of grey but of rather darker shade than usual.

(b) In addition to the proposed work to be carried out in each section, a supporting line to connect that of 6th Division on our right and that of the 5th Division on our left will be re-constructed under Divisional supervision.

(c) There has been no change in billeting areas usually reported.

Maj-Gen.

5/2/14.

Commdg. 4th Div.

WEEKLY REPORT.

12/2/15

Headquarters,
   3rd Corps.

The maps forwarded herewith show only new works, referred to in the body of the report, or in Appendix "A".

Resume.

Generally speaking the work done on the front line has consisted of revetting trenches occupied, of reclaiming portions of trench that had been previously abandoned, of constructing works of high command and of improving barbed wire entanglements. Very little work has yet been possible in the way of improving communications from front to rear, except in the case of the centre section of the Centre Sector (11th Bde), and left section of Left Sector (10th Bde), where above ground covered ways have been completed.

Work on the supporting line recently undertaken has b made good progress. Each Brigade has found large working parties both morning and afternoon (except the ~~Right~~ Left Sector (10th Bde), which has had to work at night).

RIGHT SECTOR (12th Inf. Bde.)

(a) (i) <u>Right Section</u>. At Le Touquet the gradual pushing forward through the houses, reported last week, is still going on. The 5th house is now strengthened and completed as a covered way, and officers have been forward as far as the 9th house, which is the last house before the gap. Here they have seen across an intervening space of 40 yards the German trench protected by 4 rows of barbed wire.

In the front line trenches the work of reclaiming water-logged sections, and of revetting the parapet with wood has been pushed forward with assistance of the Royal Engineers.

A complete new line of barbed wire (marked (1) on map) has been laid out. It consists of entanglements made of two crosses of wood joined by a pole and strands of wire.

In the

2.

In the second line a high command work has been completed 250 x East of Le Touquet station (2). It finishes the defensive measures connected with the collection of buildings known as North Block.

(ii) <u>Centre Section</u>. The Monmouths have been at work on a new semi-breastwork (3) to connect the right of their front trench with the Railway barricade. Owing to the closeness of the enemy progress is necessarily slow and there are still 25 yards of it to be done. This breastwork will not only give improved lateral communication, but also an increased number of fire positions.

The Monmouths are also pushing a sap forward from their support to their front trench (4).

The high command trench at Wimaer Gilde (5) has been improved by throwing back its flank.

(iii) <u>Left Section</u>. The work has chiefly consisted in recovering abandoned sections of trench and in revetting.

Wire has been improved at certain points, but the closeness of the enemy renders work difficult.

(b) It is proposed to continue unfinished work mentioned above, and, if weather permits, to commence reclaiming flooded communication trenches.

(c) No special activity has been noted on the part of the enemy.

(d) There has been a notable decrease in shelling during the past week, but sniping has increased, due possibly to our use of rifle grenades.

<u>Centre Sector (11th Inf Bres)</u>

(a) (1) <u>Right Centre Section. (E.Lancs)</u> Revetting the parapet has been the chief work in the front trench.

The second line of defence along the Le Gheer - Le Touquet road, shown last week as being in progress, has now 4 breastworks completed (see map--(6), (7), (8), & (9)).

The

3.

The covered way, running East from Le Gheer Cross roads to the defended house on the left of this section has now been improved so that it can be used by day.

(ii) Centre Section. (Hampshires) The revetting of the front trench, both front and rear, parapets has been completed and traverses constructed whereever the trace of the trench rendered this advisable. The wire in front has been considerably strengthened.

In the second line the wire has also been improved.

(b) It is proposed to continue the above work where in-completed.

(c) No activity has been noticed on the part of the enemy regarding work on his trenches.

(d) On the whole there has been no increase in the shelling, but on one day it was somewhat heavy in the neighbourhood of Ploegsteert when about 80 shells were fired. At least one of these was an incendiary shell. It took effect, destroying a hotel. Several rifle grenades have been fired at our trenches, but so far without effect.

~~Left Section.~~ Left Sector (10th Inf Brig)

(a) (i) Right Sector. The line of semi-breastworks immediately in rear of the present front line is being proceeded with and 2 sections, one short and one long, have been completed (see map (10), (11)) with sapper assistance.

Defensive measures at St Yves are finished and a covered way provided to it (12).

Hull's Burnt Farm is also completed and the Three Hun's Farm nearly so. The moat has ~~been~~ to be made to encircle it completely, whereas there is now a small gap.

(ii) Left Sector. The revetment has been improved all the way along the front trench, where required fresh wire has been put out.

The covered

The covered approach (13) has been improved so that it can be used by day.

(b)   It is proposed to continue the work in hand.

(c)   Nothing new regarding the enemy has been noticed.

(d)   During the past week the enemy has been **exceptionally** quiet. There has been shelling, but not much sniping. Incendiary shells have been used and one house was burnt down in St Yves.

New Supporting Line

This is now in course of construction. For details see Appendix "A".--Marking on map is in brown ink.

12-2-15.

Major-General
Commanding 4th Division.

APPENDIX "A"

State of Work on New Line of Defence on afternoon, 11/Feb/1915.

Reference attached maps 1/10,000 - St Yves & Frelinghien Sheets.

Approximate boundary line between 10th & 11th Brigades, as regards work on 2nd line, is the road from E of La Hutte in U/14/C to St Yvon.

10th Brig Area.

(a) Trench dug from "A" westwards, along line of road, to a point "B". This is wired as far as it is dug. Revetted as far as "C".

Trench running south from "A" is in a good state as far as "D".

(b) Le Rossignol is prepared for defence.

Farm at "E" is being prepared and should be finished in two nights.

Small farm at "F" is being prepared and will be completed about same time.

House at cross roads "A" will be arranged for defence.

(c) Westwards from Le Rossignol there is a wire fence which will be strengthened.

(d) Working Parties:- 100 men by night, in two reliefs, from 5-30 pm to 1-30 am.

11th Brig Area.

(a) Between "D" & "G" a communication trench is having firing positions made from it.

3 breastworks along hedge "G" in hand.

Breastworks along west edge of wood, south of above, will be completed tomorrow.

Breastworks at each end of Bunhill Row in hand as shown.

Breastworks parallel to Regent Street, south edge of wood, in hand.

3 breastworks will be completed tomorrow along road "H".

(b) Strong points will be made:-

In the line
(1) Where line cuts Mud Lane, near "G".
(2) Points "I" and "J".
(3) South end of Bunter Avenue.
(4) North end of road "H".
(5) Middle of same road.
(6) Touquet Berthe.
(4, 5 & 6 have had trenches dug and are wired,
 1, 2 & 3 are in hand.)

Supporting Points.
(7) Fosse Labarre not yet taken up.
(8) Ch. La Hutte in hand.

(c) Portions of front are wired, but whole will be strengthened.

(d)   Working parties--140 Infantry, in two reliefs, 100 civilians.

12/Brig Area.   --From Ploegsteert Road to River Lys.--

(a)   From Ploegsteert road trench is dug to point 2 and revetted for 200 yards.

Trench dug from "Y" to "X", 180 yards completely revetted, and 100 yards partially revetted.

About 100 yards of trench dug at "W" and "V".

(b) *Supporting Points.*
- Farm "U" is being put in a state of defence.
- Farms "T" and "R" will be started tomorrow.
- Farm "Q" and cross roads "S" to be done.

(c)   From "P" on Rabecques to "U" is a wire fence.

From "P" to Ploegsteert Road there is a wire fence on original second line which will have to be moved bodily.

(d)   Working parties   100 men in two reliefs from 12/Brigade.
     " "   25 " " " " " Cavalry.
     " "   40 " " " " " Royal Arty.

Appendix "B".

DISTRIBUTION - IV DIVISION - INFANTRY.

(Called for by G.732/3rd Corps d/- 10/2/15)

	LEFT X Brig. Sector		CENTRE XI Brig. Sector				RIGHT XII Brig. Sector		
	Left Section (DOUVE)	Right Section (ST YVES)	Right Section	Left Centre Section	Centre Section	Right Centre Section	Right Section	Left Section	Centre Section	Right Section
(a) No of Bns in front line	½ Bn*	1 Bn (less ½ Co)	3 Bns less 3 Cos 2 Each					3 Bns		
(b) No of Cos in front line	2 Cos	3½ Cos	1 Co	1 Co	1 Co	2 Cos	1 Co	1½ Cos	5 plns	3 Cos
(c) No of Cos in Bn support		½ Co	1 Co	1 Co	1 Co	1 Co	1 Co	½ Co	3 plns	1 Co
(d) No of Cos in Bn Reserve	2 Cos		1 Co	1 Co	1 Co			2 Cos	2 Cos	
(e) Strength of Brig Reserve	1 Bn		1 Co	2 Cos	1 Co	1 Co	2 Cos			
(f) Composition of and location of Divl Reserve.		1 Bn (La Creche) 1 Bn ARMENTIERES							1 Bn (Le Bizet)	

* By night 3 Cos are in the front line and the 4th Co is moved up into support.

Map sent with Weekly Report 12/2/15

FRELINGHIEN.

"A" Form. Army Form C. 2121.
MESSAGES AND SIGNALS.

TO: Capt Carton (4th Div)

Dear Carton

The Breastworks are as shown in Green completed (1)(2)(3)(4) The communication trench I am told enables you to reach the Hants trench in day time

11/2/15

G.F Boyd

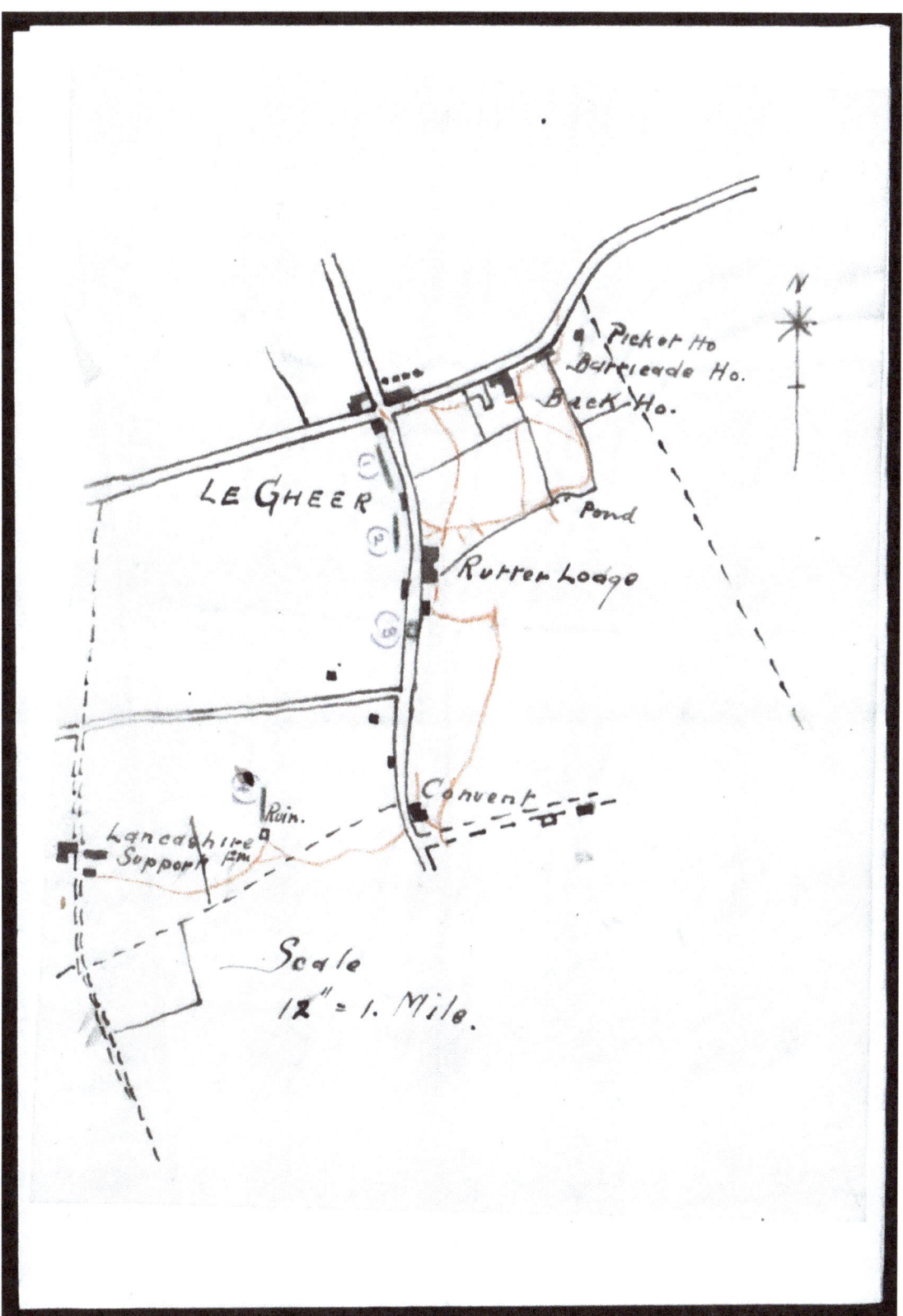

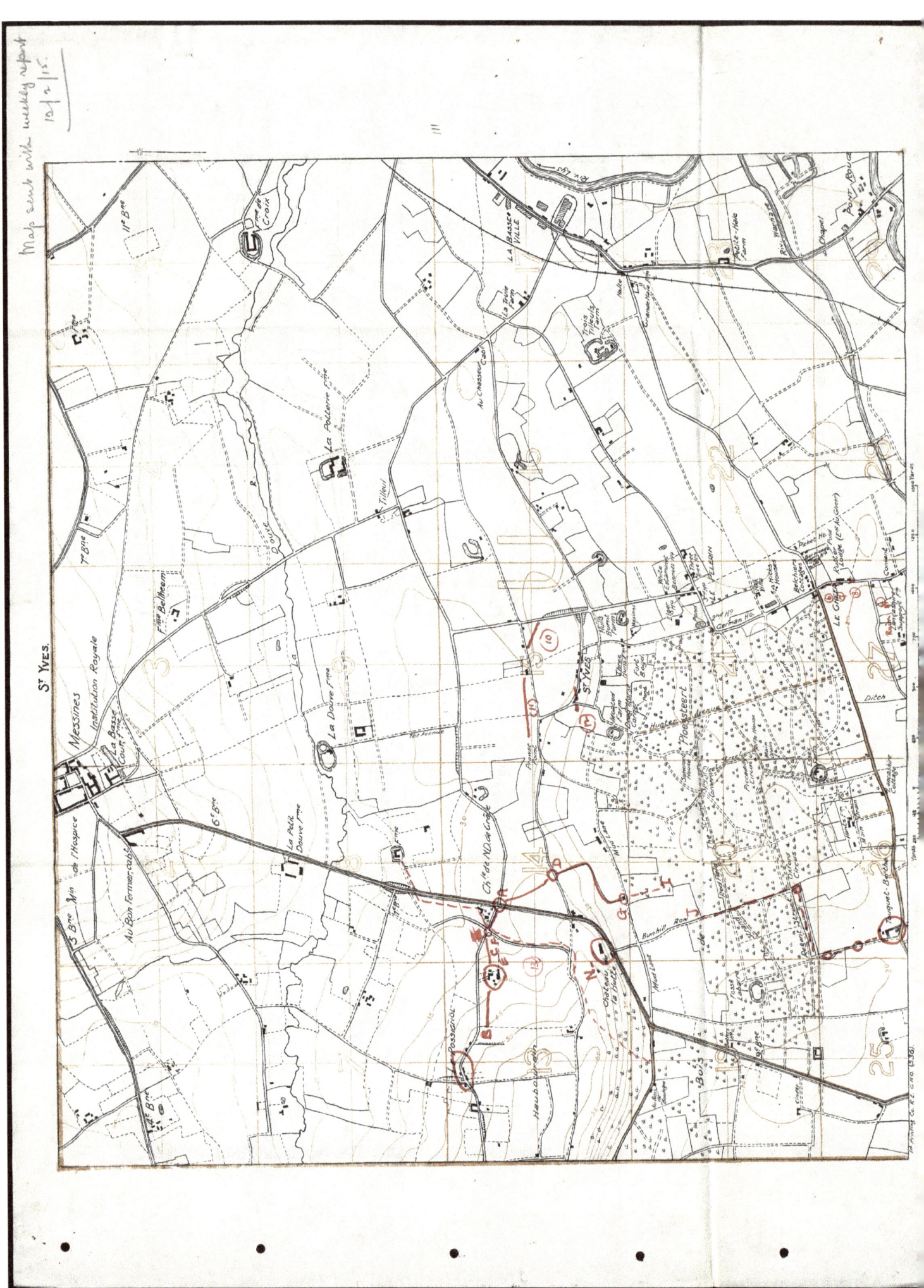

19/2/15

WEEKLY REPORT.

4/Div. GGG.28

Headquarters,

    3rd Corps.

1. <u>Resumé</u>. Owing to wet weather practically no progress has been made in reclaiming abandoned trenches. Construction of high command works all along the front has been proceeded with, and special attention has been given to strengthening the wire entanglements. In many places there now exist triple lines, especially opposite sections of abandoned trench.

    Work on the new supporting line has made satisfactory progress.

2. <u>Right Sector</u>. (12th Inf. Brig.)

(a) (i) Right Section (Le Touquet). In the Snipers' Houses a covered way has now been made to the front house and the position there strengthened. Two wing breastworks have been made with their right flanks touching the houses and facing in a N-N-Easterly direction. These would be of service in

A repelling a rush made by the enemy along the Northern side of the line of houses. This flank has also been well wired.

    All along the front of this section the wire has been strengthened and work of revetting continued.

    (ii) Centre Section (Monmouth Regt.). Closeness to the enemy has continued to hamper the work. The parapet has been strengthened and revetted.

B In the house that marks the right of this section a remarkable bomb-proof shelter has been dug. It is reached by a flight of steps in rear of the house and consists of a tunnel 7 ft deep. Inside the house there is an exit. It is a work that probably only a professional miner could achieve - certainly in the time - as it took 12 men only 8 hours and it is about 30 ft in length.

    (iii) Left Section (Essex.R.). In addition to strengthening the wire the chief work undertaken has been

C a high command work which will ultimately be about 80 yards long. It is intended primarily as a screen behind which reinforcements could be brought up. At present the main road is under fire from the German trenches at a range of under 600 yards. It may also enable the forward trenches to be reached by daylight. In front of this work a small

D fire trench has been started. It is designed to cover a section of abandoned trench which it is expected would take a considerable time to reclaim.

    The supporting line in this section is now practically complete and only requires certain additions to the wire obstacles and improvement of certain portions of the parapet. A feature of this line is the excellent arrangements made for alternative machine gun emplacements, of which there are 10 on a front of about 500 yards.

(b) No fresh works are contemplated.

(c) The enemy's artillery has been fairly quiet in front of this section. Sniping has gone on as usual.

    The enemy is reported to be constructing a pontoon bridge 15 yards below Frelinghien Bridge.

(d)

(d)   No information has been obtained with regard to the
enemy's attitude, or whether his troops have been changed
or reinforced, but neither is believed to be the case.

3.   Centre Sector.   (11th Inf. Brig.)

(a) (i) Right Section (L.R.B.).   Chief works have been
the construction of a machine gun emplacement on the banks
of the R.Warnave to fire across the front and the putting
in a state of defence of a small cottage on the other flank
of the L.R.B. line (Warnave Farm).
   (ii) Centre Section (Hamps.R.)   The main trench may
now be considered as finished. Modifications are being made
in the arrangement of loopholes, but the parapet is revetted
front and rear, traverses have been built where required and
bomb-proof bivouacs provided for the men. The wire has been
strengthened all along the front.
   (iii) Left Centre Section (Rif.Brig.).   The chief work
has been the construction of corduroy paths and entangling
the front edge of the wood which latter work is now finished.
   (iv) Left Section. (Som.L.I.).   The chief work has been
the strengthening of the defences of the Moated Farm.

(b)   Nothing new is proposed.

(c)   The only information obtained of the enemy has been
that on the 15th instant the Saxons in the Birdcage who had
been there at Xmas returned for a fortnight's tour. This
fact was volunteered by one of the enemy from his trench the
same night.

(d)   Shelling has been rather more active, especially in
Ploegsteert Wood.   ~~Sni~~ Sniping has been about the same.

4.   Left Sector.   (10th Inf. Brig.)

(a) (i)   St Yves Section.   At Hull's Burnt Fm the work
of extending the moat to complete the circle has been
continued but is not yet finished. A communication trench
leading from this farm to the eastern front trench is in
progress.
   On the northern front the new high command trench
running East from Prowse Point has made a considerable
advance in the direction of completion. A new machine gun
emplacement has been made on the road at U.15.b.d. This
enables a gun to sweep the front of the line facing East.
The wire in this section has been greatly strengthened.
   (ii) Douve Section.   The defensive measures at farm
in U.8.d are now completed. An old trench connecting the
farm in U.14.b with the Messines road has been improved
and converted into a usable communication trench. The work
of revetting the parapet and strengthening the wire has been
proceeded with.

(b)   The only completely new work in contemplation is a
communication trench of 110 yards which will connect St Yves
with the Eastern front trench.

(c)   The enemy has been quiescent along the whole front of
this sector.

(d)   On the night of the 16th a considerable noise in the
enemy's trenches, men shouting and rumble of wheels led to the
Garrison standing to arms. Nothing happened and it was
probably only a normal relief taking place.

19.2.15   Maj-Gen.
                                        Commdg. 4th Divn.

REPORT on Work on 2nd (Supporting) Line.

(1) From River Lys to Ploegsteert - Le Gheer Road.

(a) DEFENSIVE POSTS.

River farms partially prepared.--La Flencque, Grand Rabeque and London Support Farm. 2/3 rds trenches dug.

(b) Trenches of various depths dug from Railway to Le Touquet road, and thence to Ploegsteert road, with a small gap of 50 yds where line crosses Ruisseau Des Rabecques. About ¼th of this is revetted.

(c) Wiring about half completed.

(d) Working parties, as before, but civilians hampered by shelling on several days.

(2) From road to junction with 5/Division.

(a) Posts along road running N. from Touquet Berthe complete and wired.
Posts E, F, D, J, and K in hand.

(b) Trench continued with wire in front to Le Rossignol.
Trench D--G being improved, drained etc.
Breastworks G--I completed.
Breastworks along Bunter Avenue in hand.
Breastworks along Regent Street completed

(c) Wiring being done at same time.

(d) Working parties as before.

Reference 1/10000 maps St Yves and Frelinghien.

26/2/15

WEEKLY REPORT.

3rd Corps.

1. RESUME.

Throughout the week the work of consolidating the defences has gone on, and as before, consisted chiefly of strengthening the wire and revetting the parapet. Very little progress has as yet been possible in the direction of reclaiming abandoned trench, whether front line or communication. One new communication trench has been dug in the DOUVE section and, profiting by past experience, special attention has been paid to drainage.

Sniping has been much the same as usual and shelling also, except in and around PLOEGSTEERT WOOD where there has been an increase.

2. RIGHT SECTOR. (12th Brigade)

(a) (i) Right Section (Le Touquet).
The work on the snipers' houses has been continued, the walls facing the Germans have been strengthened by sandbags as well as loopholed, and the wire entanglements improved.

At the Railway Barricade (a) a breastwork has been started to connect with the one that the Monmouths are pushing out from the other side. The total length of the gap to be traversed is about 40 yards and from one third to one half of this is now done.

(ii) Left Section (WARNAVE).
The high command work at WARMAR GILDE (b) in second line is now completely revetted and several bombproofs have been made.

(c) On 19th and 20th the Germans fired a large number of rifle grenades against the Essex high command works and caused 25 casualties - mostly slight. Two days afterwards Amelia shelled the offending trenches and since then there has been no recurrence of the nuisance. Sniping and shelling have been as usual.

(d) No information has transpired concerning the enemy.

3. CENTRE SECTOR. (11th Brigade)

(a) Work has consisted of strengthening wire revetting bad sections of parapet and construction of cubby-hutches.

(c) There has been a considerable increase in shelling of this sector by the Germans. Areas affected were PLOEGSTEERT, BUNTERVILLE, LE GHEER and Hants. "T" trench. There has been very little sniping.

(d) No information about the enemy. Movements of transport occasionally reported, but nothing to show that the sound was due to causes other than the normal reliefs.

4.

4. LEFT SECTOR. (10th Brigade)

(a) (i) Right Section (ST YVES).
The B.C. trench (c) mentioned last week is still in progress as is also the work of wiring and revetting the parapet. The cutting through of the roadway into BULL'S BURNT Fm to complete the circle of the moat is nearly finished.

(ii) Centre Section (Argyle & Sutherland Highlanders).
The work done has reflected great credit on this Territorial Battalion which only took over the section 10 days ago. The defences of the farm (d) in the line have been taken in hand by Capt. Anton, a civil engineer, and carried out in a thorough manner. On the road at (e) a sandbag bombproof shelter holding a dozen men has been built in rear of the barricade. A new trench has been dug (f) to shorten the line by cutting off a corner and the revetting is making good progress.

(iii) Left Section (DOUVE).
Wiring and revetting both front and rear parapets have been continued and several bombproof shelters built.
A communication trench (g), which will shortly enable the front trench to be reached by day, and consequently facilitate the moving up of reinforcements, has been started this week. Drainage is receiving special attention.

(b) It is proposed to dig another communication trench (shown in blue) more or less parallel to the one now nearing completion.

(c) Shelling and sniping were normal and movements of transport were reported with usual regularity.

(d) A shakp belonging to a Bavarian Jaeger was picked up in neutral ground N.W. of ST YVES. This does not appear to indicate a change in hostile dispositions.

26/2/15.

Maj-Gen.
Commanding 4th Divn.

Report on 2nd (Divisional) Line of Defence.

Reference - 1/10,000 maps - ST YVES & FRELINGHIEN.

A. Right Section. R.LYS - LE TOUQUET road.
   (1) Trench nearly completed right across. Double wire fence completed. Drainage in hand. 100 yards at Le Touquet road revetted and floored. Revetting now being done on each side of railway.
   (2) LYS Fm. Trenches on 3 sides completed and revetting and wiring in progress.
   FLENCQUE Fm. Front trenches complete and revetted. Side trenches in hand.

B. CENTRE SECTION. Trench and double 12 foot wire entanglement across entire front. About 450 yards revetment completed. Drainage nearing completion.

C. LEFT SECTION. WARNETON road - LE GHEER road. Trench completed and wire fence being strengthened. Drainage nearing completion.

   Supporting Points - GRAND RABEQUE and LONDON SUPPORT Fm progressing well.

~~LE GHEER road - Junction with 5th Division.~~

D. TOUQUET BERTHE - Ch^{lle} de N.D. de Grace.
   (1) Breastworks Touquet Berthe - Regent Street and supporting points completed.
   Additional breastworks and covered communication along road in hand.
   (2) Breastworks along Regent Street completed.
   (3) Breastworks along Bunhill Row completed. Cover for garrison and traverses in hand.
   (4) Breastworks in Mud Lane and thence to communication trench completed. Communication trench from these to farm on chateau - ST YVES road, U.14.c. cleaned out and partially covered to firing trench. Chateau completed as defensive post. Wiring along Chateau - St Yves road completed.
   (5) Revetment of trench from above road to Ch^{lle} de N.D. de Grace in hand.
   Wiring in front is more than half done along the whole section.

E. Ch^{lle} de N.D. de Grace to LE ROSSIGNOL, etc.
   (1) Trench has not progressed much since last report, all efforts being concentrated on revetment which takes a lot of labour, is slow and is also absolutely necessary as trenches fall in if left only a few days.
   This is progressing satisfactorily.

F. Defence of LE ROSSIGNOL and farms in U.13.b and U.14.a 3.3 completed with wire.

   Wire entanglement completed across the whole section to junction with 5th Div.
   There is also a trench of sorts along this line.

APPENDIX "A"

The following alterations have taken place in the strength and distributions of garrisons in various sectors of the line

RIGHT SECTOR.
Add to Divisional Reserve 1 battalion, billeted at Le Bizet.

CENTRE SECTOR.
No change.

LEFT SECTOR.
Should be amended as follows:-
(a) 2 battns and 1 coy.
(b) 6½ companies
(c) ½ company.
(d) 2 companies
(e) 1 battalion and 1 company.
(f) 1 battalion (less 2 companies) Armentieres.

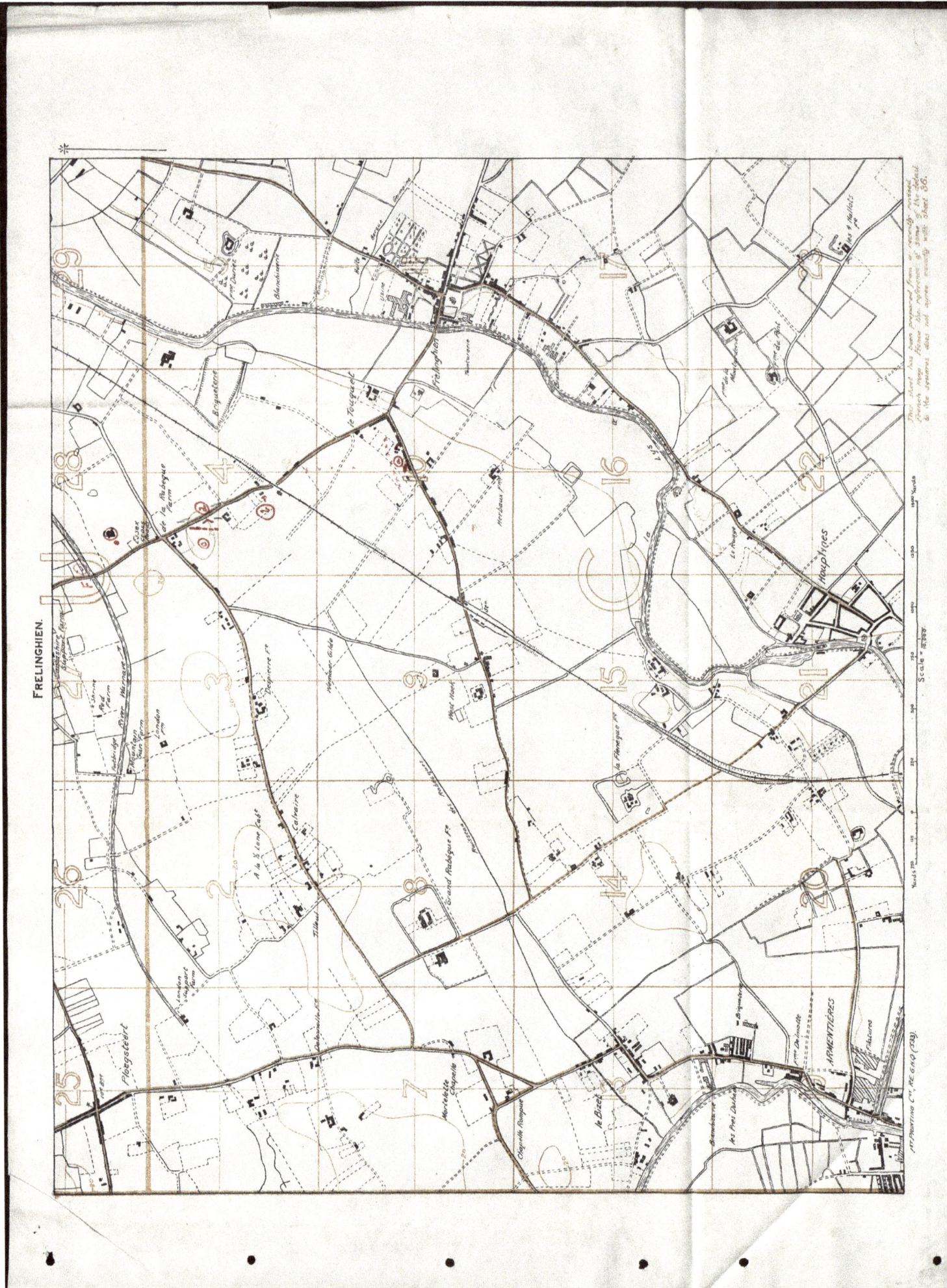

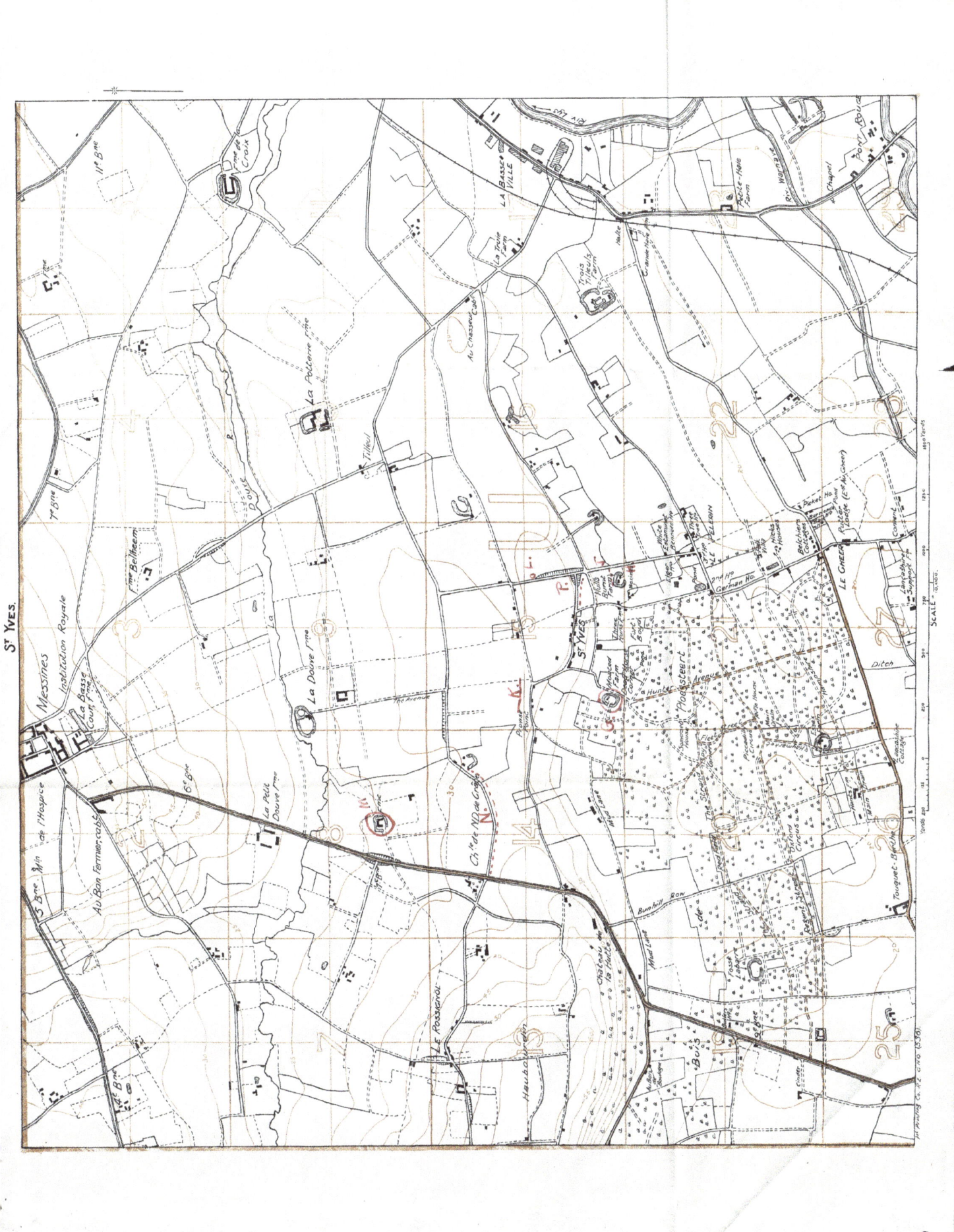

ARTILLERY REPORTS.

Wireless messages 31st heavy. on battery C 11 6 S.E. at 2pm
This was thoroughly well shelled and it is
hoped proves effect.
At 3.30 pm flashes were observed in C 2 6 d,
fire was opened on the battery and it
soon stopped work.
Produced in front by 29 4.7" at
37 Factory, 6" Hotch. on little ridge which was
using the steppes at once where hostile able
fell was seen + did up fire again
6" extreme close but thoroughly well searched in the neighbourhood establishing
135 of 32" Rde switches + suspected ? recover
station.
Ottawa wilting and used road 6.2. v.s

4th Div AA?

Very little shooting today.
14th Bde none
32nd did some registration
and shelled enemy's trenches
South of the Avenue in retaliation
also got at suspected observation
post.
29th Bde shot at enemy's snipers
and registered a road for night
firing.
31st Heavies shelled Warneton in
retaliation
37th Bde fired at a working
party near LES 4 CLOSES and
they ceased work on receipt of
Lyddite.
Warneton also shelled in
retaliation
OUL
8.2.XV

14th Bde nothing exciting

29th shelled enemys trenches & barricade in retaliation

32nd shelled trenches S.E. of Messines and interfered with a lunch party — also shelled observing station North of CHASSEURS Cabaret

37th got at a working party in N6B

4th Siege + Amelia took on Pont Rouge Bridge but failed to down it — shrapnel under own shots were all round it & perhaps hit, but it's still there —

31st Heavies shelled up Pont Rouge Brasserie with wood in retaliation

ouej
8.2.XV

G⁸. 9.5pm

14 Arty. confined itself today to two retaliations, with its 6" Howitzer, for the hostile shelling of the Le Bizet – Ploegsteert front: The two first times by landing 100 lb tokens into likely spots at Frelinghien; the third by tickling up the otherwise somnolent Bosches in the △.

2g Arty took no part in today's activity (?) beyond despatching some 3 cwt. of good English steel as ~~souv~~ – in the form of 18 pr shrapnel – as souvenirs for ultimate Consignment to ~~Baxar~~ Saxon frans.

3² Arty practically had a dies non; 13 shrapnel and 2 Trotyl representing the sum total of their part in the game, fired in retaliation of the shelling of our line from S⁺ Yves to the R. Douve –

Howitzers reminded working parties at Pottvie Farm of their vigilance,

and endeavoured to render Warneton Church uncomfortable as an observation station –

31 Heavies alone tried to be nasty, by shelling a registered battery N.W. of Pont Rouge when Ploegsteert was being shelled. But there was no evidence to show that the guns shelled were the offenders. However, they may not have been hit –

Artillery business was handicapped today through the inability of the RFC to carry out a reconnaissance –

[signature]

9·2·15

14th Bde
Amelia took a white house near railway line; the wall facing the enemy station is completely destroyed.

46

20th Bde retaliates on enemy trenches

37th Bde retaliates a bit.

31st Heavies were ranged on a battery in U 29 a.b. and gave it a good shelling
3 shots at Pont Rouge Bridge & then it got too dark to observe.

7.50 p. 10.a.40

16ᵗʰ Bde
    Aeroplane has two shots at Pont
Rouge then stopped owing to light —
Registration.

32ⁿᵈ Retaliated

29ᵗʰ fires at loopholes in farm

                    Owl
                    11-2-XV

14" Bde No shooting

32"d Bde Retaliation & on East of
Scimitar road trench by queues
of Infantry

31" Heavy nil

29" Bde Nil

37th mildly retaliated
Too thick for decent shooting

OM[?]

12.2.XV

14 Bde
Amelia hit Dartmouth on
right pier but result not
known

29. Nil

32 Retaliates + searches for
Little Willie in Donor valley

37th Retaliates at various
places —

OM[?]

13.2.XV

Aurelia' retaliated for
shelling of Hoplites
29th shelled hostile
trenches & caused a
good deal of movement
Howitzers retaliated

31st Heavens hit

3? retaliated & chased
little billie

OMK
14 2 xi

32nd Bde. Took on small guns nr BELLEVUE Fm also a house that infantry requested them

37th How. fired at digging party U 4 a N.E. also at a party in farm U 16 a (W) also at supposed battery U 33 d

14" Amelia got 2 hits out of 9 at Observing station in Frelinghein. also fired at Pont Rouge - rather bad

29th Nothing doing

[signature]
15.2.18

32nd Bde Searched for little Willie and Shot at house U16B North East where movement was seen.

29th Shot at German infantry near MILL HOUSE U14d

3)⁴ᵗʰ Shelled avenue trench

Amelia Shelled POINT ROUGE ? result

Archibald bagged an aeroplane which fell in enemies lines with a broken propeller - this is reported by Somersets & corroborated by Lt Cartland so I am informed -

16.9.W

Work done 17.2.1915

3 pm. AMELIA by way of retaliation for shelling LE TOUQUET road, fired 8 rounds at a factory S. of FRELINGHIEN bridge - 3 hits. This factory was lately put in a state of defence.

Five rounds were fired at working party in BIRDCAGE with effect. (1.2.5 RFA)

As retaliation for shelling of LE GHEER trenches were shelled.

An observing station in U 16 b was shelled from pt. 63. (32nd Brigade)

Heavies & Howitzers did not fire.

C.H.

9 pm

4 Div. Arty 19.2.15.

14th Brigade — Anzahia fired on pontoon bridge below FRELINGHIEN bridge.

29th Brigade — Fired at transport moving along road in U 24 d & flashes N 17 d of battery which shelled PLOEGSTEERT.

32nd Brigade — fired at hostile party near PETIT DOUVE.

Graham Coll.

~~4 Div Ary~~

38

6" Siege shelled artillery observing party near RED ESTAMINET. One of the few misses fell into a German trench and blew up some ammunition.
PRISCILLA retaliated on FRELINGHIEN for an indifferent attempt to shell the mountain battery section on our right.
A few retaliations on trenches by the 18pr batteries.

24.2.14

4 Div Arty 25.2.15

Little WILLIE has been very active today.
Heavies retaliated on WARNETON (50 Lyddite)
Batteries shelled in C 12 b d
        U 12 c N.W.
        C 17 a b
Various trenches and working parties shelled.
Wall destroyed near FRELINGHIEN PALACE.

DISTRIBUTION OF INFANTRY.

DISTRIBUTION - INFANTRY 4th DIVISION.

2 Coys ... in Le Bizet also 10 platoons Monmouths

	10th Brigade					11th Brigade				12th Brigade			
Dates Nights	DOUVE Trenches	ST YVES Trenches	POINT 63 Brig. Res.	LA CRECHE Div. Res.	NIEPPE (detached)	Trench line and LE GHEER	2nd line Breastworks & Houses	3rd line TOUQUET BERTHUNE Fm PLOEGSTEERT	4th line NIEPPE	Cross Roads Section	Centre Section	LE TOUQUET	LE BIZET
Feby. 1915													
31	R.I.F	R.D.F	V.R.War.R.	Sea.Highrs	7/R.Dub.F.	7/A+S.Hgrs	1 Co. L.R.B 2 " E.Lan. 1 " Hants 1 " R.B. 1 " S.L.I.	1 Co. L.R.B 1 " E.Lan. 1 " Hants 1 " R.B. 1 " S.L.I.	1 Co. L.R.B 1 " E.Lan. 1 " Hants 1 " R.B. 1 " S.L.I.	2 Cos Essex R.	6 Platoons Monmouths	Kings Own	Lan.F.
1/2	"	"	"	"	"	"				"	"	Lan. Fus.	Kings
2/3	"	"	"	"	"	"				"	"	"	"
3/4	"	"	"	"	"	"	Some distribution each night until huts in Wood are ready for occupation when THIRD LINE will be closed up.	1 Co. Nmths		"	"	"	"
4/5	"	"	"	"	"	"				"	"	"	"
5/6	R.I.F	R.Dub.F.	Sea.Hghrs	R.War.R.	"	"				"	"	Kings Own	Lan.
6/7	"	"	"	"	"	"				"	"	"	"
7/8	"	"	"	"	"	"				"	"	"	"
8/9	Sea.Hgrs	R.War.R.	R.Dub.F.	R.I.F.	"	"				"	"	Lan Fus	King
9/10	"	"	"	"	"	"				"	"	"	"
10/11	"	"	"	"	"	"				"	"	"	"
11/12	"	"	"	"	"	"				"	"	"	"
12/13	R.I.F.	R.Dub.F.	R.War.R.	Sea.Hghrs	"	"				"	"	Kings Own	Lan. F.
13/14	"	"	"	"	"	"				"	"	"	"
14/15	"	"	"	"	"	"				"	"	"	"
15/16	"	"	"	"	"	"				"	"	"	"
16/17	Sea.Hrs	R.War.R.	R.I.F.	R.Dub.Frs	"	"				"	"	Lan.Fus.	Kings C.
17/18	"	"	"	"	"	"				"	"	"	"
18/19	"	"	"	"	"	"				"	"	"	"
19/20	"	"	"	"	"	"				"	"	"	"
20/21	R.I.F.	R.Dub.F.	Sea.Hghrs	R.War.R	"	"				"	"	Kings Own	Lan. Fu.
21/22	"	"	"	"	"	"				"	"	"	"
22/23	"	"	"	"	"	"				"	"	"	"
23/24	"	"	"	"	"	"				"	"	"	"
24/25	Sea.Hrs	R.War.R.	R.Dub.F.	R.I.F.	"	"				"	"	Lan.Fus.	Kings C.
25/26	"	"	"	"	"	"				"	"	"	"
26/27	"	"	"	"	"	"				"	"	"	"
27/28	"	"	"	"	"	"				"	"	"	"
28/1	"	"	"	"	"	"				"	"	"	"

CASUALTIES.

4th DIVISION.
CASUALTIES--February 1915

Dates.	Offcrs. K.W.M.	Others. K.W.M.	Total. K.W.M.	Officers names.
1.	- 1 -	3-11 -	3 12 -	Capt. E.C. Hopkins, E.Lan.R.
2.		1 7 -	1 7 -	
3.		5 6 -	5 6 -	
4.	- 1 -	2 16 -	2 17 -	Capt. FH Hayes, Rif. Brig.
5.	- 1 -	1 5 -	1 6 -	2/Lt R.J.Woseley, E.Lan.R.
6.		11 -	- 11 -	
7.	- 1 -	3 8 -	3 9 -	2/Lt AM Blest Ess Regt.
8.	1 - -	1 8 -	2 8 -	Capt A.P.Knocker Hants R.
9		4 10 -	4 10 -	
10.	2 - -	2 7 -	4 7 -	2/Lt K.Forbes L.R.B. Lt PA Christie, Essex
11	1 - -	- 10 -	1 10 -	2/Lt EM Bent,6/R.B.(attd Som L.I.)
12.		5 7 -	5 7 -	
13.		1 8 -	1 8 -	
14		3 7 -	3 7 -	
15		3 7 -	3 7 -	
16		4 10 -	4 10--	
17.		1 17 -	1 17 -	
18.		5 10 -	5 10 -	
19.	- 3 -	2 11 -	2 14 -	(2/Lt GH Nelson,14/FAB,2/Lt Alcock,LRB, (Lt CER Bridgson, King's Own.
20.		4 27 -	4 27 -	
21		1 12 -	1 12 -	
22		7 7 -	7 7 -	
23		2 9 -	2 9 -	
24		1 10 -	1 10 -	
25		1 14 -	1 14 -	
26	- 1 -	3 13 -	3 14 -	2/Lt J.M.Round, 2/Essex.
27	- 2 -	2 11 1	2 13 1	Capt Williams Freeman,R.War R., Capt Watkins Essex R.
28	- 1 -	1 10 -	1 11 -	2/Lt Fursdon L.R.Brig.
	4.11.0	68 289 1.	72 300 1.	

CANADIANS.
(Attached 22/2/15 to 1/3/15)

1 Officer and 2 other ranks--Killed Lt DP Bell Irvine.

    10 other ranks wounded.

Major G.S.
4th Division.

CORRESPONDENCE.

CORRESPONDENCE ON THE FOLLOWING SUBJECTS WILL BE FOUND IN BOX MARKED "4th DIVISION - CORRESPONDENCE."

CANADIAN DIVISION

NORTH MIDLAND DIVISION

ANTI-AIRCRAFT

ARTILLERY

SUPPORTING LINES

OFFENSIVE ACTION

MINES

SAPPING AND MINING

PRESS CORRESPONDENTS

TRICKING ENEMY - Devices for

TRENCH MORTARS

VERMELLES - Trip to

TRENCHES - Strengthening of

ARMISTICE - Informal

MACHINE GUNS

BRIGADE ENGINEER

WEEKLY REPORTS ON WORK CARRIED OUT

GRENADES

PERISCOPES

DEFENCE SCHEME

RANGE FINDERS

PRISONERS

COUNTER ATTACKS

RELIEF OF 5th & 6th DIVISIONS

EMPLOYMENT OF R.E.

ARMOURED MOTOR CARS

LEAKAGE OF INFORMATION

ST. ELOI - Increase of Troops.

1. The ~~British Expeditionary~~ Force has now resumed offensive ~~operations,~~ after a long period ~~during which such~~ attacks as were undertaken were purely local in character. The Field-Marshal Commanding-in-Chief desires to impress upon all officers certain points which he regards as essential to success in attack.

2. The necessity for careful preparation and the general lines which such preparation should follow appear to be well understood. It is now however always understood that in trench warfare the first infantry attack takes the form of what our regulations call the final assault in a battle. Such an assault must be made in adequate strength, and be carried out simultaneously by all who are to take part in it. There is no object in forming troops in depth with a comparatively weak firing line, since this procedure has for its object the building up of a firing line for the purpose of assault. Under existing conditions this building can be carried out before the attack begins.

3. Depth of formation is still required, but not for the purpose of reinforcing the firing line. The objective of the assault can usually be determined with sufficient accuracy before the attack is launched. When this objective is reached the energy of the assaulting troops must be exhausted to some extent. To follow up the initial success a second assault is necessary, and this assault also must have a definite objective and be pushed on to it through the first assaulting party. Merely reinforcing the troops in the front line is not sufficient to carry them forward, as the difficulties of organising a further advance after the confusion of an assault and under heavy fire are usually insuperable.

4. The attack is completed by successive assaulting parties, each with a definite objective, until the enemy's various lines of defence are finally broken. Each assaulting party on gaining its objective must secure itself there in order to form an adequate support to the next party which will pass through it and to guard against counter attack.

5. It must be clearly understood that it is the first duty of everyone to push on until the allotted objective is reached. Opportunities have been missed in the past owing to officers waiting for orders, and to formations waiting on each other to gain ground. In the attack, enterprise and initiative are essential and the one inexcusable fault is inaction. Cases have occurred of officers refusing to advance when asked to do so by units on their flanks because they have not received specific orders to do so from their immediate superiors. Every delay gives the enemy time to strengthen himself, and makes ultimate success more costly and difficult. There should, therefore, be no hesitation in putting in reserves to confirm and extend success.

6. The complicated modern system of communication sometimes leaves commanders completely at a loss when it fails. It must be recognised that telephone and telegraph wires are almost certain to fail during a successful advance. The means which existed before the introduction of wires still exist, and every possible effort must be made by all leaders to retain control of their troops by such means.

7.

P.T.O.

7. Experience shows that the enemy is very skilful in bringing up machine guns rapidly, and that he frequently makes use of buildings in which to employ them. Successful attacks have frequently been held up for some time by one or two machine guns so placed. Methods of dealing with these must be thought out beforehand, and form part of every plan of attack. In close country pack artillery may be usefully employed for this purpose.

              (Sd.) W.R. ROBERTSON, Lt-Gen.

Gen. staff, G.H.Q.
British Army in the Field.   Chief of the General Staff.
Operations Section.
No. O.A.042
14/3/15.

Index

SUBJECT.

H.S. /5G

No.	Contents.	Date.

Index

SUBJECT.

III. Corps.
Second Army.

Contents.	Date.

WAR DIARY

GENERAL STAFF

4 th DIVISION

MARCH 1915.

APPENDICES

OPERATION ORDERS.

ARTILLERY REPORTS

PROGRESS REPORTS

Maps.

Summary of Information

Note: The messages mentioned in the diary will be found in a separate box marked "messages"

War Diary

March 1915

W A R   D I A R Y
1st March 1915.

NIEPPE.

Fine day until 3-30 pm when snow fell, followed by rain. Slight frsot during night.

4-25 am.	Quiet night reports forwarded to 3/Corps and exchanged with 5/6th Divisions. (H/30,BM/16,BM/1,G/155,G/238,G/87,GG/212)	
9-40 am.	Air report 7-50 to 8-15 am. Area Wez Macquart - Messines clear of movement.	IG/243
11-30 am.	Acknowledges receipt to 3/Corps of G/842/1.	G/239
12-20 pm.	Aerial observer reports that yesterday 50 or 60 trains were observed at Menin direction uncertain.	IG/1.
2-0 pm.	A woman-name unknown- reported to have crossed British lines in South-- possibly at Armentieres.	IG/2.
7-55 pm.	Evening report,,Right sector situation unchanged, little shelling. Enemy improving trenches N.W. corner Le Touquet village, Centre Sector received 40 shell and Left Sector very few, but rather more sniping. (G/7, G/245,BM/18, BM/24,H/32)	
8-15 pm.	5th Div report quiet day.	G/175
8-20 pm.	6/Div report fair amount of shelling	G/104.
11-5 pm.	Acknowledges receipt to 3/Corps of Secret G/71--Registration of Targets.)	

War Diary, Gen.Staff, 4th Division.
2nd March, 1915.

NIEPPE.   Fine day.

4.45 am   Quiet night reports as usual.
           (H39/10, BM26/11, J1/12, G10, G189/5, G109/6, GG1).

1.30 pm   Aircraft report - neighbourhood of MESSINES clear of   IG249
           movement at 10.30 am.

4.35 pm   Aircraft report - no movement for one mile behind   IG250
           enemy's lines between WEZ MACQUART and MESSINES.

6.46 pm   Quiet day reported by 5th Div.   G229/5

7.20 pm   Receipt to 3rd A.C. for their G104/1. (Registration   GG9
           of Artillery).

7.35 pm   Evening reports. Enemy very active with rifle grenades
           at Railway barricade and also against left section of
           Right Sector. About 45 shells into Left Sector. Our
           Arty. fired with effect against enemy's trenches,
           opposite Right Sector.
           (GG10, H50/10, BM38/11, BM31/12.)

8.5 pm   Evening report from 6th Div.   G119/6

10.5 pm   Secret message from 3rd A.C. G104/1 re move of 6 inch   GG11
           Hows. received and acknowledged.

WAR DIARY

3rd March 1915.

NIEPPE.

Dull day, rained most of morning and a little in afternoon.

4-45 am — Quiet night reports as usual (BM/34, H/52, BM/46, GG/12, G/742, G/129, GG/13.)

10-15 am — 12/Brig report Arty inform them that Amelia will be freely used today. They think this may cause retaliation which would affect operations in hand from Barricade to Sniper's House.   BM/40

10-16 am — 6th Siege Battery ordered to proceed under cover of darkness via Armentieres - Erquinghem and Bac St Maur to join 8/Div at Estaires tonight, and the 4/Siege Battery to move under similar arrangements tomorrow night.
    Eight 5" hows from North Midland Div (T) expected at Bailleul today and will be attached to 4/Div
    3/Corps asked to send an officer from each of the 2 North Midland Divs Howr Batteries by 8 am tomorrow, in order to take over details of zones, registered points, etc., before the departure of 4/Siege ~~Arty~~ Batty.--
--Reply from 3/Corps states that these officers will be sent. (G/104/3 & 4, BBM/24, G/16, BBM/22, GG/16, G/104/5,8,9, GG/21,24)

2-30 pm — G.O.C. held conference at 4Div H.Q. with 6/Div, 12 and 18th Inf Brigs Staffs on subject of Le Touquet & Frelinghien combined operations.

6-? pm. — 5/Div report all quiet.   G/259

7-40 pm. — Evening report - Heavy shelling by light guns, especially in Left Sector, where 150 were received; also 30 Black Maria's at Le Gheer. Sniping in front of Railway Barricade in Right Sector heavier than usual.   G/17, H/59, BM/55, BM/47

9-40 pm. — Evening report from 6/Div giving account of their Arty shoot today.   G/141, G/124/1

    The following attachments are to take place from North Midland Division for purposes of instruction:-

4th to ~~11~~ 2nd th March.
H.Q. of One Inf Brig.
One Inf Brig.
One Coy R.E.
Personnel of one F.A.B.

~~12~~ 16th to ~~19~~ 21st March

As above, with addition of
   Battery Staff of Heavy Battery.

War Diary, Gen.Staff, 4th Division.
4th March, 1915.

NIEPPE.	Fine day - much warmer but little sunshine.	
4.45 am	Quiet night reports as usual. (H63/10, BM64/11, J1/12, G18, G724/5, G142/6, G19).	
6.45 pm	3rd A.C. order the evening report to be forwarded so as to reach them by 7.30 pm. Inf.Brigs. and Div.Arty. informed that their reports should reach Div.H.Q. by 6.30 pm.	G133 GG29 GG28
7.10 pm	Receipt to 3rd A.C. for their G.130 (4.5" How.Amm.) and G131 (Reconnaissance of roads for M.T.)	GG30
7.15 pm	5th Div. report all quiet.	G311
7.50 pm	Evening report - heavy sniping round Railway barricade in Right Sector. Less shelling than yesterday. Centre Sector received about 11 shells from trench mortar or similar gun. (GG31, BM75/10, H72/10, J13/12.)	
8.20 pm	Evening report from 6th Div.	G154/6
9.10 pm	Receipt to 3rd A.C. for their secret No.G132 (Anti-aircraft movements).	GG32

WAR DIARY
5th March 1915.

NIEPPE.

Warm day but little sunshine.

4-45 am.	Quiet night reports as usual.(BM/78,H/80,BM/74,G/22,G/331,GG/23,	
		G/159)
9-25 am.	3/Corps require evening report by 7-15 pm.--Ack'd.	G/138,G/24
6-47 pm	Evening report--Increased shelling against right & Centre Sectors, and more sniping than usual against Right Sector.(G/27, H/7, BM/81, BM/91)	
6-55 pm.	5/Div report all quiet.	G/373.
7-30 pm.	6th Div--Evening report.	G/171.
	12/Brig report--	
9-35 pm.	German fatigue party observed composed of very big men who were wearing very clean or new uniforms.	J/16.

WAR DIARY
6th March 1915.

__NIEPPE.__

   Fine morning, but changed about noon, and was very wet and windy for rest of day.

4-45 am.	Quiet night reports as usual (BM/82, J/17, H/11, G/28, G/383, G/29)	
12-36 pm 1-0 pm.	3/Corps ask for sketch map, showing positions of artillery, to be forwarded at once. --Map despatched.--	G/158 BBM/57
6-55 pm.	All quiet reported by 5/Division.	G/405
7-5 pm.	Evening report - Enemy's light guns very active today. They also put ten Black Maria's into Le Bizet. Sounds of motor engine, or electric motor, heard last night and this morning by Hamps Regt. but ~~sound~~ direction of sound could not be definitely located.	G/31 BM/104 BM/89 H/25.
7-25 pm.	6/Div report a quiet day.	G/186
8-25 pm.	3/Corps inform us that the bombardment of the enemy's trenches in neighbourhood of St Eloi was successful, judging from the cries of distress heard issuing from Germans advanced trenches.	G/163
10-10 pm.	Message from 3/Corps saying that despatch rider is leaving with urgent and secret memo. No/166, This was received and acknowledged at 10-37 pm.- subject- Demarkation by Artillery and Infantry on our left.	G/167 G/32.

W A R   D I A R Y
7th March, 1915.

NIEPPE.

Wet day with short intervals of bright sunshine between noon and 4 pm.---Cold during the night.

4-40 am. Quiet night reports as usual(H/29,BM/91,BM/105,G/33,G/738,G/190,GG28

10-30 am G/61/21 re move of North Midland Division received and acknowledged. (Secret)
3/Corps asked if the move included the 5" howrs,belonging to that Div.? They replied that the howrs would remain with us and that only the party under instruction was affected. --Further instructions concerning return of North Midland Div received at 5 pm. GG/30 GG/33 G/61/24 GG/35.

12-50 pm. Brigs informed that Arty shoot would commence at 3-30 pm.   GG/34

3-15 pm. 12/Brig report that they do not think the rumours of mining near Railway Barricade are based on anything very definite or reliable.   BM/119.

In accordance with 3rd A.C. G/167 demonstration of Artillery and Infantry fire (5" howrs, 32/F.A.B. 10/Inf Brig) against trenches opposite 10/Brig took place at 3-30 pm.

6-0 pm. Asks 3rd Corps to wire instructions re broken down lorry of 4/Siege Batty.

7-) pm. Evening report--Very quiet all round.--Our bombardment of enemy's trenches reported to be very accurate.(G/35,H/50,BM/13,BM/12 126

7-0 pm. 5th Division report all quiet.   G/437

7-20 pm. 6/Div report quiet day.   G/199

7-30 pm. 10th and 12th told to send evening reports "priority" in order to ensure their arrival before 6-30 pm.   G/36

7-30 pm. 3rd Corps asked if we can have ammunition detailed for tomorrow. They replied--On the same scale as in GHQ/OAW/74 ---Div Arty informed.   G/37 G/176

10-20 pm. 10th Brigade ask if Div Arty shoot is being continued tomorrow and if so at what hour.--Replied Yes! but that definite orders would be sent tomorrow.--GOC congratulates 10th Brigade on excellent co-operation of musketry fire.   H/59 GG/38.

War Diary - 8th March 1915.

NIEPPE.

	Fine day - rather cold and windy.	
2-10 am	5th Div. report reliefs completed.	G.740
4-30 am	Quiet night reports as usual.	
	(H.61, BM.22, J.54, G.38, G.453, G.204, G.39)	
10-54 am	Inf. Brigs. informed that artillery would commence shooting at 4-30 pm.	GG.40 G.43
12-20 pm	5th Div. open a report centre at 2 pm this afternoon at A La Campagne Estaminet on Neuve Eglise - Dranoutre road.	G.463
2-30 pm	Field Marshal C-in-C visited Div. H.Q. and saw Div. Commander and Brigadiers.	G.178 GG.39
3-35 pm	Receipt to 3rd Corps for their G.182 (Sapping).	G.45
4-30 pm	Demonstration of artillery and infantry which was commenced yesterday was resumed this afternoon at 4-30 pm having for target enemy's trenches slightly West of those bombarded yesterday.	
6-55 pm	Evening report - Centre and Left Sectors received 12 and 24 shells respectively. Small working party observed near Messines wearing grey coats and red caps. Our artillery obtained 4 direct hits on Frelinghien Church tower, knocking away a large portion of the turret containing staircase.	
	(G.46, BM.30, BM.138, BM.139, SC.22)	
6-55 pm	5th Div. report all quiet along their front.	G.489
7-40 pm	6th Div. report all quiet.	G.210
10-35 pm	10th Brig. report that East Surrey Regt. now occupy trenches on their left.	H.72

WAR DIARY
9th Mar. 1915.

Fine dry, cold day, snowed slightly in evening.

4-30 am	Quiet night reports as usual.(H/75,BM/36,BM/145,G/48,G/756,G/213, (G/49.)	
12-35 pm	Aircraft report no movements observed.	IG/262
1-50 pm.	Div Arty report that 32ns FAB will, in accordance with instructions, bombard German trenches from Red Estaminet westward to La Douve Farme. 10/Brig were informed and told to co-operate with infantry fire. (BM/105,GG/44)	
3-0 pm.	10/Brig report curious trail of light observed at 4-15 am from various parts of the trenches, moving in a southerly direction.	G/52
6-0 pm.	Operation Order No 44 received from 3/Corps and acknow'd.	G/54
7-0 pm.	Evening report--Right Sector fairly heavily shelled and Ploegsteert wood shelled intermittently. Our Arty shelled German working party and Heavies registered another hit on Frelinghien Church Tower.	GG/45 BM/155 BM/51 SC/32
6-45 pm.	5/Div report all quiet.	G/515.
7-45 pm.	Inf Brigs and Div Arty told to report every two hours commencing at 7 am tomorrow.(GG/46,BM/658,BM/54, SC/34,BBM/114)	
8-30 pm.	6/Div report all quiet.	G/227
9-0 pm.	Operation Order No.22 received from 6/Div. Acknowledged and 6/Div informed that we were not issuing any Op.Orders.	GG/48

G.O.C. 3rd Corps gave verbal instructions for great activity to be shewn in pushing forward saps whereever possible. These saps not necessarily to be concealed ones as they are ordered with the deliberate intention of drawing the enemy's fire and of holding his reserves here, by threat of attack. Whatever can be done is to be calculated so as to be for future use. Above communicated by G.O.C' to Inf Brigs verbally. Div Arty instructed to fire daily the whole of their ammunition allowance, finishing it up in the evening by a deliberate pounding of some selected trench. Div Arty instructed that FAB Commanders should inform Infantry of the object selected, so that they may seize any opportunity offered by a good target.

WAR DIARY.
10th March 1915.

Fine day. Warmer than usual.

4-50 am.	Quiet night reports as usual.(H/90,BM/60,G/57,G/762,G/235,GG/50
8-53 am.	The two hourly reports ordered yesterday are to be as full as possible and should include shell and rifle fire received and delivered. Brigs and Arty informed. GG/51
10-20 am.	Message from 3rd Corps states that 8th Division and Meerut Div captured first line of German trenches at 8-20 am this morning. Units informed. G/214 G/61
10-40 am.	Copy of message sent by 3/Corps to 2nd Army re situation in 6th Division. G/215
11-10 am.	5/Div report enemy shelling Neuve Eglise.
11-42 am.	Air report-observation difficult- no movement observed. IG/265
11-50 am.	3/Corps report good progress of attacks by 8th Div in neighborhood of Neuve Chapelle. Repeated to Units. G/218 GG/54
12-50 pm.	Corps Commander wishes to see Div Commdr. at Corps HQ at 3 pm.--Acknowledged. G/220 G/66
1-0 pm.	Troops not on duty were ordered to remain in billets. GG/55
2-10 pm.	5th Div say their telephone wires in neighbourhood of Le Rossignol were cut and ask if they may send a patrol there nightly. We replied that our wires were also cut and that we were sending a patrol. G/768 GG/58
4-22 pm.	Two hourly reports not required after 9-30pm. Inf Brigs and D.Arty informed. G/224 GG/60

4-30 pm.	In order to carry out our role of keeping the enemy's reserves from being moved South, Arty and rifle fire attacks were made at 4-30pm.
	    Objectives:-Southern Group--18 pdrs-Pont Rouge Houses
	                                 5" Howrs.-Factory.
	          Centre Group.-- U/22/(a)
	          Northern Group-- Red Estaminet to La Douve Farme.
	The 11/Brig received orders to seize and place in a state of defence a burnt farm, lying between lines and our own in U/28 (a), and to run a communication trench up to this. The object being to break out saps North and South from this farm parallel to our own and thus to advance our first line in this place (South of Le Gheer) some 150 yds. (Refce 3/Corps G/205 of 9/3/15, GGG/106/2, Conference of Div (Commdes. with GOC 3/Corps.)

4-30 pm.	3/Corps report that opposite Givenchy 2nd Div captured a line of German trenches early this morning. A German counter-attack regained those trenches East and South of the village, but enemy was repulsed to the North of the village. 8th Div. reported to be doing well at Neuve Chapelle, which place they have captured. Circulated. G.225 G.68
6-24 pm	6th Div. report situation normal. G.260
6-46 pm	Prisoner taken last night says that Bavarian Corps extends as far South as the Douve. IG.269
6-59 pm	5th Div. report all quiet. G.776

6-55 pm   Report to 5th and 6th Divs. that all is quiet.   GG.64

8-40 pm   Report of good progress at Neuve Chapelle. Many
          prisoners taken.   (G.235, GG.67, G.239, GG.68)

11-35 pm 3rd Corps approved of proposal contained in our
          G.106/2 re taking of burnt-out farm.   G.242

11-50 pm 11th Brig. report that burnt-out farm 200 yards East
          of Convent occupied put in a state of defence and
          communication trench dug. Enemy took no notice.   BM.102

          Attached - Summary of two-hourly reports.

War Diary - 11th March 1915.

NIEPPE.

	Misty until about 11 am - then fine for rest of day.	
4-45 am	Night reports - All quiet excepting for half an hours shooting against left of Left Sector.	
	3rd Corps, 5th and 6th Divs. informed of the occupation by 11th Brig of burnt-out farm 200 yards East of Convent in Centre Sector which was reported late last night.	
	(BM.104, J.87, H.115, G.623, G.75, G.76, G.273)	
8-2 am	3rd Corps report total prisoners captured by 1st Army yesterday as 692. Circulated.	G.244 GG.70
8-25 am	Two hourly reports to be continued to day.	G.245
12-54 pm	Receipt to 3rd Corps for their G.247 (Secret - re Anti-Aircraft Section)	G.83
3-30 pm	News of sinking of German submarine U.12 by destroyer Ariel received and circulated.	G.260
7-8 pm	5th Div. report all quiet.	G.896
7-25 pm	Experiments were made by 12th Brig. with netting to catch rifle grenades, but report states that they did prove successful.	BM.199
7-50 pm	5th and 6th Divs. informed that we had nothing to report.	GG.75
9-58 pm	As yesterday the two hourly reports were not required by 3rd Corps after 9-30 pm. Inf.Brigs. and D.A. informed.	G.272 GG.76
8-15 pm	6th Div. report situation normal.	G.395
9-15 pm	Receipt to 3rd Corps for their Secret No. G.270 (2nd Corps movements) and G.924 (Artillery co-operation with 2nd Corps).	GG.77

Attached - Summary of to-days two hourly reports.

WAR DIARY
12/3/15

NIEPPE.

Misty until noon. Close warm day.

4-0 am.	3/Corps report that 6/Div have captured L'Epinette and that position is being consolidated.	G/279
4-20 am.	Night reports from Inf. Brigs. Enemy putting up wire in front of Monmouths and E.Lancs.- Passed to 3/Corps.	H/137 (BM/206,BM (G/91. 126
5-20 am.	6/Div report that all is well.	G/407
6-25 am	5/Div report all quiet.	G/804
7-45 am.	3rd Corps message says that 3/Div operations are postponed and that hour of commencement will be notified.	G/283.
7-45 am	5th and 6th Divs told that all was quiet on our front.	G/92
8-58 am	Prisoner taken at Neuve Chapelle states that the only troops at Lille were Landsturm.	IC/272
10-25 am	Details of 1/Army progress received from 3/Corps. Repeated to all units.	G/286,GG/80
11-30 am.	Details of attack made last night by 6/Div.	G/287
2-5 pm.	Further details of 1st Army progress-circulated.	(G/290-293-297
3-17 pm.	Message from 3/Corps says that there is strong evidence that 3/Corps front is being depleted to provide reserves against our 1st Army, and that enemy should therefore be made to hold enemy to his positions.	G/294
5-40 pm.	Orders issued that no trees or hedges had to be cut except in Ploegsteert wood, several good Arty positions, having been rendered useless owing to indiscriminate cutting and lopping.	GG/85
7-25 pm.	5/Div report all quiet.	G/737
7-45 pm.	5th and 6th Div informed that all is quiet.	G/95
9-50 pm.	Two hourly reports need not be rendered between 9 pm. and 7 am.	G/97
10-50 pm.	3/Corps report that 6th Div could hear heavy transport East at 9.pm.-direct Frelinghien.	IG/1281

Attached.- Summary of two hourly reports of 4th and 6th Divs.

Summary of Operations regarding First Army Operations.

NIEPPE

W A R D I A R Y
13th March 1915.

Fine, clear day.

4-30 am	Night reports.--All quiet excepting for a few shell fired at Douve trenches. (BM/222,BM/155,H/162,GG/88,G/846,G/98)	
9-6 am.	3rd Corps orders reports every four, instead of every two hours, unless anything of special importance occurs. Infantry Brigs and Div Arty informed.--	G/99 G/307
10-5 am.	A patrol from 6/Div discovered last night a dummy in front of German trenches which exploded on being pulled.	IG/285
10-45 am	6/Div report on exploits of bombing party.	G/458
11-0 am.	Modification of order confining troops to billets issued.	G/100
2-5 p m.	Air report 11-55 am to 12-5 pm.--No movement observed, observation difficult.	IG/287
7-2 pm.	5/Div report all quiet.	G/775
7-15 pm.	Secret memo G/320 re moves of 10th and 11th Brigs received and acknowledged.	GG/94
8-30 pm.	Inf Brigs and Div Arty informed that four hourly reports would not be required between 9 pm and 9 am.	GG/95
11/pm	5th Div asks re Southern limit of line to be taken over by him. We replied that fresh instructions were expected.	GG/94 G/106

Gen Lynden Bell GSO 3rd Corps came down at 4 pm and warned us that we might have to pull out 2 Brigs of Infantry, destination unknown.

A confirmatory telephone message to this effect was received at about 5-30 pm., and at the same moment the Brig.Gen.Comdg. 84th Inf Brig. designed to relieve 10th Brig and two Div. Staff Officers from 5/Div arrived to arrange details.

The remainder of the arrangements of the move are contained in the following papers and telegrams. G/320/3Corps, G/325, Secret 3rd Corps, GGG/110, GG/97, G/329/3Corps,and Operation Order No 42 of 5/Div attached.

Attached:- Summary of 4 hourly reports.

WAR DIARY
14th March 1915.

DIEPPE.

Fine day.

4-30 a.m. Night reports. A good deal of sniping from Avenue, otherwise all quiet. (H/188, BM/170, J/127, G/108,)

7-0 am. Nothing to report messages exchanged, with 5th and 6th G108-482 Divs. and 884.

7-30 am. Operation Order No 42 received from 5/Div. GG/98

8-15 am. 6/Div suggest that with reference to 3rd Corps G/325 G/483 (see Diary for 13th March) arrangements should be made G/109 direct between 10th and 18th Brigs and that they were G/486 sending a Staff Officer this morning to discuss matters.

9-30 am. 12/Brig told that as now arranged, front of their Brigade would not be extended beyond the Warnave, when new front is taken up. G/110.

11-25 am. 5/Div inform us that Officers of 83rd Brigs will visit trenches of 11/Brig this afternoon to reconnoitre before G/902 taking over tomorrow night. They were told that 3 pm GG/101 would be as a suitable hour, but that some of the trenches GG/104 could only be seen at night. BM/178

11-31 am. 3/Corps message says that despatch rider has just left GG/103 with Operation Orders. Recd. at 11-45 am and acknowledged. GG/337

11-45 am 10/Brig told that they would have to take over as far South as Armentieres - Lille railway on night of 16/17th G/111

12-13 pm. Air report 10-30 to 11-15 am -- No movement of enemy observed, but observation difficult owing to low clouds. IG/289

1-40 pm. 6/Div informed that the taking over of part of their line would be done on night of 16/17th by 10/Brig, and it would afterwards be divided between 10th and 11th Brigs. G/113.

1-40 pm. 3/Corps message says that four hourly progress reports are not required until further orders. Morning and evening G/343 reports to be rendered as usual. Inf Brigs and Div Arty G/114 informed.

There was nothing to report this morning at 9 am & 1 pm. at which time reports were due.

1-44 pm. 3/Corps report that they have been notified that steel bridge on Armentieres road is practically completed G/244 and ask if there is any objection to wooden bridge being removed. They were informed that the wooden bridge had been GG/106 dismantled.

3-0 pm. Arty arrangements in connection with change of front received from 3/Corps in brief. Further details to follow. G/345

3-0 pm. 4/Div Op Order No 20 issued.

4-13 pm. Secret No G/32/32 received from 6/Div & acknowledged. G/116

4-30 pm. 6/Div message amending G/32/32 received. G/499

6-30 pm. Message from 3/Corps cancels all reliefs that were to take place tonight, owing to attack now in progress against the 27th Div. Shortly afterwards orders were G/348 received by telephone that reliefs were only postponed till further orders. GG/107

6-35 pm. Units concerned were informed and told to "Stand Fast" & 108.

6-50 pm. Evening report -- Some shelling by Little Willie. Sniping more active against Centre Sector. Some good shooting by our 29th FAB. (G/118, BM/192, BM/248, BBM/218,)

7-0 pm. 11/Brig report that at 5-45 pm, Germans sent up a red rocket from the Birdcage, which fell in their communication trench behind. BM/195

7-0 pm. 6/Div evening report received. G/506

8-10 pm. In continuation of G/325 received at 2 pm. 3/Corps forward details regarding Arty moves, command, etc. (Secret) 3/A.C/G/325/2. -- Acknowledged. G/119

8-18 pm. 5/Div report all quiet. G/823

8-30 pm. 10th 11th and 84th Brigs acknowledge receipt of GG/107, and 10/Brig report that Dub Fus and half of BM/471 Argyll and Suthd Highrs are in Armentieres, but War Regt. BM/196 not yet relieved. H/205

WAR DIARY--14th Mar. continued.

8-30 pm	84th Brig message says that 13th Fd Ambce is due to take over from 10th Fd Ambce at 11 am tomorrow.	BM/481
8-30 pm	84th Brig report that War Regt. will not be relieved tonight.	BM/429
8-35 pm.	3rd Corps report all reliefs definitely cancelled for tonight.--Acknowledged.-- All concerned informed and 10th Brig warned to be prepared to march back to old billets.	G/354 GG/109 G/120 G/121
8-53 pm.	84th Brig asked to inform us immediately they had orders to return to Bailleul, suggesting meanwhile that everything stands fast.	GG/108
9-48 pm.	Acknowledgement from 84th Brig for GG/108.	BM/497
11-49 pm.	10/Brig acknowledge G/120.	H/217

In consequence of the attack on the 27th Div, mentioned above, and the subsequent postponement of all reliefs, the situation for the night was as below:-

SITUATION IN 10th BRIG AREA.

At 5-30 pm, 10th Brig handed over command of their area to 84th Inf Brig (5th Div) who were to relieve trenches that night.
½ of 7th Argyll & Sutherland Highrs moved to Armentieres before 3 pm.
Dub Fus moved to Armentieres before 3 pm.
R.Ir.Fus remained at La Creche.
Warwicks, Seaforths and ½ Arg. & Suthd Highrs remained in trenches.
4 battalions of 84th Brig had come up during afternoon from Bailleul, and then stood fast for the night about Romarin, 63 huts and North Ploegsteert on the orders for reliefs being ordered to be held in abeyance.
R.A., R.E. and 10th Fd Ambce stood fast.
11th Brig reorganization having been cancelled in view of relief by 83rd Brig (5th Div) ordered for night 15/16th.- No movement took place.
The Lon Rif Brig are still entirely out of trenches and distributed 3 Coys in Plegsteert and 1 Coy in Pont de Nieppe.

Attached--Copy of Orders for handing over stores.etc. GGG/110.

War Diary - 15th March 1915.

NIEPPE.

Fine day.

Time	Entry	Ref
4-30 am	Quiet night reports. (BM.1, G.124, BM.255, G.016, G.517, G.125)	
9-50 am	84th Brig. asked to give the position of the transport of their 4 battalions.	GG.110
10-38 am	Reply from 84th Brig. re position of transport.	SC.532
9-50 am	3rd Corps direct that any sign of increased activity is to be at once reported. Inf. Brigs. & D.A. informed.	G.374 GG.111
1-5 pm	11th Brig. report that artillery observer has reported that a 60 foot crane can be seen near Halte U.17.c. D.A. informed.	BM.5
1-40 pm	Corps Commander informs us that he will visit our H.Q. at 3-30 pm to-day and wishes to see B.G.C. R.A. D.A. informed.	G.376
3-10 pm	3rd Corps require information to identify German units in front of 2nd Army. Brigs. informed.	IG.296 GG.113
4-20 pm	3rd Corps inform us that dividing line between 2nd and 3rd Corps will be the Ploegsteert - Le Gheer road.	G.381
4-30 pm	Brigs. informed that they were to be prepared to carry out reliefs cancelled yesterday. Definite orders would be sent as soon as received.	G.126
5 pm	3rd Corps secret No. G.382 received and acknowledged. (Subject - reliefs)	G.128
5-8 pm	84th and 10th Brigs. told that definite orders for relief of 10th by 84th Brig. were received.	G.127
6-5 pm	Certain artillery movements sanctioned by Corps Commdr.	G.386
5-45 pm	11th and 12th Brigs. informed of orders for relief of 10th Brig. In event of relief of 11th Brig. being ordered, E.Lanc.R. were ordered to remain in their trenches holding as far north as Le Gheer cross roads.	G.129 BM.14 BM.270
6-30 pm	84th Brig. reported that only one battalion was not going into trenches and this would be in reserve.	BM.557
7 pm	Evening report - Little Willie fairly active. Some Black Marias at the Le Bizet. Increased sniping in front of Centre Sector. (GG.114, BM.13, BM.268, BBM.228)	
7-10 pm	6th Div. report no change.	G.541
7-10 pm	5th Div. report all quiet.	G.895
8-10 pm	3rd Corps ask when, if ever, any 18 pr guns have been captured from our Division as some British 18 prs are being used against 1st Army. Replied that 2 guns of 27th Batty were abandoned at Ligny-en-Cambressis on 25th August 1914.	G.391 GG.116
9-45 pm	6th Div. ask with reference to 3rd Corps secret G.325/3 (referred to in Diary of 13th inst) when reliefs of 18th and portion of 17th Brigs. would take place. We replied "On same nights as in para A of 3rd Corps memo under reference".	G.550 GG.117
9-55 pm	10th Brig. told to take over 1 officer and 55 other ranks of Sherwood Foresters and 54 Durhams now employed on special duty when they relieved 18th Brig.	G.130
10 pm	4th Div. Operation Order No. 21 issued.	
10-42 pm	6th Div. secret G.32/34 received and acknowledged.	GG.118
10-42 pm	3rd Corps report that 4-7 Battery lately sent to 2nd Corps is returning. D.A. informed.	G.401
11 pm	Message from 3rd Corps that two Colonels and their Adjutants, now attached to 2nd Corps for instruction in Heavy Arty., will be transferred to 4th Div. Date to be notified later.	G.405
11-55 pm	3rd Corps secret memo G.398 on ammunition economy received and acknowledged.	GG.120

WAR DIARY.
16th March 1915.

NIEPPE.

Fine day.

3-45 am.	84th Brigade report that the relief of 3 battalions of 10th Brigade completed. Reported to 3rd Corps.	BM/591 GG/121
4-30 am.	Quiet Night reports (BM/22,BM/250,G/122,G/94,G/557,GG/123)	
9-22 am.	3rd Corps inform us that the 4-7 battery from 2nd Corps is being sent to Armentieres after dark tonight. D.Arty informed.	G/411
10-0 am.	GSO 3, visited trenches that were being taken over from 17th Brig. (G/556, GG/124, G/561.)	
10-47 am.	3rd Corps report that owing to instructions from 2nd Army the 9-2 howitzer which was returning from 1st Corps would not proceed beyond Bailleul, until further orders.	G/415.
10-47 am.	3rd Corps report that with reference to their G/405 of yesterday, the officers to be attached would join today.	G/416
11-45 am.	Message No.G401 of 16th from 3/Corps repeated to 6/Div (subject--return of 4-7 battery of 28th (H) Brig) as we do not take over Arty control of Armentieres until tomorrow night.	G/132.
12-30 pm.	Under instructions from 2nd Army 3rd Corps suspend all reliefs for the present. All concerned informed.	G/420 GG/127 G/135.
1-24 pm.	3rd Corps order Arty of 3rd Cav Div and the F.ARB. & Heavy Battery of North Mid Div. to return to their respective Divisions.--D.Arty informed.	G/425
1-52 pm.	News of sinking of "Dresden" received & circulated.(G/426,GG/129)	
2-20 pm.	12th Brig acknowledge our Secret G/136, despatched at 1-0 pm. (Subject:-)	G/151
4-56 pm.	Message from 3rd Corps cancels readjustment of line ordered in G/325. Troops to return to their original fronts by night of 17th. 84th Brig placed under orders of 4th Div until relief by 10th Brig is completed.--GG/140,BM/34 All concerned informed.(BBM/242,BM/294,BM/613,)	GG/142 G/430 G/970
6-44 pm.	Evening report Little Willie again active. 24 Black Maria's in Right Sector. Our Arty shelled two working parties. (BM/36, J/153.)	GG/143, BBM/248
7-15 pm.	5th Div report all quiet.	G/985
7-32 pm.	6th Div evening report.	G/574
8-19 pm.	84th Brig report all quiet.	BM/617

WAR DIARY
17th March 1915.

NIEPPE.

Fine day, very clear. (BM/639)

4-45 am. Usual night reports. All quiet. (BM/40,J/155,G/145,G/942,G/586,G/146

7-40 am. 12th Brig report that at 5-30 am this morning as mist lifted at least 200 Germans were seen advancing against Monmouths right. They were 50 yards away, and in extended order. J/158 Rapid fire was opened and they at once dropped into reserve G/137 trench.--Reported to 3rd Corps--G.S.O.2, made further verbal BM/319 enquiries, and learnt that the Germans were 500 yards away when seen.

9-13 am. 3rd Corps send copy of orders issued to 14th Anti-aircraft Section about their returning to original arrangements and being responsible for whole of 3rd Corps line. G/445

10-58 am. Orders received that, evening report is to be rendered one hour earlier.--All informed.--(G/447,G/139,GG/148,BBM/254,H/250, (BM/42,BM/309.)

3-0-pm. Air report. All roads behind enemy's line from St.Eloi to Lys River clear of movement. IG/305

2-30 pm. Army Commdr.--Sir H.Smith-Dorrien, inspected the Sea Highrs and War Regt. as they marched through Pont de Nieppe, on their way from Armentieres to Romarin.

5-30 pm. Evening report--Sniping heavy against Right Sector. Enemy in front of right of Centre Section has put up 80 yards of heavy wire entanglement. (GG/156,BM/317,BM/49,BBM/257)

5-35 pm. Receipt from 12th Brig for our GGG/117(Mining situation) BM/326

6-20 pm. Evening reports from 5th and 6th Divisions. (G/597,G/23)

6-30 pm. Report to 5th and 6th Divs that all is quiet. GG/158.

6-15 pm. GOC issues orders for the building of a barricade across. BM/328. road East of Le Touquet Station.(GG/159,BM/323,G/140,BM/327,=BM/ G/141)

10-45 pm. 11th Brig report unusual amount of transport can be heard BM/54 moving, by Som L.I., direction not located--Repeated to 3/C.GG/160

11-35 pm. 6/Div report moving of transport. G/608

11-35 pm. 11th Brig report train also can be heard. Hamps R. confirm BM/58 movement reported above by Som. L.I. 3rd Corps informed. G/142.

NIEPPE.

WAR DIARY
18th March 1915.

Fine day--Rained late in evening.

4-30 am.   Quiet night reports received from Brigades. Relief of 84th Brigade by 10th Brigade carried out during the night.--- Reported to 3rd Corps and exchanged with 5th and 6th Divs. (BM/329, BM/59, H/260, GG/161, GG/944, G/612, G/143)

9-11 am.   3rd Corps ask for duration of movement of transport reported last night.?--Brigades were asked and replied, nearly all night.(IG/209,GG/163,GG/165, GG/166, BM/71,BM/333,BM/69)

11-0 am.   Air reconnaissance 6-45 to 7-30 am--No movement observed. IG/310

12 noon.   3rd Corps were asked if any arrangements were being made for return of 8 officers of 12th Div Arty now attached for instruction.   G/147

5-45pm.   Evening report.--A few Black Maria's behind 12th Brigade   GG/120
           H.Q. at 4 pm. and several shells from trench mortar   BM/340
           against Centre Sector. Reconnoitring patrol of Lan Fus   BM/84
           discovered that Five Gables House was not occupied by   H/278
           Germans.   BBM/263

6-0 pm.   5th and 6th Divs report all quiet.   G/627,53.

WAR DIARY
19th March 1915.

NIEPPE

Snow fell in early morning. This thawed by 9 am and there was a short interval of sunshine till about 9-30 am when snow and rain fell and continued intermittently throughout the day.--Very cold.

4-30 am.   Night reports--20 Black Marias against 12/Brig (Right G/151, Sector) last evening. All quiet otherwise.(S/28,BM/87,BM/348
                                                                              (GA/12,G/641,G/152

10-0 am.   Report from 11/Brig about Germans shouting across   BM/89
           and asking what Regts occupied trenches. Repeated   G/154
           to 3rd Corps.

12-10 pm. Arrangements for return of officers attached from
           12th Div Arty received. Div Arty informed.   G/135/10

2-10 pm.   3rd Corps told of signboard put up by ~~Germans~~ Dublins G/157
           which reads "Bread can be obtained here without tickets"

4-25 pm.   3rd Corps ask if we have a trench mortar to spare.   AQ/806
           We replied that ours were very much in use.   GG/176,G/162

5-47 pm.   Evening report--Little shelling, enemy busy in his   G/158,
           trenches, with planks, in that portion of line oppo- BM/351
           site Railway Barricade in Right Sector.(BM/94,H/291,BBM/274.

6-27 pm.   Evening report from 6th Division.   GG/660

6-42 pm.   All quiet in 5th Division.   G/85

7-0 pm.   12th Brig report that German climbed out of his
           trench and was shot by Monmouths. They also shot a
           man in civilian clothes on German parapet.   BM/352

7-5 pm.   29th FAB report considerable movement of small
           parties of Germans observed from Le Gheer. They were
           all fired at.

7-17 pm.   The above two messages repeated to 3/Corps   G/159

8-30 pm.   Message from 3rd Corps says dispatch rider is leaving
           with Operation Orders   G/481

8-50 pm.   Op. Order No.45 received and acknowledged.   G/160
             4/Div are to take over right of 5/Div line as
           far north as Messines -Wulverghem Road. 27th FAB
           of 5th Div remains stationery and comes under ~~command~~
           our command to cover this area.
             Div Area extended to Wulverghem -Neuve Eglise (excl)
           --Bailloul road.--Move to be completed by 21/22nd March.

9-15 pm.   6th Div report considerable movement of transport
           from Frelinghien towards direction of Lille.   G/664.

10-5 pm.   6th Div report further movement of transport.   G/667

10-5 pm.   Directs Brigadiers to be at Div Hdqrs at 9 am. to-
           morrow to confer with G.O.C. on readjustment of
           line in accordance with Operation Order No.45.   G/161

10-5 pm.   Ask 2nd Corps if Staff Officer of 5th Div could
           meet Staff Officer of 4th Div at 2/Corps H.Q. at
           11 am. tomorrow. ?.   G/162

11-30 pm. Reply to G/163 that Staff Officer of 5th Div would be G/85
           there.

War Diary - 20th March 1915.

NIEPPE.

	Very clear fine day.	
4-30 am	Quiet night reports.	
	(H.296, BM.95, BM.361, G.164, G.93, G.669, G.165)	
9-55 am	Air reports - 6-50 to 7-30 am. No movement observed in area Hollebeke - Menin - Lille - Ennetieres.	IG.321
	7 to 7-40 am. No movement at Quesnoy - Warneton Messines and Wytschaete.	IG.323
11-15 am	Operation Order No. 22 issued. (Extension of 4th Div. line to the Wulverghem - Messines road).	
11-45 am	Air report - 9-35 am. Column of infantry 1½ miles long between I.32.b and J.26.cd. Direction of movement uncertain - probably towards Armentieres. 11th and 12th Brigs. informed.	IG.324 G.166
1-45 pm	Air report 12 noon. Wez Macquart and Armentieres - Lille road clear of hostile movement.	IG.325
5-50 pm	Evening report - Some shelling by Little Willie and one Black Maria which fell in Le Bizet. Another man dressed in civilian clothes shot in German trenches.	
	(GG.186, BM.370, BM.118, H.32, BM.372, BBM.280)	
5-55 pm	Evening report 6th Div.	G.698
7 pm	Evening report 5th Div.	G.141
8-15 pm	3rd Corps repeat 6th Div. report on days artillery shooting.	G.494
9-15 pm	12th Brig. asked if the supporting line mentioned in para 5 of Div. Operation Order No. 22 meant 3rd line under construction by R.E. or strong points between that line and front line.	
	Replied that it meant 3rd line under construction by R.E. .	GG.188 J.210

Attached.

1. Memo showing distribution of anti-aircraft sections. No. 19 anti-aircraft section joining 3rd Corps in a few days time. G.487/3AC

2. Artillery tactical re-arrangements issued with Op. Order No. 22 to artillery units by Div. Arty.

War Diary - 21st March 1915.

NIEPPE.

Very fine warm day.
4-45 am Quiet night reports.
(BM.378, BM.125, 38, GG.190, G.968, GG.191, G.708)
11-30 am Air report 8-30 to 9 a.m. main roads clear of movements of troops. More mounted traffic observed than usual, in twos and threes, especially on Warneton - Wervicq road.   IG.334
1 pm Air report 10-45 am to 11-30 am all roads clear of movement.   IG.325
2-15 pm 3rd Corps message states that 6th Div. report German airship up.   IG.336
5-45 pm Evening report - A few Little Willies against Right Sector, also 4 Black Marias which fell in Le Bizet, otherwise no shelling. Two German balloons up - one about Commines and another in direction of St Eloi.   G.175 H.47 BM.14 BM.358
6-25pm Evening report from 6th Div.   G.722
6-48 pm 3rd Corps asked for instructions, with reference to 3rd A.C. Operation Order No. 45, regarding proposed removal of 27th F.A.B. from our area by 5th Div. Arty.   G.176
6-55 pm 5th Div. evening report.   G.177
7-18 pm 12th Brig. report that owing to less sniping they think enemy in front of them has been relieved during past few days. 3rd Corps informed & and they replied that definite information on the subject was of importance.   BM.393 GG.193 IG.342
10-14 pm Receipt to 3rd Corps for their Secret G.513 (Economy of Ammunition and G.511   G.195

WAR DIARY
22nd March 1915.

NIEPPE Fine day, rained during night.

Message received from 3rd Corps, late last night, asks if we can corroborate report from 2nd Corps that large gun flash was observed about 0/25/D/1/0.--We replied that we could not get any corroboration. GG/197 IG/232 BBM/293 IG/341.

4-30 am. Night reports:- A good deal of hammering in front of Left Sector, otherwise all quiet. Relief North of Douve completed. (H/52, BM/20, BM/398, GG/196, GA/20, G/732, G/178.)

9-20 am. 10/Brig report Germans sending up green flares. They were poor lights and 10/Brig think they were either experimental or signals. S/55 G/179 (H/63, G/181.)

9-10 am. Air reports 6-20 am to 7 am, and 11-15 am:- No movement of troops observed. IG/345 (IG/348, IG/350)

4-20 pm. Report to 3rd Corps about movements of working parties & single wagons, reported by Arty Observing Officer GG/200

6-0 pm. Evening report--30 Black Marias and a number of Little Willies fell near Le Bizet, one setting fire to a haystack near Despeere Farm. Listening patrol of 11th Brig. reported movement of transport 8-10 pm night of 20/21st, moving from N to S. and also Germans laughing and singing. 30 Rifle Grenades fired at left section. Left Sector report Germans busy with entanglements from Petite Douve to south-end of Avenue last night, sniping intermittent and apparently controlled by green flares. Building 50 yards N of Avenue Farm, U/92, appears to be a German Hdqrs of Section, as telephone lines lead to it, and men have been seen leaving it at daybreak. Artillery report 31st Heavies ranged on aeroplanes. H/73 G/182 BM/405 BM/30 GG/201 BBM/308

6-5 pm. Artillery report a wagon of 31st (H) Brig. was blown up and gun damaged at midday--Repeated 3rd Corps. G/183

6-10 pm. News received of the fall of Premzyl--circulated. (G/528, GG/202

6-10 pm. Evening report from 6/Div.--Many shells received, no casualties. Snipers active,--Successful rifle grenade combat with enemy.--Enemy very noisy, night 20/21st, opposite 18/Brig. G/746

7-15 pm. 5/Div report all quiet. G/249

7-52 pm. The damage reported by the 31st Heavies is now found to be less than originally reported.--The wagon was not blown up, but burnt out by ignition of cartridges. The damage to gun is being repaired.--No casualties. BBM.310 G/185

8-10 pm. Rifle Brig (Centre Sector) reports Enemy's equipment complete for marching off noticed on parapet between 5-30 and 6-0pm. The men were also playing and singing. Probably going to be relieved. BM/34 GG/203

Major B.F. Burnett-Hitchcock, DSO, Sherwood Foresters, who has been with the Division for 3 years, formerly as DAA & QMG, and since the 8th Sept 1914 as G.S.O.(2) left the Division on posting to the 2/London Division, and is being succeeded by:--
--Lt Col Hon L.J.P. Butler, from the 8th Brigade.

WAR DIARY
23rd March 1915.

NIEPPE.

                Fine day.

4-30 am.	Quiet night reports(H/77,J/224,BM/37,GG/205,G/265,G/754,GG/206)	
12-45 pm.	10/Brig report that no green flares were sent up last night.	78/3
1-40 pm.	3/Corps report that evidence points to the fact that Germans opposite 2/Army are side-slipping to the South. All informed.	IG/356 G/188
4-12 pm.	5/Div inform us that they are removing their trench mortars, from that part of line, taken over by 10/Brig. 3/Corps were asked if they could supply new pattern mortars to replace these, but they regretted there were none available.	G/297 GG/212 AQ/825
6-15 pm.	Evening report to 3/Corps--Little shelling by Little Willies and about 50 Rif. Grenades at Sniper's Houses. Hamps R. report enemy in front of them relieved.(G/190,BM/412,BM/41,SC/23,313.	BBM/
6-15 pm.	Evening report from 6th and 5th Divs.	(G/775,G/301)
7-35 pm.	10/Brig report 14 small groups of Germans crossed Ploegsteert - Messines road, 150 yards N.E. of La Douve River at about 6-30 pm. moving from East to West.--11/Brig informed.	SC/26 G/194 SC/27 G/195.
7-55 pm.	3/Corps asked how Hamps R. know that reliefs were carried out by Germans opposite them. Hamps say that report is based on general demeanour of enemy.--It is the quiet lot in now.--	G/193 BM/44 GG/215

WAR DIARY
24th March, 15.

NIEPPE.

Rained nearly all day.

4-50 am.   Quiet night reports. 10/Brigade report that at 9 pm formed body was heard marching down Messines Road to Douve. Horse transport heard South to North 10-40pm. G/788, G/197 for 20 minutes. Also motor transport in same direction for 10 minutes from 11-15 pm. (BM/46, J/240, H/101, GG/217, T/10

2-35 pm.   Receipt to 3/Corps for their Nos. IR/110, 179, 180, 62 and GG/222 G/553:-see Secret file)

5-18 pm.   Owing to the great difficulty in obtaining corrugated iron, Brigades were told not to use it for other than roofing purposes, except in cases of great emergency. G/203

6-5 pm.   Evening reports exchanged with 6th Div.--All quiet. G/799, G205

6-10 pm.   Evening report to 3/Corps--Right Sector enemy shelled Le Bizet all afternoon. Other sections, no shelling. Searchlight opposite left sector did not re-appear after being fired on. (G/204, BM/425, BM/61, H/113, BM318, 9.)

6-10 pm.   Div Arty report that guns in both batteries of 5th Hows have been loaded for a week, for their night lines. As   DA/22 it is impossible to extract shell they ask if guns may   GG/227 be fired so that bores may be cleaned.--Reported to 3/Corps.

6-30 pm.   Evening report from 5/Division.   G/349

7-0 pm.   32nd FAB report one battalion of enemy's infantry seen N/253 at 5-45 pm. moving North on road in O/29/c. Repeated to G/207. 3rd Corps.

8-0 pm.   Messages regarding colour etc. of enemy's uniform, received from 10th and 12th Brigades, and passed to 3/Corps (BM/426, H/114, G/208, H/116, G/209.)

WAR DIARY
25th March 1915.

NIEPPE.

Rained nearly all day. Cleared up late in the evening.

4-30 am.	Quiet night reports.(H.118,BM.67, Bm.430, G.211,GA.22,G.806,GG.129)	
2-15 pm.	3rd Corps report that message from 1st Army states that enemy opposite Rouges Bancs are either new troops, or in increased strength.--They shouted they were Bavarians.	IG.369
5-55 pm.	Evening report. Excepting that Left Sector was heavily sniped, it has been an exceedingly quiet day. No hostile movements observed.(G.214, Bm.439, Bm.13, H.122,BBM.136.)	
5-55 pm.	Evening report from 6th Division.	G.814
6-30 pm.	Evening report from 5th Division.	G.384
9-25 pm.	12th Brigade report heavy horse transport heard opposite Central Farm.--Reported to 3rd Corps.	BBM.448 G.216
10-30 pm.	32nd FAB report considerable movement of enemy's transport observed at 5-30 pm in O.24.C.--Reported to 3/Corps.N.259,G.21	

One Russian and 5 Japanese Officers visited the Division during the afternoon, and were shown round Ploegsteert Wood.

NIEPPE.

W A R   D I A R Y
26th March 1915.

Fine, until 10 am, then very dull and some rain, until about 2.pm., after, fine.

4-30am. Quiet night reports. 10th Brig. report movement of heavy horse horse transport in direction of Warneton going East.
(BM.82,279,BM.182,H.127,G.219,G.405,G.821,G.220)

8-50 am. Air report 7-15 to 7-40 am.--Country for half mile behind enemy's lines between Frelinghien and Messines clear of all movement.

9-10 am 12th Brig report that enemy show a disposition to converse with our men, and ask if it should be checked, or encouraged, J.280 with a view to gaining information if possible.? They were G.221 informed that an Intelligence Agent was being sent up who had permission to shout across, but that no other intercommunication must take place.

11-0 am. 11th Brigade report enemy shouting across to L.R.B. thinking they were the Somersets, left== The L.R.B. took over the Somersets left trench on 21st. This points to no change in enemy's units lately. 3rd Corps informed on telephone. BM/87

11-12 am. Air report 9-15 to 9-40 am. Observation difficult, owing to clouds. No movement observed. IG/378

1-0 pm. Report from 32nd Arty on observation from Barrel House. N.262 Captive balloon on canal approximately in P/27/d. Men seen G.222 drilling in same locality. Repeated to 3/Corps.

3-10 pm. Air report. 3-30 pm No hostile movement of transport or troops. Flashes observed at corner of wood J/13/a,. sheet 36, and 0/32/d, sheet 28. IG/386

5-15 pm. News of sinking of German submarine U/29, received and circulated. IG/387

5-50 pm. Evening report. Very little shelling by enemy. Som.L.I. shelled enemy snipers house with Trench howitzer. Situation unchanged.(G.224,BM.48,BM.94,H.149, BBM.531)

6-15 pm. 11th Brig report having seen two helmets of shako type in H.150 Avenue.--Repeated to 3/Corps GG.231

6-35 pm. Evening reports from 5th and 6th Divs. G.431,G.836

6-55 pm. Message from 12th Brigade states that captive balloon showed BM.465 three balls during morning and seven during afternoon. To 3rd Corps. G.225
Div Arty report about 1 Coy with transport seen marching N.264 N.W. on road in O.24.C. 3rd Corps informed. GG.232

7-20 pm. Div Arty report what appeared to be a heavy gun in three parts, on three waggons drawn by 6 horses, moving North along Ypres-Warneton road.7/5/b. Was observed from Barrel House. N.265

9-20 pm. 12th Brigade report transport moving right to left for ¼ an hour. BM.468

9-40 pm. 12th Brigade report transport moving
9-40 pm. 11th Brig report two Germans wearing shako's seen in a BM/99 trench North of St Yves. To 3rd Corps. G.228

P.T.O.

2nd page

9-58 pm. 3rd Corps ask for fuller description of balloons seen today
and compass bearings. 10th 11th and 12th Brigs and Div Arty
were asked for detail and replied saying that balloon was
yellow, and sausage shaped. They also gave bearings from   BM/102,
different points. Another ballon which was black was seen H.155,
a long way to the North.(IG.393,G.233,Bm.336,G.229,BM379,   G.233

10-15 pm. 11th Brig report that aeroplane passed over St Yves at   BM.100
9-30 pm, travelling west. 3rd Corps informed.   GG.234

10-45 pm. 12th Brig told to construct lookout post in Essex Central Farm facing towards Rly barricade.   G.230

11-30 pm. 10th Brig report much German horse transport moving along H.154
behind Messines. To 3rd Corps   G.231.

The Lincoln and Leicester Brigs of the North Midland Division
were attached to the 4th Division from 26th to 31st March 1915 as
follows:-
 H.Q. Inf Brig and Sig Section to 11th Inf Brig.
   8th Notts and Derby Regt. 10th Inf Brig.
   4th & 5th Lincolns....... 11th Inf Brig.
   4th Leicesters .... 12th Inf Brig.
   60 Div Mtd Troops........ Div Squadron.
   Coy Div Train .... 4th Div Train
   Horsed portion Fd Amb.... 10th Fd Ambce.

W A R   D I A R Y
27th March 15.

NIEPPE.

Fine day, cold wind.

4-40 am. Quiet night reports to 3rd Corps and exchanged with 5th & 6th Divs.(H.157, BM.103, BM.70, G.282, G.40, G.846, GG.235)

6-10 am. 3rd Corps report 4 trains heard in succession, moving from right to left at 3-30 am in Houplines section by 18th Brig. G.585

10-20 am. Aerial report 6-30 - 8-20 am:- Area Fleurbaix - Lille - Menin - Armentieres clear of any formed body of troops.   IG.399

9-40 am. Enemy's aeroplane has been flying over our trenches at height of 600 feet and was not shelled by anti-aircarft BM.110) guns. Also transport heard moving from S. to N.(G.234, BM.105)

12-17 pm. German shakos seen yesterday were in Southern edge of   G.237
          Avenue.   H.159

1-30 pm.) Div Arty and Brigades report yellow sausage balloons and
4-40 pm.) darker coloured balloon with balls attached were seen.
          Compass bearings were given. (H.153, BM.107, H.152, G.239, J.303,
                (G.242, GG.243, J.305, BM.340_)

5-7 pm.   No.14 Section Anti aircraft responsible for whole front of
          3rd Corps.--Previous orders regarding 19 Anti aircraft sec- G.591
          tion now cancelled.

6-5 pm.   Evening report to 3rd Corps and 6th Division. About 40
          40 little Willies at Lys farm this morning and 30 Black
          Marias near Cha.de la Hutte. Very little sniping. Arty
          report movements of transport heard during night through
          La Basse Ville, direction unknown. Our Arty fired on
          working parties in U/22/a, a German battery at Les Escluses
          and at chimney at Pont Rouge; also last night at enemy near
          Poterie farm. Germans in shouting across to units in Right
          Sector say--they are being relieved tonight by the Prussian
          Guard.(GG.245, BM 479, H 156, BBM 341, BM 117)

9-20 pm. Evening reports received from 5th and 6th Divs (G/866,G/459)

7-35 pm. Arty report a force of Germans about one battalion seen
          moving along Warneton - Ypres road accompanied by 10 trans-
          port wagons, disappearing from view behind farm in U/5/A.
          Train seen entering Warneton from North at 6-30 pm.
            Little Willies fell in single rounds at Ploegsteert,
          Rossignol and Douve trenches. Two rounds at Chateau, and
          one White Hope on trenches just N. of Wulverghem -Messines
          road. 5.9 Howzrs from direction O.33.D also fired single
          rounds at one minute intervals on 5th Div trenches.
            Apparently an explosion at Commines, more train traffic
          there than usual, also an opening made in the spire of
          Commines Church. Several flags flying in Warneton and
          Commines today. Enemy are also loopholing Avenue farm.

8-45 pm. Right Sector at 8-10 pm heard horse and motor transport
          moving N. to S. lasting over half-an-hour. (BM 484, GG 248)

10-28 pm. Arty report Germans seen in light grey uniform near
          Auchasseur Cabaret, rear of Avenue trenches and proceeding
          west along Gapaard - Messines ridge. Germans seen in
          dark uniform going N. in U/6/A, in O/2/4/C, and in U/5/A.
          This would point to Douve being dividing line between light &
          dark coats.

WAR DIARY
28th March 1915

NIEPPE.

Slight frost during night. Fine sunny day with a cold drying wind.

4-26 am. Situation unchanged. Reported to 3rd Corps that Monmouths heard considerable movement in enemy's lines opposite their trenches. From the amount of orders and talking going on, they think more than usual number of enemy in trenches. Left Sector also report considerable trans- GG/251/4 port again heard 10.pm, S.E. of ST Yves. No further particulars (BM 486/12,H/164/10,BM/1/11, BM/485/12,GA/27/5,G/875/6

8-40 am. Acknowledges receipt of 3rd Corps G.595.(Report battle of Neuve Chapelle) GG/252.

8-50 am The Monmouths saw, by means of sun glinting on bayonets, about 60 Germans leaving the firing trench line, apparently by communication trench.(G.247, BM.487)

9-10 am. Air reconnaissance--No movement Armentieres - Ennetieres - Lille - Standre - Perenchies area. IG/401

5-53 pm. Evening report:- Right sector--Nothing to report. Centre Sector - An old German seen in Birdcage wearing black greatcoat and grey coat. Left Sector quiet day. Left Section shelled with White Hopes. Small German working party located last night in U/15/a, N.E. in sap from South End of Avenue. Arty report that 14th FAB fired a few rounds at hostile trenches to prevent registration. 32nd Brig engaged new M.Guns emplacement in Avenue, and on working party in U/17/D centre. About a dozen Germans bolted from house after first round. Apaarently a howitzer in 3 parts followed by ammunition wagon seen to cross Lys into Warneton over pile bridge in U/18/a this morning: it may have been 3 limbers and a wagon. 29th Brig fired at working party working in Birdcage and 31st Heavies BBM/348) shelled hostile battery in C/12/b,d.(GG/255,BM/497,BM/11,H/166,

6-30 pm. 5th and 6th Div evening situation.--A few shell fired at Centre Section of 18th Brigade. (G/483,G/883)

7-12 pm. Artillery hostile shelling report giving approximate GG/256 number of shells received on 27th and 28th and approxi- BBM/349 mate position of guns. Forwarded to 3/Corps.

9-35 pm. Centre Sector report Green Rocket seen at 7-56 pm, compass bearing 285, from U/21/A/9,5. Left Sector report officer seen today at Dresden Farm in U/9/C/29, wearing shako like French kepi, with gold braid running from centre of crown to black polished peak. Possibly an Artillery Officer. 32nd Brig report various movements of enemy this evening:- Six 6 horse teams going North on road in U/6/B/NW. About 20 unarmed men in grey uniform entered La Poterie from Warneton direction. At 6-15 pm train arrived Warneton and at 6-25 pm half-coy infantry seen moving west of road O/24/c (G.249, BM.15,H.193,C.108,B.502)

WAR DIARY
29th March 1915.

NIEPPE.

Slight frost during night. Bright day with cold drying wind.

4-30 am. Quiet night reports received from Brigades, forwarded to 3rd Corps and exchanged with 5th and 6th Divisions.
(G/251, BM/1, J/523, H/174, G/501, G/887, G/252)

12-30 pm. Lon Rif Brig report captive observation balloon observed approximately U/16/D/64 at 10 am. On being fired at by 32/FAB it was immediately hauled down.   GG/259   BM/13

1-52 pm. Air reconnaissance--Clear of all movement to rear of German front lines, to our front.   IG/403

5-50 pm. Evening report -Quiet day except for 2 grenades fired into Snipers and Railway Barricades, and the sighting of a hostile balloon with 9 balls, by 11th Brig.
    The Arty fired on a working party at Basse Ville and shelled transport in Ypres - Warneton road (GG/266, BM/519, BM/22, (H/182, BBM/359, GG/267)

6-24 pm. 5th Div report quiet day.   G/517

6-7 pm. 6th Div report Bois Grenier and L.Epinette shelled and sniping active.   G/897

7-15 pm. Hostile shelling report from 4th Div Arty forwarded to 3rd Corps.   GG/272   BBM/362

8-40 pm. 32nd FAB report 2 German sentries outside house S.of Sucerie, and on being fired upon these 2 with 4 or 5 others from inside the house, bolted. Considerable traffic heard in Sucerie direction. Forwarded to 3/Corps.   GG.273   N.286

9-0 pm. Acknowledges receipt of G/61/81 from 3rd Corps. (Return of N.Midland Div.)   GG/274

9-28 pm 11th Brig. report aeroplane passing over St Yves travelling East to West at 7-30 pm. Forwarded to 3rd Corps.   BM.33   G.257

9-35 pm 12th Brig. report considerable transport moving in two distinct lines; one going North and one South. Repeated to 3rd Corps.   BM.526   G.258

LB

War Diary - 30th March 1915.

NIEPPE.

Hard frost during night. Bright day - cold wind.

4-30 am　　Quiet night reports received from Brigades and forwarded to 3rd Corps. Also exchanged with 5th and 6th Divs. (G.259, H.195 (BM.529, BM.37, H.189, GG.275, GA.31, GG.277, GA.30, G.904,

9-36 am　　Air report. 6-15 to 7-20 am. No hostile movement observed.　　　　　　　　　　　　　　　　　　　　　　　　　　IG.413

4-5 pm　　Acknowledges 3rd Corps Secret G.623 (Allotment of Roads) GG.278

6 pm　　Evening reports received from Brigades and summary forwarded to 3rd Corps. Very little shelling and sniping. Quiet day reports exchanged with 5th and 6th Divs.
　　(G.262, BM.48, BM.537, H.202, GG.279, BBM.366, H.914, G.12)

6-30 pm　　Report on hostile shelling received from Div. Arty. and forwarded to 3rd Corps.　　　　　　　　　　　　　　　　　BBM.369

7-0 pm　　Air reconnaissance 3-40 to 3-50 pm. Train movements observed at Commines and Menin.　　　　　　　　　　　　　　IG.419

9-40 pm　　32nd F.A.B. report fairly continuous stream of traffic moving East and and West in O.24.c between 5-45 and 6-15 pm. Probably a relief in progress. Fwded. to 3rd Corps.　　　　9-40 pm

WAR DIARY
31st March 1915.

NIEPPE.

Frost during night, dull dry day with cold wind.

Time	Entry	Ref
4-25 am	Quiet night reports from Brigades forwarded to 3/Corps and exchanged with 5th and 6th Divisions.(H.206, BM.54, BM.541, G.265, G.559	(G.944, (GG.280.)
9-25 am	G.O.C. 3rd Corps notified his wish to see Lincoln & Leicester Brigades at Road Junction North of Steenwerck at 10-35 am	G/61/84
11-2 am	Air reconnaissance 7-30 - 8-15 am Area - Armentieres - Quesnoy - Menin - Frelinghien clear of all movement of troops.	IG/424
12-0 noon	3/Corps inform us a single experimental rocket will be sent up from Mont Noir at 6-15 pm this evening.	G/635
12-35 pm	Aerial report 8-30 - 9-10 am. Observation difficult owing to clouds. No movement observed, except a few single vehicles.	IG/427
12-40 pm.	10/Brig report two Germans seen yesterday just West of Dresden House in U/12/a centre, with grey caps. One with a dark band, the other with a dark peak to cap.	H.208
5-25 pm.	A patent listener forwarded to 12th Brigade for use of a trained listener from the miners of the Monmouths, as the L.R.B. in 11th Brig think the Germans are mining from White Estaminet in centre of U/21/b.	GG/284
5-55 pm	Evening report to 3/Corps--Quiet day. Very little shelling or sniping. Germans active in strengthening parapets, wire and trenches.(G276, BM.557, BM/76, H.219, BBM/373,375)	
6-35 pm.	Quiet day reports exchanged with 5th and 6th Divs.(GG/57, G.277, G/607)	
6-27 pm.	12th Brig inform us Germans fired 3 shells, near junction of Ploegsteert - Le Bizet and Essex Road. It is thought with a view to registering, as it is not a usual place to shell.(BBM/559, GG/288)	
7-0 pm.	10th Brigade report 20 H.E. shell burst along Steenbecque trenches, numbers 6 and 7, in U/1/b centre, about 4 pm. The first ten fired at closer range and at 15 minutes interval.	G/279 H/220 H/221
7-25 pm.	Arty forward Hostile Shelling Report for the day. Forwarded to 3/Corps. (GG/289, BBM/376, N/298)	

Considerable aerial activity on the part of the enemy was reported from many sources. Aeroplanes or airships dropped signal lights in the early hours of 2 - 4 am, and several observation balloons and sausages were seen during the day - Messages attached.

attached :- List of casualties for month of March.
Programme showing distribution of Infantry Battalions.
Copy of orders for troops in reserve in billets.
Map showing trench line

Operation Orders

SECRET.   Copy No. 1

OPERATION ORDER No. 20
by
Maj-Gen. H.F.M.Wilson, CB, Commdg. 4th Divn.

NIEPPE.
14/3/14.

1. The Division has been ordered to take over a new line from the Perenchies - Armentieres Railway (incl) to the River Warnave, the line now held by the 10th and 11th Brigs being taken over by the 83rd and 84th Brigs of the 5th Div.

2. The 84th Brig will relieve the 10th Brig to-night (14th/15th). [10th Brig will go into billets as shown in the attached table.]

3. The 10th Brig will take over the trenches now held by the 18th Brig. and part of the 17th Brig on night of 16th/17th.

4. Detailed arrangements for taking over the trenches from 17th and 18th Brigs on night of 16th/17th will be made direct by the 10th Brig with the Brigs concerned.

5. As soon as it can be arranged the 11th Brig will take over ¼ of the line which the 10th Brig take over on night of 16th/17th. Point of demarkation and date will be communicated later.

6. The 83rd Brig will relieve the 11th Brig on night of 15th/16th. The 11th Brig will, on relief, move into billets as shown on attached table.

7. The dividing line between the 4th and 5th Divs will be the Warnave - Ploegsteert (excl to 4th Div) - Romarin (excl to 4th Div) - Rabot (excl to 4th Div).

8. Div. Arty. will remain in its present position and for tactical purposes will be under order of the Div. Commdr. in whose area they are situated.

9. 12th Brig will continue to hold its present line.

10. The 7th Fd. Co. and West Lancs Fd Co will remain in their present billets. The 9th Fd Co will move to billets near Houplines. Details as regards time and place will be communicated direct to O.C. 9th Fd Co by C.R.E.

11. 11th and 12th Fd Amboes remain in present stations. 10th Fd. Amboe. will be relieved by 13th Fd Amboe on 15th and will move to billets in Armentieres under orders from A.D.M.S.

12. There will be no change as regards the Train, The Follies, The Cinema, The Baths and Div. Hd. Qrs.

AAMontgomery

Colonel,
General Staff, 4th Divn.

Issued at 3 p.m.

	14/15.	15/16.	16/17.
Night.			
10th Brigade, H.Q.	21 Rue Nationale, ARMENTIERES.	21 Rue Nationale, ARMENTIERES.	
R. Warwicks,	H.Q. & 2 Coys. Ecole de Musique Rue Nationale. and 2 Coys. Rue Butin, ARMENTIERES.	Ecole de Musique, Rue Nationale and Rue Butin.	TAKING OVER TRENCHES.
Dublin Fusiliers,	Billet F (Factory Dansette) ARMENTIERES.	Billet F (Factory Dansette)	
A. & S. Highlanders, Irish Fusiliers,	Blue Factory, ARMENTIERES. LA CRECHE (to be cleared by 10 a.m. 15th)	Blue Factory. H.Q. Hotel d'Egmont (opposite rly. station), 2 coys in station goods sheds, 2 coys. in station and houses near.	
Seaforth Highlanders,	Romarin (to be cleared by 10 a.m. 15th)	H.Q. and 2 coys. Hospice Mahieu, Place de Republique, 2 coys. in houses in Rue de St. Jean.	
11th Bde. H.Q.,		75 Rue de la Gare, NIEPPE.	SAME AS FOR 15/16.
East Lancs.,		NIEPPE.	
Hants,		PONT DE NIEPPE.	
Somerset L.I.,		PONT DE NIEPPE.	
Rifle Brigade,		Brasserie Droulers and present coy. billet ARMENTIERES.	
London Rifle Brigade.		Factory where coy. is billeted and houses near, ARMENTIERES.	

Copy No. 27

O P E R A T I O N   O R D E R   No. 21
by
Maj-Gen. H.F.M.Wilson, CB, Commdg. 4th Divn.

NIEPPE.
15/3/15.

1. The Division has been ordered to take over a new line from the Perenchies - Armentieres Railway (incl) to Le Gheer barricade;* the line now held by the 10th and 11th Brigs being taken over by the 83rd and 84th Brigs of the 5th Div. and the 12th Brig.

*(incl)

2. The 84th Brig relieves the 10th Brig to-night (15/16th). 10th Brig will go into billets as shown in the attached table.

3. The 10th Brig will take over the trenches now held by the 18th Brig and part of the 17th Brig on night of 17/18th.

4. Detailed arrangements for taking over the trenches from 17th and 18th Brigs on night of 17/18th will be made direct by the 10th Brig with the Brigs concerned.

5. As soon as it can be arranged the 11th Brig (less E.Lan.R) will take over ½ of the line which the 10th Brig take over on night of 17/18th. Point of demarkation and date will be communicated later.

6. The 83rd Brig will relieve the 11th Brig on night of 16/17th, except the part held by the E.Lan.R. The 11th Brig (less E.Lan.R.) will, on relief, move into billets as shown on attached table.

7. 12th Brig will take over up to Le Gheer barricade (incl), the E.Lan.R. coming under orders of 12th Brig.

8. The dividing line between the 4th and 5th Divs will be Le Gheer barricade (incl to 4th Div) - Ploegsteert (excl to 4th Div) - Romarin (excl to 4th Div) - Rabot (excl to 4th Div)

9. Div Arty will remain in its present position and for tactical purposes will be under order of the Div Commdr in whose area they are situated.

10. The 7th Fd Co and West Lancs Fd Co will remain in their present billets. The 9th Fd Co will move to billets near Houplines. Details as regards time and place will be communicated direct to O.C. 9th Fd Co by C.R.E.

11. 11th and 12th Fd Ambces remain in present stations. 10th Fd Ambce will be relieved by 13th Fd Ambce on 16th and will move to billets in Armentieres under orders from A.D.M.S.

12. There will be no change as regards the Train, The Follies The Cinema, The Baths and Div. Hd. Qrs.

13. Operation Order No. 20 of 14th instant is cancelled.

a.a.Montgomery
Colonel,
General Staff, 4th Divn.

Issued at 10 pm.

Nights of

	15/16th	16/17th	17/18th
10th BRIGADE H.Q.	54 Rue de Lille, Armentieres.	54 Rue de Lille, Armentieres.	
R.War.R.	HQ & 2 Cos Ecole de Musique Rue Nationale. 2 Cos Rue Butin, Armentieres.	Ecole de Musique, Rue Nationale and Rue Butin.	
Dub.Fus.	Billet F.(Factory Dansette) Armentieres.	Billet F.(Factory Dansette)	
A.& S. Highrs. Ir.Fus.	Blue Factory, Armentieres. La Croche (to be cleared by 10 am 16th)	Blue Factory. HQ. Hotel d'Egmont (opposite railway station). 2 cos in station goods sheds, 1 Co Dulac factory Rue du Strasbourg, 1 Co Mahieu warehouse Rue de la Gare.	Taking over trenches.
Sea.Highrs.	Romarin (to be cleared by 10 am 16th)	HQ. and 2 Cos Hospice Mahieu Place de Republique, 2 Cos in houses in Rue de St Joan.	
11th BRIGADE H.Q.		75 Rue de la Gare, NIEPPE.	Same as for 16/17th
E.Lan.R.		Remain in their present trenches and billets.	
Hamps.R.		Pont de Nieppe.	
Som.L.I.		Pont de Nieppe.	
Rif.Brig.		Brasserie Droulers and present Co billet Armentieres.	
Lon.Rif.Brig.		Factory where Co is billeted and houses near Armentieres.	

4th. Div. No. A/84.

Troops in reserve in billets.

(1). Not more than one quarter of the personnel of any Unit or Detachment in reserve are to be away from their billets at any one time, with the exception that :-

    (a). Such numbers as are required for exercising horses may be taken out for the purpose.

    (b). When a Unit or Detachment is washing in Nieppe, it may proceed to the Baths as a whole, but will do so armed and equipped under charge of an Officer.

    (c). When attending Divine Service a Unit or Detachment may proceed as a whole, but will be armed and equipped (without packs).

    (d). A whole Unit or Detachment may proceed without Arms or equipment to the Divisional Cinema or Follies, but will be accompanied by an Officer. Similarly, individuals need not be armed or equipped when going to these Shows.

(2). Except as referred to above, all parties leaving quarters will be armed, equipped and under proper charge.

(3). Individuals are not allowed to proceed more than half-a-mile from their billets without a Pass signed by the Officer Commanding the Unit or Detachment, specifying their destination and purpose.

(4). All N.C.O.'s and men, not on duty or attending a Divisional Performance, will be in their billets by 8 p.m.

(5). All Quarter-guards will include a Bugler. Should it be necessary to summon troops to return to billets the "Alarm" will be sounded by all Buglers on guard, and every Officer, N.C.O. and man will at once return to billets.

    The "Alarm" will only be sounded on receipt of a written order from Divisional or Brigade Headquarters, but will be taken up at once by all Buglers on guard.

F.P.S. Taylor, Lt.-Colonel,
A.A. & Q.M.G. 4th. Division.

18-5-15.

SECRET.

Copy No. 1

3rd CORPS OPERATION ORDER No.45.

Headquarters,
3rd Corps,
19th March, 1915.

1. Under instructions received from 2nd Army, the 3rd Corps will extend its line to the WULVERGHEM - MESSINES ROAD up to and including TRENCH No.7.

2. The 4th Division will extend its line in accordance with the above on the night of 21st/22nd March, and will be completed by the morning of the 22nd instant.

All arrangements in connection therewith will be made direct between the 4th and 5th Divisions.

Preliminary arrangements will be made on the night of 20th/21st March.

3. The MESSINES - WULVERGHEM - NEUVE EGLISE ROAD will be the dividing line between the 2nd and 3rd Corps, but NEUVE EGLISE is allotted to 2nd Corps for billeting purposes, with the exception of certain buildings to be arranged direct between the 4th and 5th Divisions.

4. The artillery supporting the new portion of the line to be taken over by the 4th Division will remain in its present positions. The 27th Brigade, Royal Field Artillery, will come under the orders of the 4th Division from 6 pm., 21st March, for tactical purposes, but not for administration.

A. LYNDEN BELL. Br.General,
General Staff.

Issued at 7.45 pm.

Copy No. 1 to   4th Division.
        2 to   6th Division.
        3 to   North Midland Division.
        4 to   5th Sqdn., R.F.C.
        5 to   2nd Corps.
        6 to   5th Division.
        7 & 8 General Staff.
        9.   D.A. & Q.M.G.
       10 & 11 A. and Q.
       12.   R.A. & R.E.
       13.   O.i/c Signals.
       14 - 16 Spare (filed by G.S.).

SECRET.   Copy No. 1

OPERATION ORDER No. 22
by
Maj.Gen.H.F.M.Wilson, C.B. Commdg. 4th Div.

NIEPPE.
20/3/15.

1. The 4th Division will extend its line to the left up to the Wulverghem - Messines road up to and including trench No.7. The extension to be completed by the morning of 22nd March.

2. (a) The 12th Brig. will take over from 11th Brig. up to and including the road running from U 27 b - U 26 d. This move to take place night 20/21st.
   (b) The 11th Brig. will take over from 10th Brig. up to and including St.Yves - La Hutte road.
        Prowse Pt. (1/10000 map) inclusive to 11th Brig.
        Move to take place night 21/22nd.
   (c) The 10th Brig. will take over from 14th Inf.Brig. up to Wulverghem - Messines road including Trench 7.
        Move to take place night 21/22nd.

3. The Messines - Wulverghem - Houve Eglise road will be the dividing line between 4th and 5th Divisions.

4. The Artillery supporting the new portion of the line to be taken over by the 4th Division will remain in its present positions. The 27th Brig. R.F.A. coming under orders of 4th Division from 6 p.m. 21st March for tactical purposes.

5. In the supporting line the 12th Brig. is allotted from the Lys to the Warnave, 11th Brig. from the Warnave to the St.Yves- La Hutte road (incl)* La Hutte Cha., 10th Brig. St.Yves - La Hutte road (excl) to Wulverghem - Messines road.

* and to include

Issued at 11/15 a.m.

A.A. Montgomery
Colonel,
Gen.Staff, 4th Division.

BBM 279

For information

4th. Division

Artillery Instructions, issued in connection with 4th: Div: Operation Order No.22.

1. From 6 p.m. 21st. March, the existing Artillery Tactical arrangements cease to operate, and units of and attached to 4th. Divisional Artillery will be redistributed as under.-
2. Reference Maps Scale 1/20000.

Formation.	Position of H.Q.	Units comprising the formation.	Tactical Employment.	Zone.	SAA Ammn: supplied to:-
14th:Arty.	Day-LE TOUQUET Stn: Night-No:307 LE BIZET.	14th:F.A.B. 1 Section:2nd: Derby(How) Battery.	Supporting 12th:Inf: Brig:	FRELINGHIEN to road running N.E. from C.4.a. centre.	12th: Inf: Brig:
29th:Arty:	PLOEGSTEERT Village. U.25.c.(S.E.)	29th: F.A.B.	126.Bty: supports 12th: & 11th:Inf: Brigs:, remainder support 11th:Inf:Brig:	From road running N.E. from C.4.a., to a North-easterly line through St. YVON.	11th: Inf: Brig:
32nd:Arty:	Farm T.23.b.	32nd:F.A.B.	135.Bty.supports 11th: Inf:Brig:, remainder support 10th: Inf:Brig:	From St.YVON -HALTE to ROSSIGNOL-MESSINES road.	10th: Inf: Brig:
27th:Arty:	Farm T.15.d. (West)	27th:F.A.B. (less 1 Bty).	Supports 10th:Inf: Brig:	From North easterly line through LA PETITE DOUVE to WUL-VERGHEM - MESSINES road.	-
Hows:	Farm T.23.c. (North).	1/4 N.Mid: How:Bde:(TF) (less 1 Sec: 2nd:Derby Bty)	2nd:Derby Bty:(less 1 Sec:)supports 11th: Inf:Brig:	From R.WAR-NAVE to road junctions U. 16.b.(N.E.)	-
			1st:Derby Bty:support 10th:Inf: Brig:	From road junctions U. 16.b.(N.E.) to road junction 0.32.c. (South).	
Heavies.	LA BRAND Farm. B.18.a.	31 Heavies.	Counter-Battery.	FRELINGHIEN to GAPAARD.	-
No:2 Mtn: Battery.	NIEPPE. (Rue de la Gare)	No:2:Mtn:Bty: (less 1 Sec:)	1 Sec:attd: 11th:Inf: Brig: 1 Sec:in reserve.	-	-
Div:Am: Column.	(a)NETERIE. (b)PONT de NIEPPE. (Ammn:refilling point).	4th:Div:Am: Column.	-	-	-

(a) Divisional and Divisional Artillery Signal Cables will be laid as follows, from 5p.m. 21st instant :-

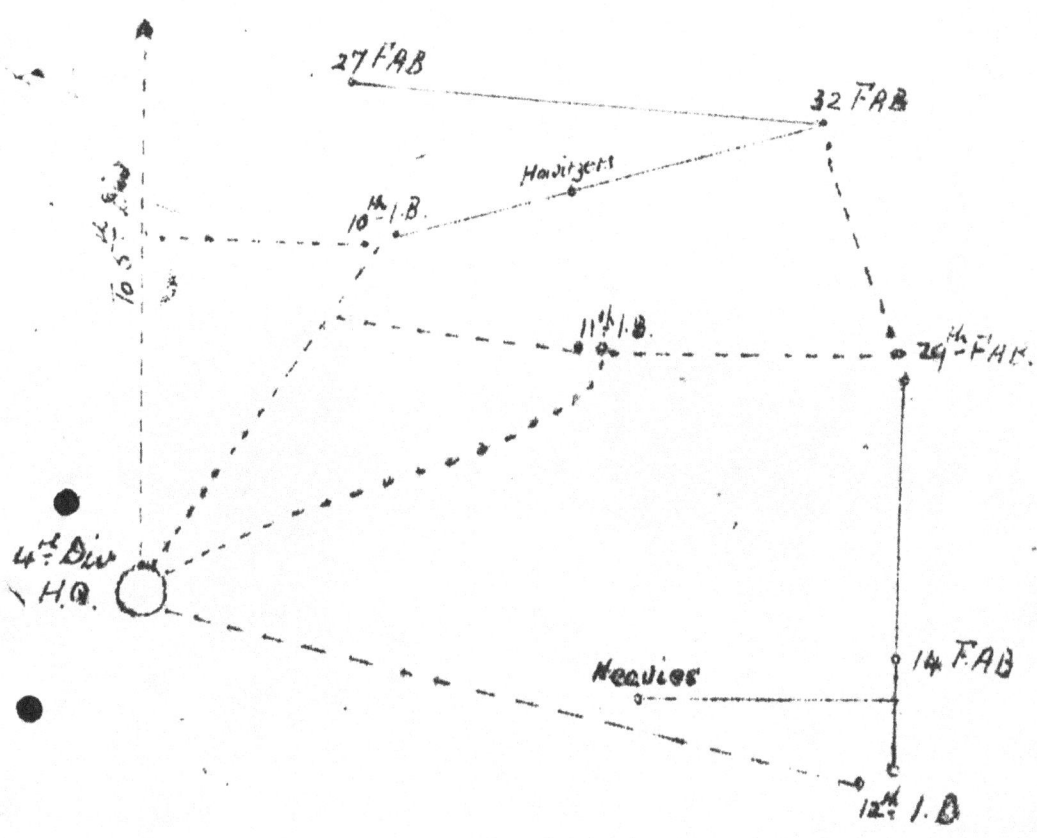

(b) Cables represented by dotted lines are laid, operated and maintained by Signal Company №.

Cables represented by continous lines (less that connecting 27 and 32 F.A.Bs), though laid by Signal Company will be operated and maintained by R.A.

Issued at ^p.m.
20/3/15,

E.H.G.LEGGETT, Major,
Brigade Major, 4th Divisional Artillery.

Artillery Reports

G.S.

A quiet day.
Aerial gun reconnaissance was asked for but not carried out.

14 F.A.B. reregistered certain points with a section that had been moved slightly.

29 F.A.B. One battery shelled a Working Party East of Le Gheer, & another retaliated against certain points ESE of Le Gheer on account of hostile fire against our trenches.

32 F.A.B. All three batteries retaliated in their zones for ~~bomb~~, and 134 battery shelled some german guns south of the Gapaard-Messines Road.

4th Siege Bty. Shelled a large house at Halte & also the Basse Ville Sucrerie.

31 Heavies nil.

1/4 N.M. Bde was engaged in taking over its positions, zones & duties.

4/3/15.

G.S.   5/3/15. 19

Hostile guns fairly active along front;
de Bizet, Ploegsteert & Hill 63 shelled.

1) 5" Hows at de Bizet registered &
retaliated against Frélinghien.

2) 29 F.A.B. retaliated for the shelling of
Ploegsteert and 127 battery fired on
a posn. of infantry U.23. cal. apparently
with good effect.
Paris shelling Ploegsteert were
mostly 96 mm Field guns & 10.5 cm.
Field Howitzers.

3) 32 F.A.B. Our battery fired East of
St Yvon & stopped the hostile sniping
& rifle grenades.
Another battery engaged & silenced
temporarily two batteries along the
Gapaard - Wervicq road.

4) 1/4 N. midland How'rs. were
engaged in registering.

5) 31 Heavies searched two

old gun positions East and
North East of Frélinghien from where
it was thought enemy were shelling
de Bizet.

No air reconnaissance was
carried out.

6.30 pm
5/3/15

[signature]
Bde.

G.S.

There has been a continuance of the shelling of our line today, and a considerable artillery duel on the immediate left of our front.

1) 32nd FA.B carried out local retaliations + fires on two batteries along the Gapaard - Wervicq road. Also shelled the big farm just NE of St Yvon at- inquest of Warwicks.

2) 29th F.A.B shelled enemy's trenches in retaliation for the hostile fire against Ploegsteert and Engaged the flanks of guns east of Basse Ville. This latter battery has been giving a good deal of trouble lately, but owing to aerial work having been carried out, it has not yet been definitely located.

3) 14th F.A.B shelled guns at Les Echelles which opened on our heavier, and also retaliated against the enemy's trenches.

4) Howitzers continued their registration.

5) 31 Heavies fired 64 lyddite and 10 shrapnel against Warneton, Beaumont and Les Echelles from said last place hostile guns attempted to counter-

DHSL

6 3/15.

G.S.

A diminution in the shelling of our line today. No aerial work done. Visibility fair.

1) 14" F.A.B. did not fire, but its Howitzers continued registering.

2) 29th F.A.B. registered a part of the Pont Rouge - Basse Ville road, and fired a few rounds at a working party near Halle.

3) 32nd F.A.B. hardly fired, except during the afternoon bombardment of the trenches S.E. Herenies as ordered; for which 180 rounds were fired in conjunction with the Howitzers. Also shelled guns S.E. of the Spanbroek - Herenies road.

4) 31 Heavies did not fire. They observed a considerable amount of smoke, apparently from railway engines, moving from Werviq to Comines "and thence north".

5) Howitzers continued registration during the morning, and 1st

Derby battery took part in the afternoon trench bombardment, with apparently good results.

7/3/15

E.T.L.
Bde.

32A

G.S./
A quiet day. No air reconnaissance done.

1) 14 F.A.B. The 5" Hows. tried to help in demolishing Frelinghien Ch: Tower but without success.

2) 29 F.A.B. fired at the german works about Basse Ville, and also at Deulemont, for the instruction of Young Officers.

3) 32 F.A.B. reports that one of the batteries which have lately been in evidence near the Papegoed - Warneton road moved away today. One gun was seen moving along the Warneton road. At 4.20 p.m. fire was opened against the trenches S & S.E. of Messines, as ordered.

4) 31 Heavies shelled Frelinghien Ch: Tower today, & got four direct hits, but with little effect that a largish portion of the round turret containing the staircase was knocked away.

5) Howitzers registered certain Points, shelled the trenches on the left of La Petite Douve Farm and participated in the afternoon bombardment.

[signature]
Br.

8-3-15.

"A" Form. Army Form C. 2121.
MESSAGES AND SIGNALS. No. of Message

Prefix	Code	m.	Words	Charge		Recd. at	
Office of Origin and Service Instructions			Sent		This message is on a/c of :	Date	
			At	in.	Service.	From	18
			To			By	
			By		(Signature of "Franking Officer.")		

TO   3 Corps   From 10 Brig 9.9 am
                                                 No H81. 9...
Sender's Number | Day of Month | | In reply to Number | AAA
  952 | Ninth | | |

Forwarded

10 Brig **Copy**

A curious trail of light was observed this morning at 4.15 am from various parts of our trenches aaa It was moving across the sky horizontally to the East of us in a Southerly direction aaa The moon was up at the time & there was practically no wind aaa No sound was heard aaa One Offr. reports it a long way off but another says it covered a very large arc in such a short time that it would appear to have been not very far though it was otherwise impossible to estimate distance.

Sea Hghrs 8.45 am
9/3/05

Further message ~~Did not look like a searchlight aaa~~ ~~might have been airship~~ but there was no sound and appeared to travel much too fast for one at a great distance aaa Thought you might have had other reports which might have helped to solve mystery 11.52 am

From 4 Div
Place
Time 3.25 pm
The above may be forwarded as now corrected.   (Z)
                                                Censor. Signature of Addressor or person authorised to telegraph in his name
*This line should be erased if not required.
3502 M. & Co. Ltd. Wt. W929/549—100,000. 6/14. Forms C2121/10.

G.S.

A fairly quiet day, as far as the shelling
down here was concerned.
Air reconnaissance went out, but
could locate no guns between Sea
between and Warneton, altho' it is
known that guns are in that area.
A disappointment.

1) 14" F.A.B. — Howitzer shelled the factory
in Frelinghien. A working party
was shelled N.E. de Touquet, and
the German trenches opposite the
brewery were retaliated upon by
field guns.

2) 29" F.A.B. — The big farm 500ˣ West of
Halle was well shelled; also
a working party 1000ˣ S.W. of
Pont Rouge. 127 Battery fired 60
shell into a fairly extended at-
100 strong moving towards
Basseville from Pont Rouge
seemingly with good effect.

3) 32ⁿᵈ F.A.B. Left battery retaliated against
the Douve Trenches.
The other two batteries bombarded
trenches from Red Potamine/
to La Douve Farm at 4·30 p.m.

(1452)

4) 31 Heavis. Shelled a battery 1000ˣ
NE of Frelinghien, which has been
dropping shells towards le
Bizet. It then turned on to
Frelinghien Church Tower, knocking
down the top half and a good
portion of the walls a good way
up.

5) 1/4 N. Midland How: Shelled the new
breastwork near Tilleul a
machine gun near la Petite Douve
repaired captain fourth, and
took part in the 4·30 p.m.
bombardment, with 32 r.g.p.s

S H L

9/3/15.

			"A" Form.	Army Form C. 2121.
		MESSAGES AND SIGNALS.		No. of Message _____

Prefix ___ Code ___ m.	Words.	Charge.	This message is on a/c of:	Recd. at ___ m.
Office of Origin and Service Instructions.	Sent			Date
	At ___ m.		___ Service.	From
	To ___			(51)
	By ___		(Signature of "Franking Officer.")	By

TO	4th Division			
Sender's Number	Day of Month	In reply to Number		AAA
* BBM.218.	10.			
6.15pm	report			
14 FAB	Shelled hostile trenches N.of Le Touquet			
	& Les Eclusas with 18 prs. 5" Hows. shelled			
	the Triangle.			
29 FAB	Shelled German trench 53 J to Sheer			
	destroying parapet + wire entanglement.			
	Also most of the fortified farms in its zone.			
32 FAB	Retaliated for the shelling of our front			
	trenches + for trench mortars – Also engaged			
	a trotting mean Messines at 6 pm.			
31 Heavies	Searched for guns from Fort Jones to			
	Halte & shelled a battery 1000 N. of			
	Fort Rouge.			
Hows.				

From	Fourth	Div	Arty	
Place				
Time		6-15 pm		

The above may be forwarded as now corrected. (Z)

Censor. Signature of Addressee or person authorised to telegraph in his name

* This line should be erased if not required.
(24473). M.R.Co.,Ltd. Wt.W4843/541. 50,000. 9/14. Forms C2121/10.

	"A" Form.			Army Form C. 2121.
	MESSAGES AND SIGNALS.			No. of Message _____

Prefix ___ Code ___ m.	Words.	Charge.	This message is on a/c of:	Recd. at ___ m.
Office of Origin and Service Instructions.	Sent			Date ___
	At ___ m.		___ Service.	From ___
	To ___			
	By ___		(Signature of "Franking Officer.")	By ___

TO	4th Division			34

Sender's Number	Day of Month	In reply to Number		
*BBM 228	15			AAA

6.15 Report

14 FAB. Shelled enemy's trenches South of "twin cottages" also a black hut near LES ECLUSES also LONG BARN AAA. 5" Howitzers shelled enemy's earthworks in C 4 d. AAA.

29 FAB. Shelled an enemy working party in U 22 A and another near enemy's front line trenches in U 28 A. AAA Also shelled road in V 17 C, covered way in U 26 D and farm in V 24 A. AAA

32 FAB. Shelled South wall of PETIT DOUVE farm AAA Engaged guns East of MESSINES last night AAA Shelled enemy's working party near CHASSEUR CABARET, searched for "LITTLE WILLY" and retaliated on enemy's trenches

From			
Place			
Time			

The above may be forwarded as now corrected. (**Z**)

Censor. | Signature of Addressor or person authorised to telegraph in his name

* This line should be erased if not required.

"A" Form.　　　　　　　　　　　　　　　　Army Form C. 2121.
MESSAGES AND SIGNALS.　　No. of Message _____

Prefix ____ Code ____ m.	Words.	Charge.	This message is on a/c of:	Recd. at ____ m.
Office of Origin and Service Instructions.	Sent			Date ____
	At ____ m.		____ Service.	From ____
	To ____			
	By ____		(Signature of "Franking Officer.")	By ____

TO { Page 2　　　　　　　　　　　　　　　　34

| Sender's Number | Day of Month | In reply to Number | AAA |

3 Heavies Engaged two batteries registered in U30D
as 68th Bty. reported being shelled from direction
of LES ECLUSES AAA Enemy retaliated
by firing on our guns and near LE BIZET
from the direction of FRELINGHEIN
Hows. Fired at enemy's sap in "avenue", trenches
South of TILLEUL AAA Also farm in
V 16 D. S.W., and at working party in V 16 D
S.W. AAA

From　Fourth Div Arty
Place
Time　6.30 p.m.

The above may be forwarded as now corrected.　(Z)　J M [Lount] Lt for
　　　　　　　　　　　　　　　　　　　　　　　　　　　　M/5
　　　　　　　　　　Censor. Signature of Addressor or person authorised to telegraph in his name
　　　　　　　　　　　　　　　　　　　　　　　　　　　　Bde.

"A" Form.   Army Form C. 2121.
MESSAGES AND SIGNALS.   No. of Message_____

Prefix____Code____m.	Words.	Charge.	This message is on a/c of:	Recd. at____m.
Office of Origin and Service Instructions.				Date_____
_____	Sent		_____Service.	From
_____	At____m.			
_____	To____			
_____	By____		(Signature of "Franking Officer.")	By

TO { Fourth Division

| Sender's Number | Day of Month | In reply to Number | AAA |
| * BM.248. | 16th | | |

6.30 pm Report.

29th FAB. Shelled working party on left of Le Gheer-Halle road and men by Basse Ville, & in Birdcage. Also a working party near R. Warnave (U.28.0.58). Also trenches & farm opposite St Yves.

14th FAB. Shelled german trenches with guns & howitzers. Enemy fired a few rounds at our trenches about 5 pm.

32nd FAB. Shelled a hostile Observing Stn.

31 Heavies Nil.
Howitzers fired a few rounds at Tilleul.

Very misty — no aerial work.

(F 37)

From Fourth Div Arty
Place
Time   6-30 pm
The above may be forwarded as now corrected.   (Z)   E H Leggett Major
Censor.   Signature of Addressor or person authorised to telegraph in his name
* This line should be erased if not required.
(24473). M.R.Co.,Ltd. Wt.W4843/541. 50,000. 9/14. Forms C2121/10.

"A" Form.   Army Form C. 2121.

MESSAGES AND SIGNALS.

TO: 4th Division

Sender's Number: BBM.257. Day of Month: 17

5.15 p.m. report.

14 FAB. Enemy working party observed heightening their parapet between A and railway. Enemy shelled our working party near G^d Rabecque Fm.

29 FAB. Fired a few rounds at men moving south of Halle.

32 FAB. Shelled Avenue Farm at request of our Infantry, owing to hostile movement there.

31 Heavies } NIL
How^r.   }

5.40 p.m

From: Fourth Div Arty
Place:
Time: 5-15 p.m.

"A" Form. Army Form C. 2121.

MESSAGES AND SIGNALS.

Prefix ___ Code ___ m.	Words.	Charge.	This message is on a/c of:	Recd. at ___ m.
Office of Origin and Service Instructions.				Date
	Sent		Service.	From 35
	At ___ m.			
	To			
	By	(Signature of "Franking Officer.")	By

TO: 4th Division   5.30 p

| Sender's Number | Day of Month | In reply to Number | AAA |
| BBM 263 | 18th | | |

5.15 pm Report.

14. FAB — Shelled a working party near △. Enemy fired a few light shell at our trenches + a few heavy ones this afternoon towards Le Bizet

29 FAB — 125 By engaged working party and trench mortar near Birdcage

32 FAB — Shelled enemy's trenches Avenue + N.E. of St Yves

Hows. NIL

31' Heavies — This afternoon searched the Basse-Ville — Pont Rouge road. A hostile 15 cm battery replied from E. of Frelinghien and our guns replied by engaging it.

From: Fourth Div. Arty
Place:
Time: 5.20 pm

The above may be forwarded as now corrected. (Z) E.H.G. Leggett Major
Censor. Signature of Addressor or person authorised to telegraph in his name

* This line should be erased if not required. BM.

(24473). M.R.Co., Ltd. Wt. W4843/541. 50,000. 9/14. Forms C2121/10.

"A" Form. Army Form C. 2121.
MESSAGES AND SIGNALS. No. of Message _____

Prefix ___ Code ___ m.	Words.	Charge.	This message is on a/c of:	Recd. at ___ m.
Office of Origin and Service Instructions.	Sent			Date (30)
	At ___ m.		____ Service.	From
	To			By
	By	(Signature of "Franking Officer.")		

TO	4th Division			
Sender's Number	Day of Month	In reply to Number	AAA	
BBM 274.	19th			

5.15 pm Report —

14 FAB — Carried out some further registrations & shelled working party near Briquetrie.

29 FAB — Registered and shelled a working party opposite Birdcage.

32 FAB — Registered and shelled a house near Au Chasseur Cabaret where movement was seen.

Howitzers } NIL
Heavies }

(5.41 p)

From: Fourth Div Arty
Place:
Time: 5.15 pm

The above may be forwarded as now corrected. (Z) E H S Legge ? Major

"A" Form. Army Form C. 2121.
MESSAGES AND SIGNALS.

| TO | 4th Div |

Sender's Number	Day of Month	In reply to Number	AAA
BM 280	20th		

5.15 pm	Report
14 FAB	Enemy fired a few light shell behind the railway at 12.15 pm - We retaliated with 2 shell.
32 Arty	Two large fires seen East of Basse Ville at 3.35 pm - Batteries registered - Balloon up.
Howitzers	Nil
Heavies	Aeroplane had accident & did not work. Shelled a chimney S of Pont Rouge from which enemy are thought to observe our Flasters [?] near to Big [?].
29 FAB	Fired a few rounds at people moving along communication trench & in Birdcage.
4.30 pm	One gun, some transport & stragglers seen moving north on road O.35.a.

From: Fourth Div Arty
Time: 5.20 pm

BM

25

quietest
Nothing ^ to report.
Windows of BIRCHEN Farm have been
blinded which looks suspicious
31st Heavies tried to range on battery
near ABLINCOURT but aeroplane
had to come down with engine trouble
21.3.XV   OW

5.15 p

"A" Form. Army Form C. 2121.
MESSAGES AND SIGNALS. No. of Message _____

Prefix ____ Code ____ m.	Words.	Charge.	This message is on a/c of:	Recd. at ____ m.
Office of Origin and Service Instructions.	Sent			Date ____
	At ____ m.		Service.	From 25
	To ____			By ____
	By ____		(Signature of "Franking Officer.")	

TO { Fourth Division

| Sender's Number | Day of Month | In reply to Number | A A A |
| BBM 308- | 22 | | |

Nothing to report
except 31st Heavies ranged
with Aeroplane

From Fourth Div _____
Place
Time

The above may be forwarded as now corrected. (Z)

Censor. Signature of Addressee or person authorised to telegraph in his name

* This line should be erased if not required.

for BM

"A" Form. Army Form C. 2121.

MESSAGES AND SIGNALS. No. of Message _____

Prefix ____ Code ____ m.	Words.	Charge.	This message is on a/c of:	Recd. at ____ m.
Office of Origin and Service Instructions.	Sent			Date ____
	At ____ m.		Service.	From ____
	To			By ____
	By		(Signature of "Franking Officer.")	

TO { 4" Division

Sender's Number	Day of Month	In reply to Number	AAA
* BBM 313	23rd		

5-15 p.m.	Report-	
2 FAB.	Left battery retaliated for the shelling of Douve trenches. Centre bty fired on house at N. end of Avenue said to be a Sec" Headquarters.	
Howitzer.	NIL	
14 FAB.	Enemy fired a few light shell behind our trenches about 3 p.m. -	
Heavies	Engaged a battery just S. of Halte.	
29 FAB.	Column of transport seen moving N. from Pont Rouge but light too bad to see details. Flash seen somewhere about Gapaard - A field gun from about U22d, rather troublesome -	
27 FAB.	121 Bty retaliated twice against enemy's trenches as ours were being shelled - Neuve Eglise was shelled at 4 pm.	

From	Fourth	Div	Arty
Place			
Time	5.30	pm	

The above may be forwarded as now corrected. (Z) E H Theogate Major

Censor. | Signature of Addressor or person authorised to telegraph in his name

* This line should be erased if not required.

"A" Form. Army Form C. 2121.

MESSAGES AND SIGNALS.

No. of Message _____

Prefix __ Code __ m. Office of Origin and Service Instructions.	Words.	Charge.	This message is on a/c of: Service. (Signature of "Franking Officer.")	Recd. at ____ m. Date ____ From ____ By ____
	Sent At ____ m. To ____ By ____			

TO { 4 Div

Sender's Number	Day of Month	In reply to Number	AAA
* BBM 318	24th.		

5.15 pm. report.

14th Arty – Nothing to report

29th Arty – fired a few rounds at communication trenches on road near PONT ROUGE.

32nd Arty – 134 fired at machine gun emplacement in AVENUE – 135 at German billet in U.16.D & trenches E of St YVES.

Hows – No firing to day.

Heavies – Nothing to report

2y Arty – Nothing to report

From 4th Div Arty
Place
Time

The above may be forwarded as now corrected. (Z)

Censor. Signature of Addressor or person authorised to telegraph in his name

Major

* This line should be erased if not required.
(24473). M.R.Co.,Ltd. Wt.W4P43/541. 50,000. 9/14. Forms C2121/10.

"A" Form.   Army Form C. 2121.
MESSAGES AND SIGNALS.   No. of Message_____

| Prefix____ Code____ m. | Words. | Charge. | This message is on a/c of: | Recd. at____ m. |
| Office of Origin and Service Instructions. | Sent At____ m. To____ By____ | | _____Service. (Signature of "Franking Officer.") | Date____ From 25 By____ |

TO { 4th Div.

| Sender's Number AAM 326 | Day of Month 2 Feb | In reply to Number | A A A |

5.15 Report.

7 AB. NIL.
29 FAB Fired on a working party in Birdcage – Grey greatcoats only seen
32. FAB. Shelled new breastwork near Petite Douve Fm.
27 F.AB Shelled a house in Messines where movement was seen
Howitzers Grey greatcoats only observed –
31 Heavies NIL.

5.45 p

From: 4th Div Arty
Place
Time: 5-35 pm   Sturgess   Major B.M.

The above may be forwarded as now corrected. (Z)
Censor. Signature of Addressor or person authorised to telegraph in his name
* This line should be erased if not required.
(24473). M.R.Co.,Ltd. Wt.W4843/511. 50,000. 9/14. Forms C2121/10.

"A" Form.   Army Form C. 2121.
MESSAGES AND SIGNALS.   No. of Message _____

Prefix ___ Code ___ m.	Words.	Charge.	This message is on a/c of:	Recd. at ___ m.
Office of Origin and Service Instructions.	Sent At ___ m. To ___ By ___		Service. (Signature of "Franking Officer.")	Date ___ From ___ By ___

TO   4th Division

Sender's Number	Day of Month	In reply to Number	AAA
*BM-336.	26th		

5.15 pm Report -

14 FAB   NIL

9. FAB   All quiet - Fired a few rounds on one or two working parties.

32 FAB.   Engaged a machine gun emplacement in Avenue. 10 germans with light coats seen "Au Chasseur Cabt". Except for one single 15pr, all guns which fired on our front left Sector today were north of the Messines - Gapaard ridge.

31 Heavies.   Engaged guns at Les Ecluses, whose flash had previously been seen from Le Gheer.

Howitzers   Emptied guns at (a) an observation St" in Messines (b) farm 11.16.d, east of St Yves.

27 FAB.   (a) Lenwerck Fm. T.10.d. was shelled this morning apparently by 10 cm howitzers. (b) New trench dug on unmetalled path running S.E. in U.2.c (10th I.B. informed) (c) Wulverghem + Neuve Eglise were shelled. 10 rds fired as retaliation.

From	Fourth	Div	Arty
Place			
Time		5.25 pm	

The above may be forwarded as now corrected.   (Z)

Censor.   P H G Leggett   Major

Signature of Addressor or person authorised to telegraph in his name

*This line should be erased if not required.

BM

"A" Form. Army Form C. 2121.
MESSAGES AND SIGNALS. No. of Message _____

Prefix ___ Code ___ m.	Words.	Charge.	This message is on a/c of:	Recd. at ___ m.
Offic. Origin and Service Instructions.	Sent			Date ___
	At ___ m.		_____ Service.	From ___
	To ___			
	By ___		(Signature of "Franking Officer.")	By 52

TO { 4th Dw

| Sender's Number | Day of Month | In reply to Number | AAA |
| * BBM-336. | 26th | | |

At 12 noon, 27 FAB reported balloon bearing 74°
from farm T.16.b.9.5. aaa
At 1.45 p.m, 27 FAB reported two balloons, bearing
49° and 69° from Le in Le Pressignol U.13.a
aaa
At 5 p.m. 29 FAB reported that balloon had been
up most of the day apparently just behind
Basse Ville.
At 6 p.m, 31 Heavies reported having seen a
balloon bearing 2° right from farm V.15.b
as seen from Le Bizet Church C.19.b

No information re colour or balloonist.

From Fourth Div Arty
Place
Time 10.30 p.m.

The above may be forwarded as now corrected. (Z) E H Glaggett Major
Censor. Signature of Addressor or person authorised to telegraph in his name

* This line should be erased if not required.

(24473). M.R.Co.,Ltd. Wt.W4F43/541. 50,000. 9/14. Forms C2121/10.

"A" Form.   Army Form C. 2121.
MESSAGES AND SIGNALS.   No. of Message _____

Prefix ___ Code ___ m.	Words.	Charge.	This message is on a/c of:	Recd. at ___ m.
Office of Origin and Service Instructions.	Sent			Date ___
	At ___ m.		___ Service.	From 35
	To			By ___
	By		(Signature of "Franking Officer.")	

TO { 4th Division 3.55p

| Sender's Number | Day of Month | In reply to Number | AAA |
| * BM. 340. | 27 | | |

Division Report.
10.20 a.m. One balloon up, reported in P.30.b. or P.13.
11.50 a.m. Two balloons reported to have been up. Bearings
            4° & 11° Right of Messines Church from 11.13.a.b (north)
            A second bearing of one of these balloons gave
            72° from form T.16 as centre
12 noon   Balloons reappeared bearing 35° & 118°
            from U.13 a.b (north).

From   Fourth   Div   Arty
Place
Time   3-45 pm

The above may be forwarded as now corrected. (Z)   E H Clegg (?)   Major
                                          Censor.   Signature of Addressor or person authorised to telegraph in his name
* This line should be erased if not required.   PM.

"A" Form.				Army Form C. 2121.
MESSAGES AND SIGNALS.			No. of Message	

Prefix	Code	m.	Words.	Charge.	This message is on a/c of:	Rec'd. at	m.
Office of Origin and Service Instructions.			Sent			Date	
			At	m.	Service.	From 42	
			To				
			By		(Signature of "Franking Officer.")	By	

TO	4th Division 5·50

Sender's Number	Day of Month	In reply to Number	AAA
*BRM·341.	27		

5·15 pm	Report.
14 FAB	NIL
29 FAB	Movement of transport reported during night through LA BASSE VILLE - direction unknown AAA German field guns fired about 75 rounds at farm in U.27.C North probably for East of PONT ROUGE AAA. Two small German anti-aircraft guns fired at our aeroplane from NE of LA BASSE VILLE AAA. German battery in U.17.D shelled LA HUTTE with about 15 4·2" shells. Our guns engaged working parties in U.22.A. Very little sniping to day.
32 FAB	Last night shelled enemy moving near POTERIE from AAA To day

From	Fourth
Place	
Time	

The above may be forwarded as now corrected. (Z)
Censor. Signature of Addressee or person authorised to telegraph in his name
* This line should be erased if not required.

"A" Form.   Army Form C. 2121.
MESSAGES AND SIGNALS.   No. of Message _____

Prefix___Code___m.	Words.	Charge.	This message is on a/c of:	Recd. at___m.
Office of Origin and Service Instructions.	Sent			Date___
	At___m.		___Service.	From___
	To___			
	By___		(Signature of "Franking Officer.")	By___

TO {		Page 2		42
*	Sender's Number	Day of Month	In reply to Number	A A A

registered with 135 Battery AAA shelled hostile working party and checked gun lately overhauled

~~Howitzer~~
~~2 Heavy~~ ~~Hows. Img~~
Hows/Gns Nil

3″ Heavy Shelled German battery at LES ECLUSES reported to be firing at LE GHEER. AAA Fired at PONT ROUGE chimney but no direct hit obtained.

27 FAB Enemy were shelling our trenches so retaliated on german trenches.

From Fourth Div Arty
Place 5.50 pm
Time ~~5.45~~

"A" Form. Army Form C. 2121.
MESSAGES AND SIGNALS.

TO	4½ Division		

Sender's Number	Day of Month	In reply to Number	AAA
BM 34F	28th		

5.15pm Report.

14th FAB — Fired a few rounds at hostile trenches to check registration. AAA

32nd FAB — Shelled enemy trenches in retaliation to German shelling of our trenches AAA Engaged new machine gun emplacement in the AVENUE AAA. Fired at working party near house in J17D centre. About a dozen Germans bolted from the house after first round AAA Less movement than usual has been observed today AAA What appeared to be a howitzer in three parts followed by an ammunition wagon was seen to cross the LYS into WARNETON over the pile bridge in U18A this morning, but it might possibly have been three limbers and a wagon

From
Place
Time

"A" Form. Army Form C. 2121.
MESSAGES AND SIGNALS.

TO: Page 2

Sender's Number	Day of Month	In reply to Number	AAA
29th FAB	Fired at working party in the "Birdcage" AAA. No movement seen today.		
Hooitzus	Nil		
31 Heavies	Shelled hostile battery in C 12 B D AAA. Aeroplane ranged Left section on battery U 30 B.		

From: Fourth Div Arty
Time: 5.15 pm

"A" Form. Army Form C. 2121.
MESSAGES AND SIGNALS. No. of Message _____

Prefix ___ Code ___ m.	Words.	Charge.	This message is on a/c of:	Recd. at ___ m.
Office of Origin and Service Instructions.	Sent			Date
	At ___ m.		___ Service.	From (23)
	To			
	By		(Signature of "Franking Officer.")	By

TO { Fourth Div.   6.50 p

| Sender's Number | Day of Month | In reply to Number | AAA |
| * RBM 349 | 28th | | |

Hostile shelling report :-

27/3/15.

6.5pm Two 'white lights' fired from direction of MESSINES ridge fell just N of LA HUTTE chateau AAA.

28/3/15

7 am. Four 4.2 inch Howitzers fired about 40 shell at a British aeroplane over LE GHEER. Direction of guns unknown

12.15 pm. Two field gun shells passed near house in C 3 B.D apparently going towards LE BIZET. It has not been discovered where these shell fell and the direction from which they were fired is not known

From			
Place			
Time			

The above may be forwarded as now corrected. (Z)

Censor. Signature of Addressee or person authorised to telegraph in his name

* This line should be erased if not required.

"A" Form.   Army Form C. 2121.

MESSAGES AND SIGNALS.   No. of Message _____

Prefix ___ Code ___ m.	Words.	Charge.	This message is on a/c of:	Recd. at ___ m.
Office of Origin and Service Instructions.				Date ___
	Sent		Service.	From (23)
	At ___ m.			
	To ___			By ___
	By ___		(Signature of "Franking Officer.")	

TO { Page 2

Sender's Number	Day of Month	In reply to Number	AAA
* BBM 349.			

1.40 pm } 2 shrapnel burst high above trenches
and 13.10 pm } 100 yards west of MESSINES PLOEGSTEERT
road. Direction from which fired unknown
AAA

2.15 pm to } Single field gun shrapnel every 2 or 3
3.15 pm } minutes fell on front E4909 (U 8 D)
and on our trenches near this farm.
The shell appeared to be fired from the
MESSINES — ___ ridge. AAA

From   4ooth Div Arty.
Place
Time   6.45 pm

The above may be forwarded as now corrected.   (Z)   _____
                                                                                Major
                         Censor.   Signature of Addressor or person authorised to telegraph in his name

* This line should be erased if not required.

"A" Form.
Army Form C. 2121.

MESSAGES AND SIGNALS.

Prefix	Code	m.	Words	Charge			Recd. at	m.
Office of Origin and Service Instructions.			Sent		This message is on a/c of:		Date	
			At	m.		Service.	From	27
			To					
			By		(Signature of "Franking Officer.")		By	

TO   4" Division   5.42

Sender's Number	Day of Month	In reply to Number	AAA
B239 359	27		

S.B. Report

14 FAB — NIL.

29 FAB — Fired on working party, house at Basse Ville. No hostile firing & little sniping. No movement seen. From R. Warnave northwards enemy have recently strengthened & raised their parapets by 2 courses of sandbags. Birdcage also strengthened and more barbed wire erected. Considerable work has been done on 2nd line in U.28.d. Judging from fire at our aeroplanes, there are several machine guns in houses at Basse Ville.

32 FAB — Shelled transport on Ypres-Warneton Road: & fired on front trenches to stop sniping opposite Argylls. 135 Bty fired at Sausage Balloon, N.E. of Warneton, and it immediately descended.

Howitzer — NIL.

From
Place
Time

The above may be forwarded as now corrected (Z)

"A" Form.   Army Form C. 2121.
MESSAGES AND SIGNALS.   No. of Message

Prefix ____ Code ____ m.	Words	Charge	This message is on a/c of :	Recd. at ____ m.
Office of Origin and Service Instructions				Date ____
	Sent		Service ____	From ____
	At ____ m.			
	To			
	By		(Signature of "Franking Officer.")	By ____

TO | 2ⁿᵈ | | |

| Sender's Number | Day of Month | In reply to Number | A A A |

31 Heavies. Tried to register Warneton Station + Papaard X roads with aeroplane, but had no success.

27 FEB.

From Fourth Div Arty
Place
Time 5.30 pm

The above may be forwarded as now corrected

E H S Legrell Major

Censor. Signature of Addressor or person authorised to telegraph in his name

*This line should be erased if not required.

"A" Form. Form C. 2121.

MESSAGES AND SIGNALS.   No. of Message

Prefix	Code	m.	Words	Charge		This message is on a/c of :	Recd. at	m.
Office of Origin and Service Instructions			Sent			Service.	Date	
			At	m.			From	25
			To				By	
			By			(Signature of "Franking Officer.")		

TO   4ᵗʰ Division   5·5⁵

Sender's Number	Day of Month	In reply to Number	AAA
*BBM.366.	30		

5.15 pm	Report		
14 FAB	NIL		
Howitzers	NIL.	No movement seen today.	
29 FAB	Very little sniping & no movement seen. Shelled observation house at Basse Ville, farm in U.15.d, and working party near Au Chasseur Cabaret.		
32 FAB.	Fired on party of Officers near Poterie Fm and working party Basse Ville. Some trenches are reported on ridge P5 and P6.		
31 Heavies	Shelled a section of (?) 7ld. Hows. northeast of Basse Ville Sucrerie with aeroplane observⁿ.		
27 FAB.			

(5.55)

From   Fourth   Div   Arty
Place
Time   5.55 pm

The above may be forwarded as now corrected   (Z)
Censor.   Signature of Addressor or person authorised to telegraph in his name

"A" Form.   Army Form C. 2121.

MESSAGES AND SIGNALS.   No. of Message

Prefix___Code___m.	Words	Charge	This message is on a/c of :	Recd. at___m.
Office of Origin and Service Instructions.				Date___
	Sent			From
	At___m.		Service.	**29**
	To			
	By		(Signature of "Franking Officer.")	By

TO — 4ᵗʰ Division

| Sender's Number | Day of Month | In reply to Number | AAA |
| BBM 36 g | 30ᵗʰ | | |

Hostile Artillery Report.

9.30 a.m. — About 6 field gun shells fell near Gᵈ Rabecque Farm (do [illegible]). Thought to have been fired by single gun from E or NE of Brelington Poscill, D.7. a same gun fired again at same place about 5 p.m.

3 p.m. to 4 p.m. — Vicinity of La Haute Chᵉᵉ shelled by a section of Fld guns, probably situated about Gapaard Cross Roads.

4.25 p.m. — Same place shelled by a single Fld Howitzer, also thought to be near Gapaard Cross Roads.

2.55 p.m. — ? 6 pdr Fld Hows shell reported to have fallen near La Haute Chᵉᵉ, from Wameton. Probably fired by the section in U.18.d (N) which 31.(4) engaged this afternoon.

(To 3/Corps [illegible])

From: Fourth Div Arty
Place:
Time: 6.30 p.m.

The above may be forwarded as now corrected (Z)

Censor.   Signature of Addressee or person authorised to telegraph in his name

"A" Form.
MESSAGES AND SIGNALS.
Army Form C. 2121.

Prefix	Code	m.	Words	Charge		This message is on a/c of :		Recd. at	m.
Office of Origin and Service Instructions			Sent					Date	(44)
			At	m.		Service.		From	
			To					By	
			By			(Signature of "Franking Officer.")			

TO — Fourth Div.

Sender's Number	Day of Month	In reply to Number	AAA
BBM 373	31		

5.15pm report.

14th FAB — Nil.

29th FAB — Fired at german working parties AAA. Very little movement along the front of this brigade during the day AAA. Considerable activity all day in East side of 'Birdcage', a good many planks being carried along; also a lot of new earth thrown up on North side of 'Birdcage'.

32nd FAB — Last night fired at battery whose flash came from V4A AAA. Today fired at machine gun emplacement in AVENUE and at working parties including one in V17A which scattered on being fired at.

From ~~Fourth Div Arty~~
Place
Time — 5.32

The above may be forwarded as now corrected (Z)

"A" Form. Army Form C. 2121.

MESSAGES AND SIGNALS.

Prefix	Code	m.	Words	Charge	This message is on a/c of:	Recd. at	m.
Office of Origin and Service Instructions.			Sent			Date	
			At	m.	Service.	From	(44)
			To				
			By		(Signature of "Franking Officer.")	By	

TO — Page 2

Sender's Number	Day of Month	In reply to Number	AAA
BBM373			
Howitzers } Nil.			
31 Heavies }			

From   Fourth Div Arty.
Place
Time   5.15 p.

The above may be forwarded as now corrected. (Z)

BM

Army Form C. 2121.

MESSAGES AND SIGNALS. No. of Message

Code	m.	Words	Charge	This message is on a/c of:	Recd. at	m.
		Sent			Date	
and Service Instructions		At	m.	Service	From	
		To				
		By		(Signature of "Franking Officer.")	By	

TO — 4ᵗʰ Div.

Sender's Number	Day of Month	In reply to Number	AAA
BBM 375	31		

In continuation of 5.15 pm report (BBM 373)

27ᵗʰ FAB. Fired at enemy's trenches as germans in those trenches were firing at our aeroplane AAA. ~~Fired at~~ Also fired at enemy's trenches in retaliation for their shelling our trenches

From   Fourth Div Arty.
Place
Time   6.45 pm

The above may be forwarded as now corrected   (Z)

Censor.   Signature of Addressor or person authorised to telegraph in his name

BM

*This line should be erased if not required.
2662 M. & Co. Ltd. Wt. W929/549—100,000. 6/14. Forms C2121/10.

Army Form C. 2121.

AND SIGNALS. No. of Message

Prefix	Code	m.	Words	Charge		This message is on a/c of :		Recd. at	m.
Office of Origin and Service Instructions.			Sent					Date	
At		m.				Service.		From	66
To									
By					(Signature of "Franking Officer.")		By		

TO — Fourth Div.

Sender's Number	Day of Month	In reply to Number	AAA
BBM 376	31		

Hostile shelling report

4·50 a.m. — Battery apparently North of FRELINGHEM fired 12 light shell at the LE TOUQUET – LE BIZET road AAA.

8 a.m. — Enemy anti-aircraft guns fired at one of our aeroplanes over LE GHEER. AAA

9·20 a.m. and 10·35 a.m. — A few field gun shell fell in ARGYLL'S trenches. Direction from which fired not known AAA.

2·52 p.m. to 3·10 p.m. — One 15cm. gun fired 5 rounds at NEUVE EGLISE.

3·35 p.m. — The same gun fired 2 more rounds at NEUVE EGLISE. From the sound the gun was behind MESSINES–GAPAARD ridge.

From ~~Fourth Div. Arty.~~
Place
Time 7·10 p.m.

The above may be forwarded as now corrected (Z)

Censor. Signature of Addressee or person authorised to telegraph in his name

*This line should be erased if not required.

Army Form C. 2121.

...ES AND SIGNALS. No. of Message

Prefix	Code	m.	Words	Charge	This message is on a/c of :	Recd. at	m.
Office of Origin and Service Instructions.			Sent			Date	
			At	m.	Service.	From	65
			To				
			By		(Signature of "Franking Officer.")	By	

TO — Page 2

| Sender's Number | Day of Month | In reply to Number | AAA |
| BB19 376 | 31st | | |

3·40 pm to 4 pm. — Eleven 10 cm. howitzer shell fell in our left two trenches. The rounds were fired in pairs and from the sound appeared to come from behind the MESSINES - WYTSCHAETE ridge AAA.

5·10 pm — Six heavy howitzer shell fell round LE BIZEE - PLOEGSTEERT road, four bursting on percussion and one in the air. They seemed to come from the neighbourhood of LES ECLUSES

From Fourth Div Arty
Place
Time 6·35 pm

Progress Reports

WEEKLY REPORT.

4th Div.No. GGG/28.

5/3/15

Head Quarters,

Third Corps.

Weekly Report.

1. Resume.   Another quiet week leaves very little to
report. The only fresh work of any note undertaken has
been a trench close behind the Railway barricade which
will act as a retrenchment. This is an important matter
because the barricade, owing to its closeness to the enemy,
is a front where a rush might be expected. Elsewhere
revetting and wiring had been proceeded with and in one
or two places the line has been shortened by cutting off
a corner. Work has begun in earnest on several waterlogged
communications which it is hoped shortly to reclaim.

Under headings (c) and (d) there is practically
nothing to report in any of the sectors. In the left
sector the enemy has commenced a new communication trench
west of the Messines road in U.2.b. Sniping has been the
same all along the line. The village and wood of Ploegsteert, also the trenches in the left sector, have been
shelled daily but without effecting material damage.

2. Right Sector. (12th Brig.)

(a) The retrenchment referred to above has been
started but the enemy's snipers, profiting by the moonlight
nights, were able to prevent the work from making much
progress.

The barricade to join up the Monmouth House with
the Railway barricade has been gone on with.

Defences in the snipers' houses are still being
consolidated.

(b) Nothing new is proposed.

3. CENTRE Sector. (11th Brig.).

(a) In the East Lancs section, Picket Ho., which
marks the extreme left of the line held by this Regt., has
been provided with a Machine Gun emplacement skillfully
concealed in front of the debris of the house.

There is under construction a communication trench
which will link up the Lancashire support farm with the
Convent.

In the Hants section the communication trench
joining the T trench with Ploegsteert wood is now being
reclaimed.

In the Somerset section a fire trench has been
dug North of Moated Fm. to give protection in this direction
to 2 Mountain guns whose emplacements are alongside the
farm.

(b) A new work strengthening the angle where the 10th
and 11th Brigs. join is proposed and will be commenced
when labour is available.

4. Left Sector. (10th Brig.)

(a) Progress has been made with the semi-high command
work along the ridge West of ST.YVES.

The

The trench designed to shorten the line held by the A. and S.Highrs. by cutting out an angle is now finished.
The communication trench from the Messines road to the right of the Douve section is now completed.
(b) The new communication trench referred to last week in the Douve section has not yet been started and is still in contemplation.

5th March, 1915.

Major General,
Commanding 4th Division.

Report on progress of work on 2nd line.

February 4th.

R.LYS - PLOEGSTEERT - LE GHEER Road.

(a) R.LYS - TOUQUET Road.
From river to railway and 150 yards beyond railway - trench and revetment completed, flooring in hand.
100 yards near LE TOUQUET road, revetment completed.
Remainder trench completed, drainage and revetment in hand.
Wire fence with apron completed.
SUPPORTING POINTS. River Farm. Trenches ¾ completed.
                                  Wire ½ completed.
                   Flanque Fe. Trenches completed about ¾
                                  revetted. Flooring in hand.

(b) TOUQUET Road - WARNETON Road.
Trench and drainage complete. Revetment half done. Wire complete. Flooring in hand.
SUPPORTING POINT. Rabecques Farm. Trenches and drainage complete. Revetment and wire half done.

(c) WARNETON Road - LE GHEER Road.
Trench complete. 100 yards more revetment to do. Drainage in hand. Wire fence nearly completed.
SUPPORTING POINT. LONDON Farm. Defences completed. Redoubt between London Farm and Rabecques traced but not yet commenced.

LE GHEER Road - Junction with 5th Division.

(a) Road - Wood. Houses fortified, breastworks built and wire entanglement completed.
Communication and overhead cover in hand.

(b) Bunhill Row to Mud Lane. Breastworks completed. Communications, wiring, screening, headcover, machine guns platform in hand.

(c) U.14.c. 5.2 to U.14.c. 8.8. Trenches being dug, drained and revetted, about 70% completed.

(d) U.14.c. 8.8 to U.14.a. 5.4. Trench dug, drainage and revetting in hand.

(e) U.14.a. 5.4 to U.13.b. 6.8. Trench completed, drained and revetted.

Trench being continued westwards. It has been found useless to dig trench unless revetted at once. Some further trenches have been dug but have fallen in.
Supporting points as far as LE ROSSIGNOL completed.

1st Line Work.
Seaforths section. Practically all trenches revetted and fitted with firing step.
Warwicks section. New trench N.W. of St.YVES, about ¼ done.
Kings Own section. Complete revetment of trenches in hand.

The distribution called for under 3rd A.C.No.G732, dated 10th February, 1915, and forwarded with weekly report on 12th February, 1915, should be amended as follows-

Right Sector. (12th Brig.)

(a) No. of Bns. in front line 2
(b) No. of Coys. in firing line ... 6 Coys.(less 1 P.)
(c) No. of Coys. in Bn. support ... 1 P.
(d) No. of Coys. in Bn. reserve ... 2 Coys.
(e) No. of Bns. in Bn. reserve ... 2 *
(f) Composition of and location of Divisional reserve. .. 1 Bn. Le Bizet.

* Includes 5th South Lancs. which has always some platoons in trenches undergoing instruction.

WEEKLY REPORT.

RIGHT SECTOR. (12th Brigade)

(a) A trench has been dug in the garden beside the forward Sniper's House, 18 yards are completed. Defences of these buildings have been further consolidated by backing the walls with sandbags.

The retrenchment at the Railway Barricade, referred to last week, has been completed to a length of 50 yards.

The communication trench from Le Touquet station to the Sniper's houses has been reclaimed for 200 yards and is being boarded. All along the front revetting and putting out wire entanglements has continued.

It is proposed to continue the work in progress.

(b) Sniping and shelling have been as usual. Rifle grenades have been much used by the enemy against the Sniper's Houses, upwards of 20 being fired a day.

(c) No information is available as to any changes in the hostile dispositions.

CENTRE SECTOR. (11th Brigade).

(a) The E.Lancs seized and have strengthened a farm in front of their line and it is now garrisoned night and day. This marks a definite advance towards the hostile trenches.

A Machine Gun emplacement has been made in front of Picket House. The Hants Regt. has reclaimed a large ~~portion~~ part of an abandoned communication trench. This will give a second means of reaching the forward trench.

The Somersets pushed a sap from their right trench towards the Birdcage.

(b) It is proposed to continue the work in hand.

(c) Sniping and shelling have been about the same as usual. Since the attack of the First Army our demonstrations have lead to recriminations; but not more than might have been
expected

expected.

(d) No information has been obtained about the enemy.

LEFT SECTOR. (10th Brigade)

(a) The work reported last week is still in progress. The high commands across the front of the right section (St Yves) are now about 2/3rds on the way to completion (260 out of 400 yards).

The defences of St Yves have been consolidated.

In the Douve section the communication trench referred to last week is completed and this section can be reached by day.

A second trench has now been constructed parallel to the first.

Three saps were broken out from the trench East of St Yves

Revetting and wiring have continued.

(b) It is proposed to still further consolidate the defences of St Yves. Other work in hand will be continued.

(c) The Douve section has been ~~shelled~~ shelled rather less and the St Yves section rather more than usual. Sniping, generally speaking, less.

(d) There is no information about the enemy.

Major General

12/3/15.   Commanding 4th Di

REPORT on 2nd Line, 4th DIVISION.

(a) RIVER LYS - TOUQUET ROAD.

Trench completed and also 500 yards of flooring. Wire (double) fence being improved. Drain being made.

POSTS, LYS FARM. (ROBARDERIE)

Revetment of trenches in hand. Communication trenches in hand.

Flanque Farm. Trenches complete. Some flooring, barricading and communication trenches made, wiring commenced.

(b) TOUQUET ROAD - WARNETON ROAD.

Trench, wiring and drainage complete. About 300 yards revetment to be done. Flooring and Machine Gun emplacements in hand.

RABECQUES FARM.

Trench and drainage complete. Revetment and flooring ⅔ths done. One wire fence all round, 2nd fence in hand.

(c) WARNETON ROAD - LE GHEER ROAD.

Trench and revetment complete. Wire being strengthened, additional drains being made.

LONDON FARM.

Complete.

POST, near TILLEUL.

Just commenced.

(d) LE GHEER ROAD - WOOD.

Completed except some filling in of intervals between breastworks, to furnish continuous cover.

(e) South edge of wood.

Complete except for wiring around posts and head cover for 4 breastworks.

(f) BUNHILL ROW.

Wire entanglement completed. Head cover in hand. Pathway half done.

(g) SOUTH of MUD LANE.

Wire entanglement completed. Headcover not yet commenced.

(h) U/14/C/5.2. - U/14/C/3.3.

Communication and fire trenches being revetted.

(i) U/14/C/3.3 - U/14/a/5.4.

Revetting of fire trench in hand.

(j) U/14/a/5/5 to ROSSIGNOL.

Completed except for 100 yards.

────────────────────────

Reference.- St Yves and Frelinghien sheets. 1/10,000.

Weekly Report.

19/3/15

Resumé.

In the Right Sector work has chiefly consisted in re-opening communications and increasing retrenchments behind the Railway barricade. In the Centre and Left Sectors, owing to the relief of the brigades concerned which was contemplated and, in the case of the 10th Brig., carried out, there has been practically no work done.

RIGHT SECTOR.

(a) The communication trench from the LE TOUQUET Railway Station to the Sniper's Houses has now been boarded for a distance of 200 yards. The communication trench leading from the same place towards the Railway barricade has been largely reclaimed and an officer has been along it by day. In the front line the new retrenchment that crosses the line about 100 yards South of the barricade is now about 150 yards in length. In the Sniper's Houses the trench mentioned last week that was started from the Northern corner of the most advanced block of buildings and was to pass in front of the House of the Seven Gables is now completed. It is 70 yards in length and increases the length of front held here to about 100 yards. The garrison for this trench is to be accommodated in bomb proof shelters in the Seven Gables, which is about 20 yards in rear. Of these shelters one is completed so far as the walls are concerned. A plan of the Sniper's Houses is attached which shows part of the above trench. Bomb proof shelters are being made in several places but they are not yet completed.

(b) It is proposed to continue work on the communications and bomb proofs.

(c) Shelling has been rather more pronounced. On 2 or 3 occasions the GRANDE RABEQUE Farm has been shelled but no damage done. Also LE BIZET and yesterday a house near 12th Brig. H.Q. was demolished.

(d) With reference to the enemy – no information is available.

CENTRE SECTOR.

(a) As already stated work has been hampered by the move that was projected, though not carried out.

(b) It is proposed to continue work of re-opening communications.

(c) There has been a marked diminution in shelling as compared with the 2 previous weeks.

(d) A train was reported to have been heard at WARNETON Sta. but at such a distance information obtained in the trench is necessary unreliable. Movements of wheeled transport were also heard. This occurs at intervals and is as likely to be due to normal reliefs as to the arrival or departure of troops. In this Sector the front line of defence is now very strong and a method of blinding loopholes has been successfully attained so that we are at last more than able to hold our own with the enemy's snipers and instances frequently occur where these are silenced.

LEFT SECTOR.

(a) Owing to the relief of the 10th Brig. by the 84th Brig. little work was done. The communication trench leading from the forward Estaminet to Seaforth H.Q. has been used by day. The breastwork on the ST.IVES ridge across the left front of this Sector made some progress.

(b) It is proposed to continue this work and to strengthen the enciente defences of ST.IVES. A trench exists and could

be used but it is capable of considerable improvement which the dryer weather will now permit.
(c) There has been the normal amount of shelling.
(d) Continued movements of transport were heard on the night of 17/18th but its direction could not be accurately determined.

4th Division.

Report of Progress on Second Line.

Ref: 1/10,000 Frelinghien & St Yves.

1. RIGHT SECTION.

(a) <u>R.Lys - Le Touquet Road.</u>

<u>Trench</u> work has been continued on the flooring and drainage and on machine gun emplacements. About 300 yards of flooring and draining still to be done.

<u>Communication trenches</u> have been commenced.

<u>Lys Farm.</u> Fire trenches deepened, parapets thickened, wire entanglement improved and communication trenches made.

<u>La Flenecque Fm.</u> Trenches complete except flooring. Communication trenches and wire entanglement in progress.

(b) <u>Le Touquet - Warneton Road.</u>

Wire and drainage complete. About 50 yards of trench still to revet and 1,000 yards to floor. Machine gun emplacements being made.

<u>Farms in square C.14.b</u> - Trench almost complete.

<u>Grand Rabeque Fm.</u> ¾ trench finished. Drainage complete. Barricades being made. Machine gun emplacements made. Wire entanglements strengthened.

(c) <u>WARNETON - LE GHEER road.</u>

Drainage and flooring of trenches in progress. Wire entanglement strengthened and doubled all along.

<u>Tilleul Fm.</u> Trenches complete. Wire entanglement almost complete. Wall being loopholed.

<u>London Support Fm.</u> Complete.

2. LEFT SECTION.

Practically no change - on account of moves.

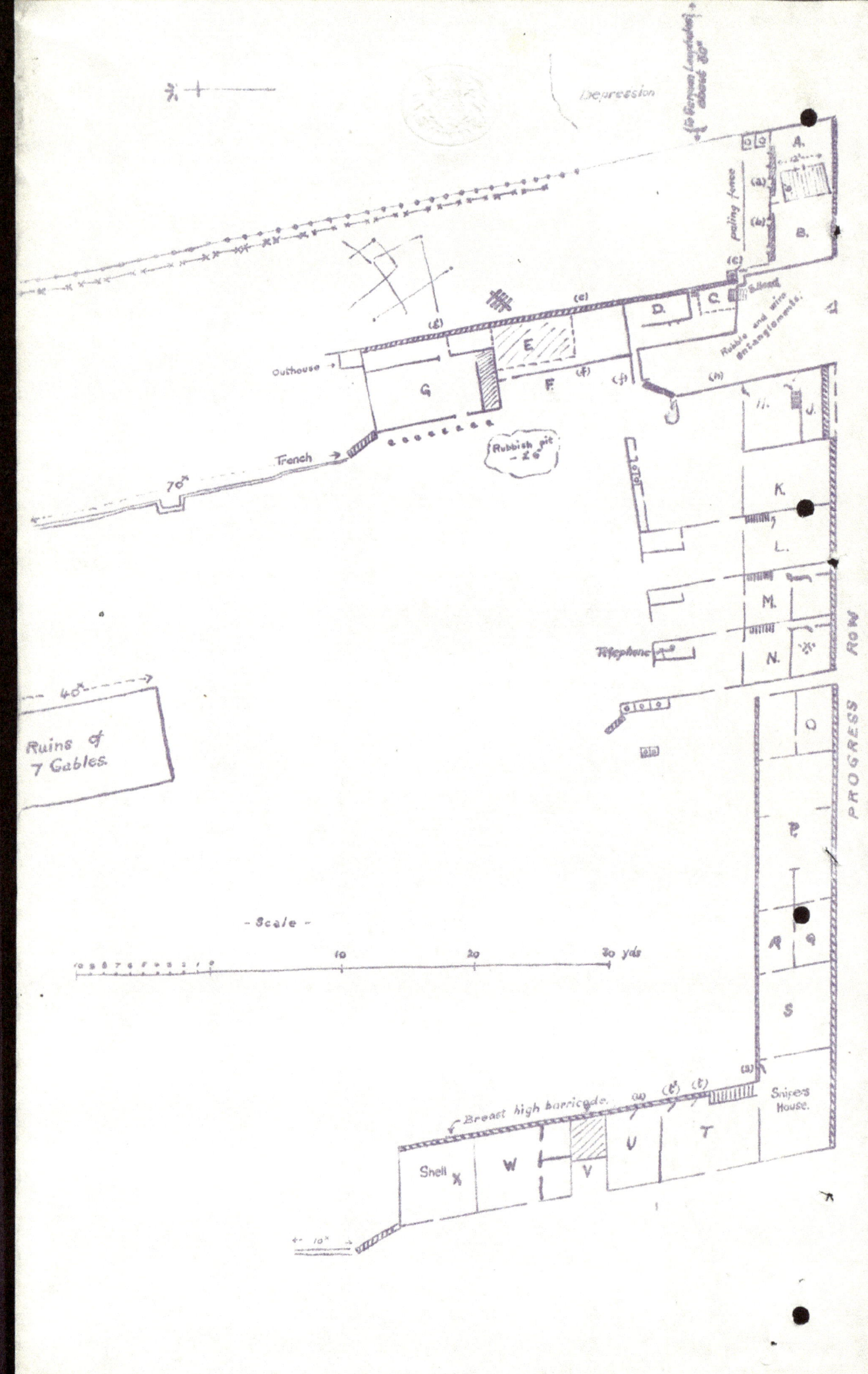

WEEKLY REPORT.   26/3/15

3rd Corps.

RESUME.

In the right sector communications have received chief attention, and the trench to the Snipers' Houses from Le Touquet is now finished.

In the centre sector the St Yves section has been taken over and communications have been improved at the edge of the wood to facilitate intercommunication between supporting points and also the debouching of a force engaged on a counter attack.

In the left sector trenches beyond the Douve have been taken over and improving of the wire obstacles which were considered to have been quite inadequate were at once taken in hand.

RIGHT SECTOR. (12th Inf. Brig.)

(a) The following communication trenches have been completely dug :-

Le Touquet Station - Snipers' Houses (see map (a)) boarded and finished.

Le Touquet Station - Railway Barricade (see map (b)) boarding in progress.

Despierre Fme - Essex Central Fm. (see map (c)) boarding in progress.

The gap between the Le Touquet and Warnave sections (i.e. between Railway Barricade and Monmouth Houses) which was 40 yards, has at last been closed by overlapping high commands (see map (d)). This work has been attended with considerable delay owing to the proximity and activity of the enemy's snipers. The retrenchment 50 yards in rear which consists of semi-high command works thrown out from either side so as to overlap is now nearing completion (see map (e)).

A new high command in rear of the Essex Central Fm. about 100 yards in length acts as a further retrenchment to this part of the line.

(b) It is proposed to continue the work in hand.

(c) Sniping has been as usual. Shelling, especially of the Le Touquet section, more pronounced. The enemy has caused some loss and considerable annoyance with rifle grenades. This has been particularly noticeable since the shortage has made it impossible to reply.

(d) No information is available concerning enemy.

CENTRE SECTOR.

CENTRE SECTOR. (11th Inf. Brig.)

(a) The Brigade took over the St Yves section from the 10th Brigade. A general reorganization throughout the Brigade was therefore rendered necessary. It was considered that the St Yves section was not as strong relatively as other parts of the front and special attention is being given to improving each detail of the defences. A new fire trench has been commenced on the North flank of the St Yves village.

In the second line the communication trench from the Three Huns Fm to the trenches on the East front is completed.

The communication trench to the Hants. "T" trench from Ploegsteert Wood has now been re-opened.

(b) The following work is proposed.

In Ploegsteert Wood: Improvement of communications to enable supports to move up and debouch from the wood for counter-attack on St Yves. Clearing of wire and hedges outside the wood. Improvement of accomodation in Somerset left trench (A) so as to have more men at the salient opposite the White Estaminet.

Le Gheer: Work on sap (B) with a view to straightening the line as soon as ground is dry enough.

St Yves: As a retrenchment to the St Yves defences it is proposed to make a line of works from Barricade House (C) to the road North of Moated Fm. with the object of assisting the deployment of the counter attack.

(c) Shelling and sniping have been about the same as last week.

(d) Various indications concerning the enemy do not lead to the belief that other than normal reliefs have been taking place. It is thought from the absence of Black Marias shell that the artillery in front has been depleted.

LEFT SECTOR. (10th Inf. Brig.)

(a) The communication trench to point 100 yards North of Seaforth House (D) is now completely boarded and the one leading directly to Seaforth House is dug through but not yet boarded. The rain has interfered with the work.

In the trans-Douve trenches it was found that between two fire trenches echelloned one in front of the other, there was a gap from front to rear of 200 yards. The flank of the forward trench appeared dangerously exposed. This has now been refused and heavily wired and wire entanglements placed across the gap. (E)

(b) It is proposed to continue consolidating the defences of the trans-Douve and especially strengthening the wire entanglements so as to bring them into line with the remainder of the front of the 4th Div.

(c) Shelling and sniping have been as usual.

(d) A report that dark blue great coats had been observed South of the R.Douve suggested a change in the units to our front. However, further enquiries revealed the fact that similar greatcoats have been observed from time to time in small numbers at various points along the front.

26th March, 1915.

for Maj.Gen. Commanding 4th Divn.

Summary of Information

Orders for handing over stores, etc.

1. Hand Grenades - Hand over all in trenches and carriers with battalions.
   Move brigade reserve (200) and carriers (100)

2. Rifle Grenades - Hand over all.

3. Telephone Lines - Hand over.
   Instruments - Move.

4. Cable lines - Hand over any of use to relieving brigade and move others.

5. Sandbags   )
   R.E. Stores   ) - Hand over.

6. Tools - Equipment Mob: Vehicles - move; hand over remainder.

7. Pumps - Hand over except private ones and R.E. Mob. equipment.

8. Gum boots - take away (battn stores)

9. Very pistols - Take away (battn stores)
   "   lights - hand over.

10. Loophole plates - hand over.

11. Handcarts - hand over half / half half.

12. Machine gun
    Amm. carriers - take away
    Hyposcopes   - take away

13. Periscopes - take away.

14. S.A.A. at trenches - hand over
15. Reserve depot of rations near trenches - hand over

Jarvis -

FIRST ARMY SUMMARY OF INFORMATION.

The enemy with whom we were engaged to-day was the VII German Corps.

The location of the units of the Corps at dawn to-day was as given in sketch in margin.

The 158th Regt. was withdrawn from the trenches four days ago and has gone either to HAUBOURDIN or away from this area altogether.

The 53rd Regt. appears to be in corps reserve near Don.

Prisoners state that two heavy batteries of the VII Corps have been moved from this area during the last few weeks.

Our attack this morning was a complete surprise to the enemy. At LILLE there are only reserve formations. So far as can be made out the enemy has no further large body of troops which he can throw into the fight during the next few days.

The prisoners taken number about 800. The 3rd battalion of the 16th Regt. has been all either killed or captured.

According to prisoners statements there is no line of trenches between that taken by us to-day and the LILLE defences running through ENGLOS.

The villages are entrenched.

Following Headquarters located:

VII Corps   - LAMADELEINE.
14th Div.   - DON.
13th Div.   - FOURNES (?)
Railhead   - DON.

11 p.m.

10th March, 1915.

(sd)   J. CHARTERIS, Major,

General Staff, 1st Army.

4th Division
6th Division

INFORMATION 4th and 6th DIVISIONS, 10th March, 1915.

Time	4th Division.	6th Division.
8.5 a.m.		16th Bde. carried out bursts of fire for 15 minutes at a time early this morning followed by neighbouring Coy. cheering AAA 17th Bde. maxims and Cos. ordered bursts of rapid fire.
9.50 a.m.	No movement observed in any Sector opposite 4th Div.	6th Div. report a good deal of hostile sniping.
10.30 a.m.		18th Bde. Art. commenced at 7.30 a.m. on enemy's new trenches near PONT BALLOT with good effect AAA Enemy replied with a few shell no effect AAA 17th Bde. sniping and burst of fire 16th Bde. salient North of RUE DU BOIS shelled with good effect heavy sniping and bursts of fire at RUE DU BOIS AAA Enemy appears to be distinctly dominated there AAA 19th Bde. report enemy has not replied as yet to any of the fire attacks AAA Our barrels were dropped down LYS early this morning awaiting report from Westminsters as to effect AAA All inhabitants in area HOUPLINES - ARMENTIERES - L'ARMEE and LA VESEE confined to their houses between 2 p.m. and 8 p.m. to-day.
12.20 pm.	4th Div. report 11.30 am. AAA Right sector no movement seen AAA Germans fairly busy with earth and timber in front trenches AAA One of our aeroplanes fired on fairly heavily by rifles and artillery AAA Centre sector no movements very quiet to their front AAA Left sector no movements AAA Artillery report no movement. AAA	6th Div. report special work of which you are aware progressing vigorously AAA Fresh activity all along line except in 17th Bde. will re-commence at 2 pm. AAA 17th Bde. has special scheme on AAA 2nd F.A.Bde. and right section Heavy Batty. gave a burst of fire on FRELINGHIEN at 10.30 am. AAA 42nd Batty. fired at trenches at PONT BALLOT AAA 24th Bde. shelled trenches on front L'EPINETTE WEZ MACQUART and batteries firing from LA BLEUE and I 23 a. at 10 a.m.
2.25 pm.	4th Div. report AAA Right sector no hostile movements observed AAA Centre sector normal AAA Left sector no movement AAA Our artillery put 6-18 pdr. shells into enemy's trenches AAA Enemy shelling Pt.63 and St.YVES intermittently AAA	6th Div. report 16th and 19th Bdes. supported by 38th F.A.Bde. delivered burst of fire between 11 and 11.30 am. on German salient in front of RUE DU BOIS and on trenches opposite centre of 18th Bde. AAA Germans fired some bombs in reply AAA Right Section 18th Bde. co-operated with artillery in fire attack on hostile trenches at 11.30 am. AAA Opposite centre and left

INFORMATION 4th and 6th DIVISIONS, 10th March, 1915.

Time.	4th Division.	6th Division.
Contd. 2.25 pm.		sections 18th Bde. enemy refuses to reply to systematic sniping AAA 42nd Batty. shelled PONT BALLOT trenches at 11.30 am. 43rd and 53rd and 1 section heavy Batty. fired with good results on house in FRELINGHIEN AAA Heavy Batty. also fired at train at QUESNOY station which left hurriedly and also obtained 5 direct hits on house at LA HONGROIE and 2 on one in I 17 reported to be observation post AAA 42nd and 110th Battys. engaged enemy's guns North of LE FRESNELLE.
3.55 pm.		6th Div. report 3.30 pm. that 19th Bde. have continued their rifle and machine gun fire at enemy trenches enemy replying with a few shells AAA Enemy's infantry small reply AAA Enemy active opposite 16th Bde. with grenades AAA 18 H.E. shells over our right company of this Bde. no damage AAA Our artillery engaged farms at South end of FRELINGHIEN one battery shelled PONT BALLOT AAA 2 Batteries shelled trench N. of LILLE road and a trench mortar which was silenced AAA 34th Batty. engaged a Batty. at FLEUR DE COSSE and RUE DU BOIS Wood with apparently good effect.
6.20 pm.	4th Div. report no movement observed AAA Left sector was shelled intermittently since 2.30 pm. AAA Brass band heard in the distance opposite left sector AAA Reported that enemy have established depot for planks and barbed wire just S. of LA POTTERIE FARM AAA Also that a good deal of entanglement has been removed from in front of German trench running from U 15 b. to point about 300 yards East of South end of avenue U 9 c. AAA This is being verified AAA Only the base of FRELINGHIEN Church remains.	6th Div. report that 18th Bde. drew machine gun fire in three places and machine guns were silenced effect thought to be good AAA Sniping active and our rifle grenades having good effect at RUE DU BOIS and on left of 18th Bde AAA

INFORMATION 4th and 6th DIVISION, 10th March, 1915.

Time.	4th Division.	6th Division.
7.10 pm.	Reference my G.232 the battalion in section concerned report that German wire on both sides of RED ESTAMINET in U 15 b. is cut but they attribute this to shelling of our artillery AAA German wire in front of right and centre companies is intact.	
8.15 pm.	4th Div. AAA No movement observed AAA Right sector received a few light shells round railway barricade and enemy fired six rifle grenades on LYS section AAA Centre sector received 47 light shells AAA Left sector quiet AAA It is reported that our artillery made excellent practice in German trenches in which and machine gun co-operated AAA The enemy made no reply to this AAA	6th Div. AAA Artillery shelled enemy's salient at RUE DU BOIS his trenches at PONT BALLOT and South of FRELINGHIEN also house at LA HONGROIE AAA Heavy Batty. and 43rd Batty. engaged guns at HOUPLINES and 110th Batty. engaged gun in I 12 b. AAA 111th shelled LA PREVOTE AAA Infantry maintained fire on enemy's trenches but have nothing special to report.

INFORMATION - - 4th and 6th DIVISIONS, 10/11th March, 1915.

Time.	4th Division.	6th Division.
10.50 pm.	4th Div. report no hostile movements observed AAA Centre sector report our shrapnel burst accurately on enemy's parapet and blew away portion of German Barricade in WARNETON ROAD and to which enemy's field guns replied on edge of PLOEGSTEERT WOOD AAA	6th Div. AAA 16th Bde. report enemy apparently anxious as very large numbers of flares are being sent up AAA Enemy firing MINENWERFER in reply to rifle grenade fire AAA 18th Bde. report another explosion occured 7.30 pm. same place as last night AAA Explosion preceded by 2 blasts on a whistle AAA Durhams report their converging fire on part of line apparently very effective.
8.25 am.	4th Div. report all quiet no movement of enemy observed AAA	6th Div. AAA 18th Bde. right section opened rapid fire at 5 am. left section heavy sniping during night drawing more fire than usual AAA Enemy in 18th Bde. front seemed rather jumpy last night AAA Explosive expert thinks that explosion reported in my G.241 sounded like H.E. used for demolition.
10.15 am.	4th Div. report that owing to mist very little can be seen AAA Right and Centre sectors nothing observed AAA Enemy worked hard in avenue in U 9 a. and strengthened wire in front of DUBLINS East of RED ESTAMINET U 15 b.	6th Div. report 16th Bde. in co-operation with 24th Batty. opened fire on breastwork I 22 a. at 5 am silencing a maxim AAA At 5.15 am. 87th Batty. turned some snipers out of SNIPERS HOUSE by road junction I 22 a. AAA Patrolling all along the line AAA Enemy sent out no patrols but continue active sniping which was dealt with by bursts of rapid fire AAA All his trenches appear fully manned as usual AAA A very loud explosion occured in enemy's trench just N. of FRELINGHIEN during the night AAA
12.34 pm.	4th Div. report AAA No movements observed AAA Left sector report that Germans have repaired all their wire in front of right section near St. YVES.	6th Div. report as follows AAA 16th Bde. report one patrol which came back late got on to a German working party with magazine fire dispersed the party and caused some casualties AAA Enemy have made little reply to our fire only a few shells near WATER FARM in 19th Bde. AAA
2.25 pm.	4th Div. report no movement observed AAA Some shells fell in trenches and left sectors AAA Our howitzers made good practice on avenue in U 9 a. AAA	6th Div. report continued hostile sniping along the line AAA Very misty and artillery can do little AAA Hostile artillery not replying.
4.30 pm.	4th Div. report that enemy trying to push out barbed wire attached to trestles in front of trenches opposite WARNAVE section of right sector otherwise no movements centre sector reports our artillery good range	6th Div. report that 16th Bde. fired 4 rounds with new mortar at German house with great effect sniper's house by the road junction I 22 a. was shelled with effect AAA Enemy reported more active in front of No.2 section 18th Bde. sniping continues all along the line AAA

INFORMATION - - 4th and 6th DIVISIONS, 10/11th March, 1915.

Time.	4th Division.	6th Division.
Contd. 4.30 pm.	enemy retaliating with 60 light shells no harm done AAA Enemy shelled St.YVES heavily from 12.30 to 1.15 pm. AAA Little damage AAA Our artillery retaliated at 1 pm. with good effect several Germans bolted from factory when fired on also FME DE LA CROIX well shelled.	
5.50 pm.	4th Div. have nothing to report in right and left sectors AAA Centre sector report during Howitzer bombardment about 12 Germans moved from BIRDCAGE to man trench and were fired upon by our machine guns AAA Sniping normal AAA An F.A.Bde. fired 30 rounds per battery at enemy's trenches AAA Germans retaliated on our trenches near LE TOUQUET.	6th Div. report Germans have made little artillery reply all day but are still sniping actively AAA
6.45 pm.	4th Division report right sector no movement observed AAA Centre Sector Hants report enemy unusually quiet; from smaller number of fires observed it is thought enemy's trenches to their front not so strongly held as usual AAA Considerable rifle fire in front of Irish Fus. in left sector AAA Germans in firing light shells in DOUVE Valley obtained three direct hits on their own trenches.	6th Division report enemy showing no activity in front of 19th Brigade AAA In front of 16th Brigade enemy shelled DES PLANQUE FARM and towards CHAPELLE D'ARMENTIERES AAA 18th Bde. report enemy more responsive than usual opposite their left AAA

L'EPINETTE captured during the night - no details yet.

C.H.Harington Lt Col

INFORMATION - - 4th & 6th /DIVISIONS, 12th March, 1915.

Time.	4th Division.	6th Division.
8.5 am.	4th Div. report no hostile movement observed AAA Working party seen opposite centre sector was fired on AAA Enemy's transport on move at 10.30 pm. opposite centre sector direction unknown.	6th Div. report 17th Bde. maintains position no signs of enemy being active elsewhere AAA
10.50 am.	4th Div. report no hostile movement observed AAA German wiring party fired on by infantry in centre sector.	Details of attack last night as follows AAA At midnight the right of 18th Bde. opened a brisk fire to which Germans responded by sending up a lot of lights opposite 18th AAA 17th Bde. troops detailed for attack advanced in 2 columns converging and obtained first 8 houses easily AAA The last 3 were very heavily wired and enemy got away by communication trenches while our men getting through wire AAA Enemy fired a lot but very wild and high AAA Our casualties 5 officers and 30 AAA Net results advanced 300 yards on a front of ½ a mile AAA No prisoners taken AAA Understand arrangements made by 17th Bde. worked well AAA
12.35 pm.	4th Div. report small working party in ruins of BIRDCAGE dispersed by rifle fire and a few small shells at DOUVE trench otherwise Germans quiet.	6th Div. report Germans all quiet AAA
1.45 pm.	4th Div. report no hostile movement observed AAA Centre sector shelled very slightly otherwise all quiet AAA	6th Div. report 17th Bde. entrenching strongly AAA Still very misty no artillery on either side firing all quiet except for heavy sniping all along the line.
4.6 pm.	4th Div. report no hostile movement observed AAA Some shelling of LE TOUQUET section and avenue in T 12 AAA Our artillery retaliated on ruined farm in U 15 d. & U 33 c. & U 33 d. AAA	6th Div. AAA Enemy have been shelling new trenches of 17th Bde. at L'EPINETTE AAA Our artillery retaliated on enemy's battery and trenches opposite AAA Enemy's fire active opposite right and centre of 18th Bde.
6.25 pm.	4th Div. no movements to report AAA Enemy shelling LE BIZET with medium shell at 5.30 pm. AAA Left sector our artillery making good practice AAA	6th Div. report our guns fired few shrapnel and lyddite on enemy's trenches near L'EPINETTE AAA otherwise nothing to report.
10.10 pm.	4th Div. report many flares going up in front of their centre sector otherwise nothing to report	6th Div. report AAA 17th, 18th, 19th Bdes. nothing to report AAA 16 Report enemy's sniping more active and used a small field gun or Minenwerfer against their left AAA

INFORMATION 4th DIVISION. 13th March, 1915.

7-28 am. Enemy put 16 shell round ST YVES about 3-45 am. Also shelled MESSINES road and DOUVE trenches from 2 am, and are still shelling. Our Artillery opened with effect on PETITE DOUVE Farme and vicinity at 4-15 am, keeping up the fire till 5 am.. During this time heavy rifle fire was heard, apparently opposite 2nd Corps.

9-15 am. No hostile movement observed. Shelling of Left Section which was going on when last report was made has now ceased. A few rifle grenades have been fired against the Right Section of this Sector, otherwise all quiet.

1-30 pm. No hostile movement observed. Saps in Right Section of Left Sector progressing. Artillery fired on working party N.W. of Birdcage.

5-26 pm. Right Sector report RABEQUE Farme set on fire by incendiary shells about 4-30 pm. Centre Sector sniping rather more active in front of Rif Brig. Left Sector report St Yves and left trenches shelled about 1-30 pm. 31st Heavy Battery searched for the German battery.

9-25 pm. All quiet and no hostile movement observed. A few Little Willies H.E. in Centre Sector and a few shells landed behind Central Farme on left of Right Sector. A German battery near the Sucerie shelled St Yves and was engaged by 31st Heavies. Enemy also put a few shells near the Station at Le Touquet.

CORRESPONDENCE ON THE FOLLOWING SUBJECTS WILL BE FOUND IN BOX MARKED "4th DIVISION - CORRESPONDENCE."

Jan-March 1915

CANADIAN DIVISION

NORTH MIDLAND DIVISION

ANTI-AIRCRAFT

ARTILLERY

SUPPORTING LINES

OFFENSIVE ACTION

MINES

SAPPING AND MINING

PRESS CORRESPONDENTS

TRICKING ENEMY - Devices for

TRENCH MORTARS

VERMELLES - Trip to

TRENCHES - Strengthening of

ARMISTICE - Informal

MACHINE GUNS

BRIGADE ENGINEER

WEEKLY REPORTS ON WORK CARRIED OUT

GRENADES

PERISCOPES

DEFENCE SCHEME

RANGE FINDERS

PRISONERS

COUNTER ATTACKS

RELIEF OF 5th & 6th DIVISIONS

EMPLOYMENT OF R.E.

ARMOURED MOTOR CARS

LEAKAGE OF INFORMATION

ST. ELOI - Increase of Troops.

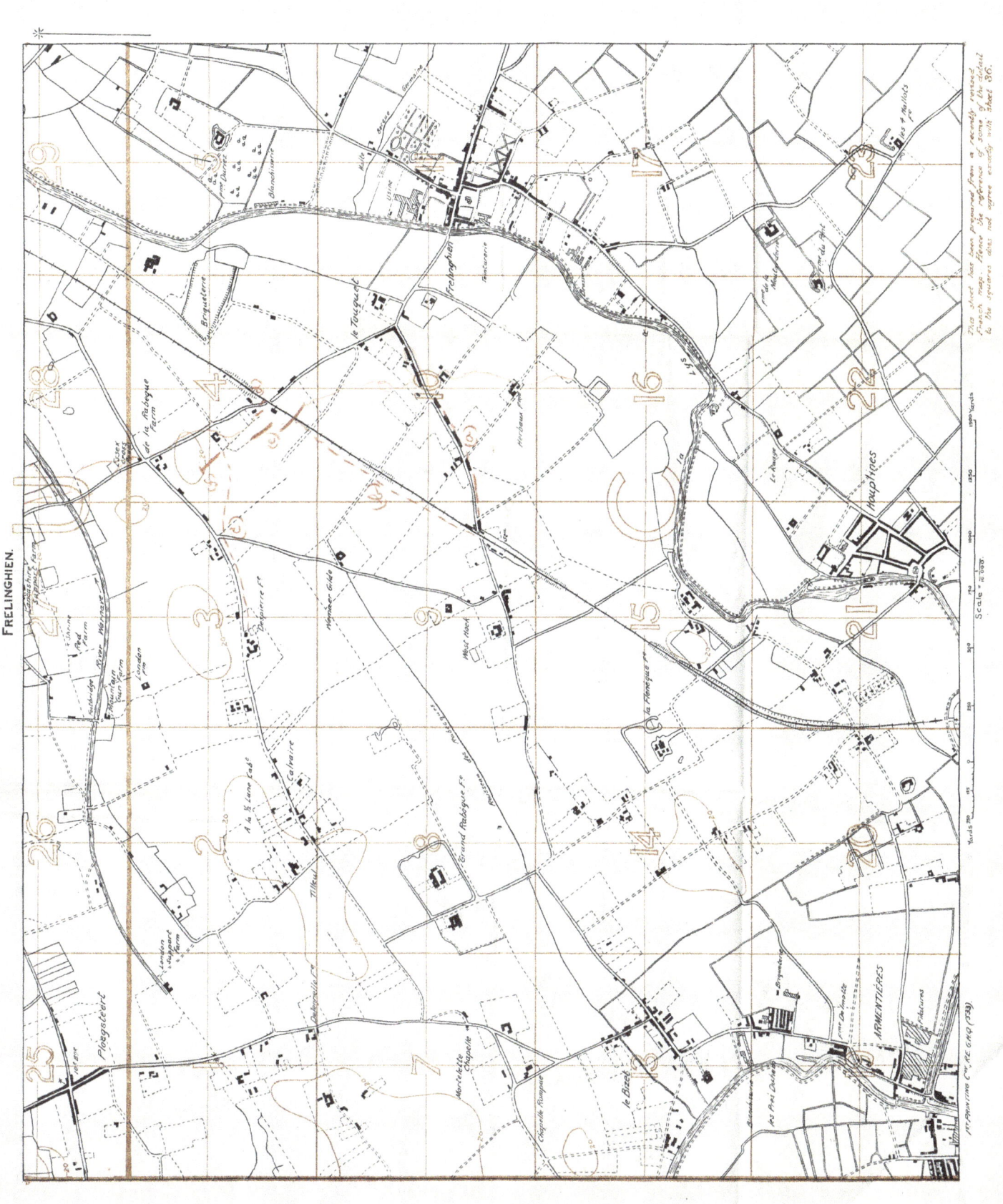

3rd Edition - 1st Feby 1915.

NOTES with reference to VERMELLES:

1. SHORT STATEMENT OF FRENCH ACTION AT VERMELLES:

The village of Vermelles lies on both sides of two parallel roads that run N-N-E on the western slopes of a gently sloping spur running N-N-E from high ground that lies S-W of the main Bethune-Noyelles-Lens road. Towards the north of the village the principal street runs S-E uphill across the above two roads. In this street stand the Brewery and the Church and from its south eastern end on the high ground across the railway a good view of the present German position can be obtained. To the west of the village the ground falls for 450 yards in a gentle slope to a small stream - the Courant de Bully - whence the ground rises steadily westward to a ridge some 1000 yards away from the village, whence it falls slightly to the Rivière de la Font^e de Bray, and rises again to the Sailly ridge which is nearly two miles from Vermelles.

The western face of Vermelles gives an almost ideal position for defence:

(1) A splendid open field of fire down to the stream and up to the first ridge,

(2) A good extent of front to give free use of numbers in the firing line,

(3) Good lateral communications.

The weak point of the village is the pronounced salient that its southern (S-S-W) end forms.

The French 131st Brigade, under the command of Colonel Gadel, was brought up by motor bus on the 13th October, 1914 to form the right of an attack on the German position in the vicinity of Vermelles. The French attacked on the 14th and 15th October with their left on Annequin, and their right on Mazingarbe. Their left attack, which was their main attack, advanced over the above mentioned open slopes against the west face of the village. It reached a line west of the Courant de Bully.

The right attack carried out by the 131st Brigade came in on Vermelles from the south and south-west, one regiment astride each of the two parallel roads mentioned at the beginning of this

paper

paper. This attack succeeded in getting close up to the Brewery and Church. Here however it was counterattacked and driven back. Owing to the personal efforts of a good battalion Commander the retirement was checked at the south end of the village and the French managed to establish themselves in the Cemetery and in the extreme S-S-W houses of the village and to dig themselves in in trenches in line with thses houses facing N-N-E.

The Germans were thus thrown back both on the west and south and their line was left with a very pronounced salient at Vermelles.

Note the power of a good battalion or company leader and the importance of checking a retirement at the earliest moment. These end houses gave the French good supporting points from which to work forward. If they had fallen back further and the Germans had got these end houses the French would have had to advance over open ground in any attempt to capture the village.

From the 15th October, the French steadily pressed on their enveloping attack against the village. The progress on the open slopes to the W-N-W was very small, but the progress from the south-west from house to house along both roads was satisfactory until the regiment on the left road reached the close proximity of the chateau, a well built little modern villa with capacious cellars.

Its grounds (about two acres) were surrounded by a brick wall. The Germans made the chateau very strong with trenches behind the walls and very deep communicating trenches radiating all over the grounds from the cellars where they slept. Against this position in the chateau the French could make no progress above ground. They therefore commenced mining.

On 1st December the French exploded two mines under the front of the enclosure wall of the chateau of Vermelles and under cover of the confusion caused by this explosion they rushed forward in ten columns of twenty men each, each column being headed by some men of the Moroccan troops of the Active Army, who were brought specially to Vermelles for this duty. It was considered that the young men of the Active Army (i.e. men under 30) who had not been employed in trench work, were better suited for leading columns, though the older men (i.e. the Reservists men over 30) were better for maintaining a position when once it was gained. During the night of the 30th November the walls of the houses, and gardens that the French were holding were broken in ten places for the ten columns, the holes being built up again with loose bricks so that these breaches might not be apparent to the enemy.

The attack took place at 11 a.m. on 1st December after the men had had a good meal and were in the best fighting spirit

When the mines exploded the stormers pushed down the loose bricks covering them and dashed forward to the assault. The Germans were so demoralised by the explosion of the mines that they precipitately retired from the chateau grounds and adjacent trenches. Not a shot was fired by them for about ten minutes. The French were therefore able to advance with very slight loss and were able to establish themselves in the chateau and along the north wall of the chateau grounds.

After strengthening and consolidating their position at the chateau the French again pressed on utilising a mountain gun to fire into the houses that still held out. This threat from the south-west combined with the pressure of the French on the north, west and south caused the Germans to evacuate Vermelles and to go back to a position which they had previously prepared nearly two miles further East.

2. FORMATION OF BRIGADE:

1. The 131st Brigade is formed of the

    280th) Regiments of Reservists
    281st)   i.e. men over 30
    296th)

with a battalion of Territorials (i.e. men over 40) attached to the Brigade. Each of these regiments consists of two battalions.

2. The Brigade now holds a front of about three kilometres about two miles beyond Vermelles. This front is divided between these three regiments and the territorial battalion.

The battalions of each regiment are alternately (a) in reserve and (b) in the front line and support for four days.

The battalion not in reserve has two companies in front line and two companies in support. The supporting companies change places with the firing line companies at the end of two days. The territorial battalion has one company in the front line, xxx one in support, and two in reserve.

3. DETAILS OF MINES:

The right mine was about 128 metres long, and the left mine was about 80 metres long. The bottom of each mine was about 6 metres below the surface. Each mine was charged with 400 kilos (say 900 lbs) of black powder.

A mine that was exploded in November when charged with 200 kilos of melinite was not a success as it expended all its energy below ground and made no crater on the surface.

4. POINTS PARTICULARLY WORTHY OF NOTICE:

(1)   The very large amount of work done both by the French and by the Germans.

(2)   The patient and methodical way in which the attack was carried out step by step and from house to house. The attack lasted 52 days.

(3)   The very small losses incurred by the French in this methodical advance is noticeable.

(4)   The experience of Vermelles agrees with our own experience of the houses held by the Germans east of Ploegsteert Wood, and shows clearly that if a house is properly prepared and everything inflammable removed it can be defended by determined men whatever artillery fire be brought to bear on it.

(5)   The great number of communication trenches (boyaux) and their depth.

(6)   The advantage taken of the shelter of houses to make the communication trenches straight whereever possible - protecting them by "blinded traverses" i.e., timbers across the trench over which are planks and over the planks earth

(7)   The type of deep trench used by the Germans in their "semi-circular trench" which was exposed to fire from an arc of

over

180 degrees. It would not be good in any other position.

(8)   The German overhead cover in many places is clever especially where it has been made as a protection against enfilade and reverse fire.

(9)   The local resources which the Germans used especially in their revetments - barrels used as gabions, local corn sacks used as sandbags.

(10)   The siting of machine gun emplacements by the Germans especially those placed in front of the line of trenches.

A tunnel is dug under the parapet and comes up outside to just below the ground level. The gun fires over the latter and the detachment kneel out of view. The gun can thus fire to front or flanks and when shelled can be drawn back into the tunnel.

(11)   The method of bomb-proofing the German Commander's cellar at the north end of the village; (a) earth and iron railings on the floor; (b) big beams put across from wall to wall the outer ones about 3 feet, the centre one about 5 feet above the floor; (c) these beams being in turn covered with iron pipes so as to explode any shell before it could reach the roof of the cellar, and so as to protect the roof of the cellar in case the top of the house fell in.

(12)   The utilisation of the ground underneath a partially demolished haystack for a battalion Commander's residential dug-out consisting of staircase, hall, parlour and bedroom complete with bedstead and other furniture with pictures hung round the earth walls. From this commander's dug-out the communicating trenches to the fire trenches started, and near by were dug-outs evidently intended for the battalion staff.

(13)   The dug-outs behind the parapet and built into it; very good and comfortable, with wooden sides and front doors and windows.

(14) Note: The absence of wire entanglements is due to the fact that the French have removed both German and French wire for use in front of their present trenches. I understand however that the wire on both sides was very indifferent.

(15)   The accuracy of the French 75 millimetre artillery fire which we were told was at first observed from the spoil heaps back near the batteries, but afterwards always observed from the front trenches in close proximity to the enemy.

(16)   The extensive use made by the French of their 80 millmtr mountain gun firing a ~~lyddite~~ *high explosive* shell. This gun was constantly brought up into the front line trenches. One of its emplacements is still to be seen S.W. of the village.

(17)   The moral effect of the discharge of a gun firing High Explosive at short range both at trenches and at houses

To get this moral effect the Germans on one occasion brought up a field gun into the middle of the village within 30 yards of the French by night, fired four rounds rapidly and then removed the gun still under cover of darkness.

---

(18)   The details of the construction of the mines.

(19)   The difficulty of disposing of the "spoil" i.e. the earth excavated from the mines, and the great amount of labour in carrying the earth from the head of the mine out to the spoil heap in little baskets.

(20)   The difficulty of placing the mines in the right place owing to the impossibility of measuring the distance to the enemy's position. It will be noticed that both the French mines were exploded 10 feet short of the wall instead of being immediately under the wall.

(21) Note: It was found best to employ local coal miners for mining rather than the reservist soldiers who were not trained as miners. The men of the 131st Brigade all come from the south of France near Narbonne, where there is no mining.

A Hunter Weston
M.G.

Cont'd (22) over.

(22)   The small _material_ damage caused by big mines is remarkable and instructive.

Most troops when first confronted by a new form of offence are apt to be terrified.   Some of our troops were at first alarmed by Black Marias and other large calibre explosive shells.   Now they do not much mind them unless they land fair on their heads.   As an example notice the splendid behaviour of the men in the Hants front trench when that trench was so accurately shelled by our own 6" howitzers.   Though several men were killed, no man was alarmed or showed any signs of wishing to run away.

It is the same with mines.   If the Germans had been used to mines or had really good courage, the explosion of these mines (which apparently killed not more than two or three men) would not have terrified them, and caused them to retreat precipitately out of the Chateau, Chateau grounds, and adjacent trench.

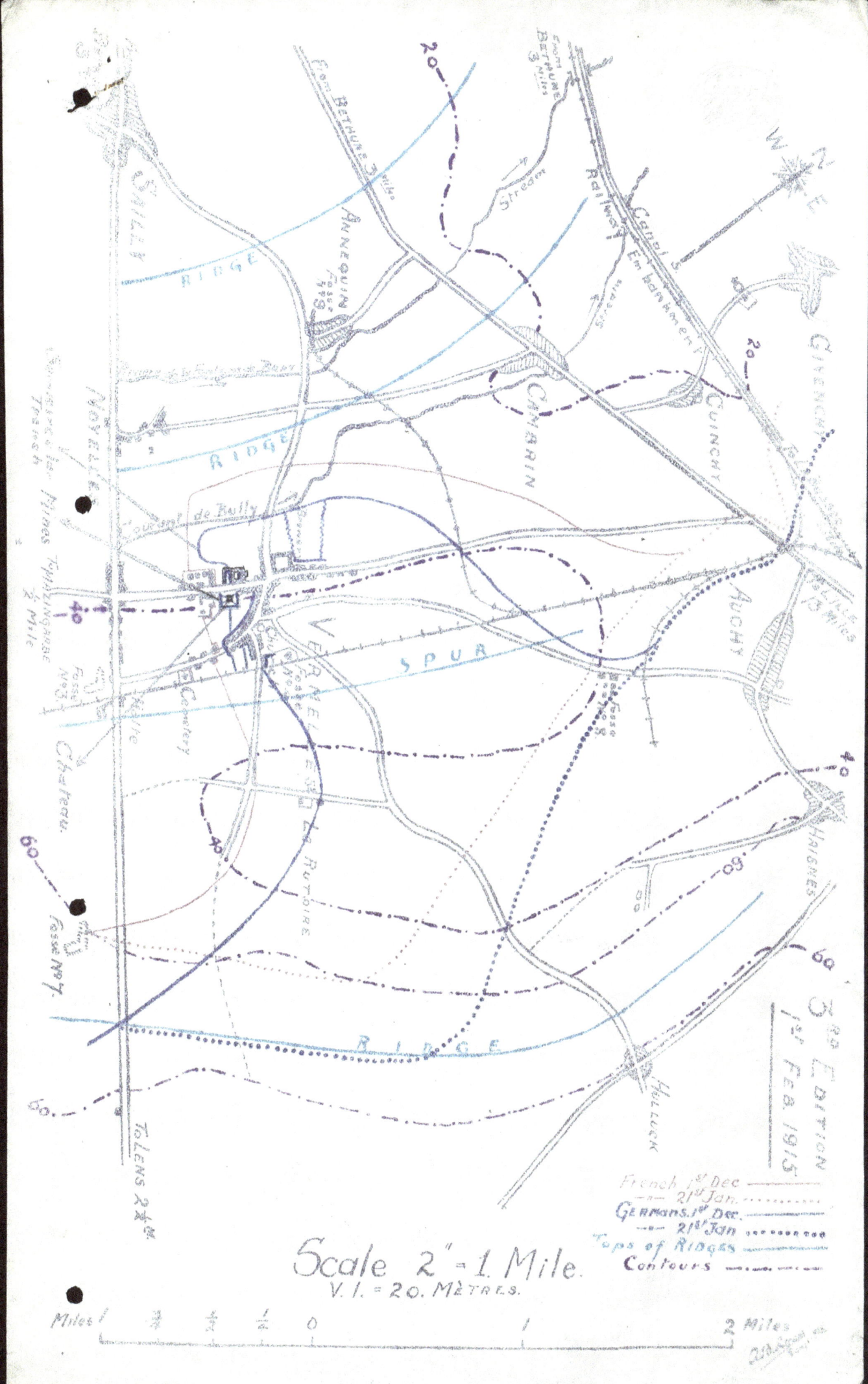

3rd Edition - 1st Feby 1915

NOTES with reference to VERMELLES:

1. SHORT STATEMENT OF FRENCH ACTION AT VERMELLES:

The village of Vermelles lies on both sides of two parallel roads that run N-N-E on the western slopes of a gently sloping spur running N-N-E from high ground that lies S-W of the main Bethune-Noyelles-Lens road. Towards the north of the village the principal street runs S-E uphill across the above two roads. In this street stand the Brewery and the Church and from its south eastern end on the high ground across the railway a good view of the present German position can be obtained. To the west of the village the ground falls for 450 yards in a gentle slope to a small stream - the Courant de Bully - whence the ground rises steadily westward to a ridge some 1000 yards away from the village, whence it falls slightly to the Rivière de la Fonte de Bray, and rises again to the Sailly ridge which is nearly two miles from Vermelles.

The western face of Vermelles gives an almost ideal position for defence:

(1) A splendid open field of fire down to the stream and up to the first ridge,

(2) A good extent of front to give free use of numbers in the firing line,

(3) Good lateral communications.

The weak point of the village is the pronounced salient that its southern (S-S-W) end forms.

The French 131st Brigade, under the command of Colonel Gadel, was brought up by motor bus on the 13th Oct. 1914 to form the right of an attack on the German position in the vicinity of Vermelles. The French attacked on the 14th and 15th Oct. with their left on Annequin, and their right on Mazingarbe. Their left attack, which was their main attack, advanced over the above mentioned open slopes against the west face of the village. It reached a line west of the Courant de Bully.

The right attack carried out by the 131st Brigade came in on Vermelles from the south and south-west, one regiment astride each of the two parallel roads mentioned at the beginning of this paper

paper. This attack succeeded in getting close up to the Brewery and Church. Here however it was counter-attacked and driven back. Owing to the personal efforts of a good battalion Commander the retirement was checked at the south end of the village and the French managed to establish themselves in the Cemetery and in the extreme S-S-W houses of the village and to dig themselves in in trenches in line with these houses facing N-N-E.

The Germans were thus thrown back both on the west and south and their line was left with a very pronounced salient at Vermelles.

Note the power of a good Battalion or Company leader and the importance of checking a retirement at the earliest moment. These end houses gave the French good supporting points from which to work forward. If they had fallen back further and the Germans had got these end houses the French would have had to advance over open ground in any attempt to capture the village.

From the 15th October the French steadily pressed on their enveloping attack against the village. The progress on the open slopes to the W-N-W was very small, but the progress from the south-west from house to house along both roads was satisfactory until the regiment on the left road reached the close proximity of the chateau, a well built little modern villa with capacious cellars.

Its grounds (about two acres) were surrounded by a brick wall. The Germans made the chateau very strong with trenches behind the walls and very deep communicating trenches radiating all over the grounds from the cellars where they slept. Against this position in the Chateau the French could make no progress above ground. They therefore commenced mining.

On 1st December the French exploded two mines under the front of the enclosure wall of the chateau of Vermelles and under cover of the confusion caused by this explosion they rushed forward in ten columns of twenty men each, each column being headed by some men of the Moroccan troops of the Active Army, who were brought specially to Vermelles for this duty. It was considered that the young men of the Active Army (i.e. men under 30) who had not been employed in trench work, were better suited
for

for leading columns, though the older men (the Reservists i.e. men over 30) were better for maintaining a position when once it was gained. During the night of the 30th November the walls of the houses and gardens that the French were holding were broken in ten places for the ten columns, the holes being built up again with loose bricks so that these breaches might not be apparent to the enemy.

The attack took place at 11 a.m. on 1st December after the men had had a good meal and were in the best fighting spirit.

When the mines exploded the stormers pushed down the loose bricks covering them and dashed forward to the assault. The Germans were so demoralised by the explosion of the mines that the precipitately retired from the chateau grounds and adjacent trenches. Not a shot was fired by them for about ten minutes. The French were therefore able to advance with a very slight loss and were able to establish themselves in the chateau and along the north wall of the chateau grounds.

After strengthening and consolidating their position at the chateau the French again pressed on utilising a mountain gun to fire into the houses that still held out. This threat from the south-west combined with the pressure of the French on the ~~north~~, west and south caused the Germans to evacuate Vermelles and to go back to a position which they had previously prepared nearly two miles further East.

2. FORMATION OF BRIGADE:

1. The 131st Brigade is formed of the

    280th)   Regiments of Reservists
    281st)   i.e. men over 30.
    296th)

with a battalion of Territorials (i.e. men over 40) attached to the Brigade. Each of these Regiments consists of two battalions.

2. The Brigade now holds a front of about three kilometres, about two miles beyond Vermelles. This front is divided between these three Regiments and the territorial battalion.

The battalions of each regiment are alternately (a) in reserve and (b) in the front line and support for four days.

The

The battalion not in reserve has two companies in front line and two companies in support. The supporting companies change places with the firing line companies at the end of two days. The territorial battalion has one company in the front line, one in support, and two in reserve.

3. DETAILS OF MINES:

The right mine was about 128 mètres long, and the left mine was about 80 mètres long. The bottom of each mine was about 6 mètres below the surface. Each mine was charged with 400 kilos (say 900 lbs) of black powder.

A mine that was exploded in November when charged with 400 kilos of melinite was not a success as it expended all its energy below ground and made no crater on the surface.

4. POINTS PARTICULARLY WORTHY OF NOTICE:

(1) The very large amount of work done both by the French and by the Germans.

(2) The patient and methodical way in which the attack was carried out step by step from house to house. The attack lasted 52 days.

(3) The very small losses incurred by the French in this methodical advance is noticeable.

(4) The experience of Vermelles agrees with our own experience of the houses held by the Germans E of Ploegsteert Wood, and shows clearly that if a house is properly prepared and everything inflammable removed it can be defended by determined men whatever artillery fire by brought to bear on it.

(5) The great number of communication trenches (boyaux) and their depth.

(6) The advantage taken of the shelter of houses to make the communication trenches straight whereever possible - protecting them by "blinded traverses" i.e. timbers across the trench over which are planks and over the planks earth.

(7) The type of deep trench used by the Germans in their "semi-circular trench" which was exposed to fire from an arc of over 180 degrees. It would not be good in any other position.

(8) The German overhead cover in many places is clever especially where it has been made as a protection against enfilade and reverse fire.

(9) The local resources which the Germans used especially in their revetments - barrels used as gabions, local corn sacks used as sandbags.

(10) The siting of machine gun emplacements by the Germans especially those placed in front of the line of trenches.

A tunnel is dug under the parapet and comes up outside to just below the ground level. The gun fires over the latter and the detachment kneel out of view. The gun can thus fire to front or flanks and when shelled can be drawn back into the tunnel.

----

(11) The method of bomb-proofing the German Commander's cellar at the north end of the village; (a) earth and iron railings on the floor; (b) big beams put across from wall to wall the outer ones about 3 feet, the centre one about 5 feet above the floor; (c) these beams being in turn covered with iron pipes so as to explode any shell before it could reach the roof of the cellar, and so as to protect the roof of the cellar in case the top of the house fell in.

(12) The utilisation of the ground underneath a partially demolished haystack for a Battalion Commander's residential dug-out consisting of staircase, hall, parlour and bedroom complete with bedstead and other furniture with pictures hung round the earth walls. From this commander's dug-out the communicating trenches to the fire trenches started, and near by were dug-outs evidently intended for the battalion staff.

(13) The dug-outs behind the parapet and built into it; very good and comfortable, with wooden sides and front doors and windows

----

(14) Note: The absence of wire entanglements is due to the fact that the French have removed both German and French wire for use in front of their present trenches. I understand however that the wire on both sides was very indifferent.

----

(15)

(15) The accuracy of the French 75 millimetre artillery fire which we were told was at first observed from the spoil heaps back near the batteries, but afterwards always observed from the front trenches in close proximity to the enemy.

(16) The extensive use made by the French of their 80 millmtre mountain gun firing a ~~lyddite~~ *high explosive* shell. This gun was constantly brought up into the front line trenches. One of its emplacements is still to be seen S.W. of the village.

(17) The moral effect of the discharge of a gun firing High Explosive at short range both at trenches and at houses.

To get this moral effect the Germans on one occasion brought up a field gun into the middle of the village within 30 yards of the French by night, fired four rounds rapidly and then removed the gun still under cover of darkness.

----

(18) The details of the construction of the mines.

(19) The difficulty of disposing of the "spoil" i.e. the earth excavated from the mines, and the great amount of labour in carrying the earth from the head of the mine out to the spoil heap in little baskets.

(20) The difficulty of placing the mines in the right place owing to the impossibility of measuring the distance to the enemy's position. It will be noticed that both the French mines were exploded 10 feet short of the wall instead of being immediately under the wall.

(21) Note: It was found best to employ local coal miners for mining rather than the reservist soldiers who were not trained as miners. The men of the 131st Brigade all come from the south of France near Narbonne, where there is no mining.

Cont'd (22) over.

(22)   The small <u>material</u> damage caused by big mines is remarkable and instructive.

Most troops when first confronted by a new form of offence are apt to be terrified. Some of our troops were at first alarmed by Black Marias and other large calibre explosive shells. Now they do not much mind them unless they land fair on their heads. As an example notice the splendid behaviour of the men in the Hants front trench when that trench was so accurately shelled by our own 6" howitzers. Though several men were killed, no man was alarmed or showed any signs of wishing to run away.

It is the same with mines. If the Germans had been used to mines or had really good courage, the explosion of these mines (which apparently killed not more than two or three men) would not have terrified them, and caused them to retreat precipitately out of the Chateau, Chateau grounds, and adjacent trenches.

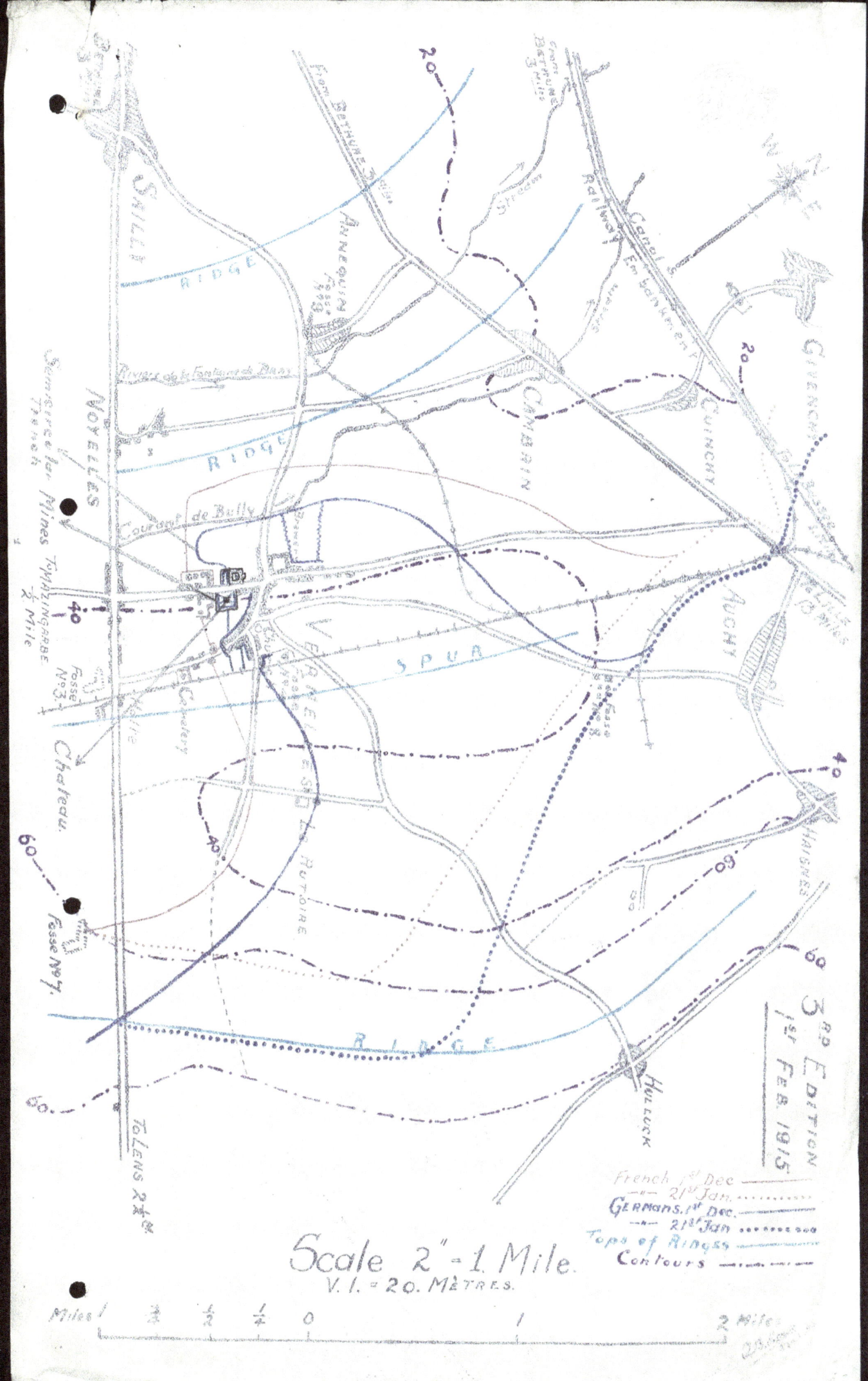

ST YVES.

TRANSLATIONS.

Auberge, Aub^{ge}	Inn.
Bac	Ferry.
Cabaret, Cab^{t}	Inn.
Carrière	Quarry.
Cheminée	Factory Chimney.
Déversoir	Weir.
Écluse	Lock.
Étang, E^{tg}	Pond.
Fontaine, Font.	Spring.
Gué	Ford.
Marais	Marsh.
Moulin, M^{in}	Mill.
Nacelle	Ferry.
Puits	Well, Shaft.
Source	Spring.

BELGIUM AND FRANCE.
("B" SERIES).
SHEET 36 N.W.

WAR DIARY
4th DIVISION
March 1916

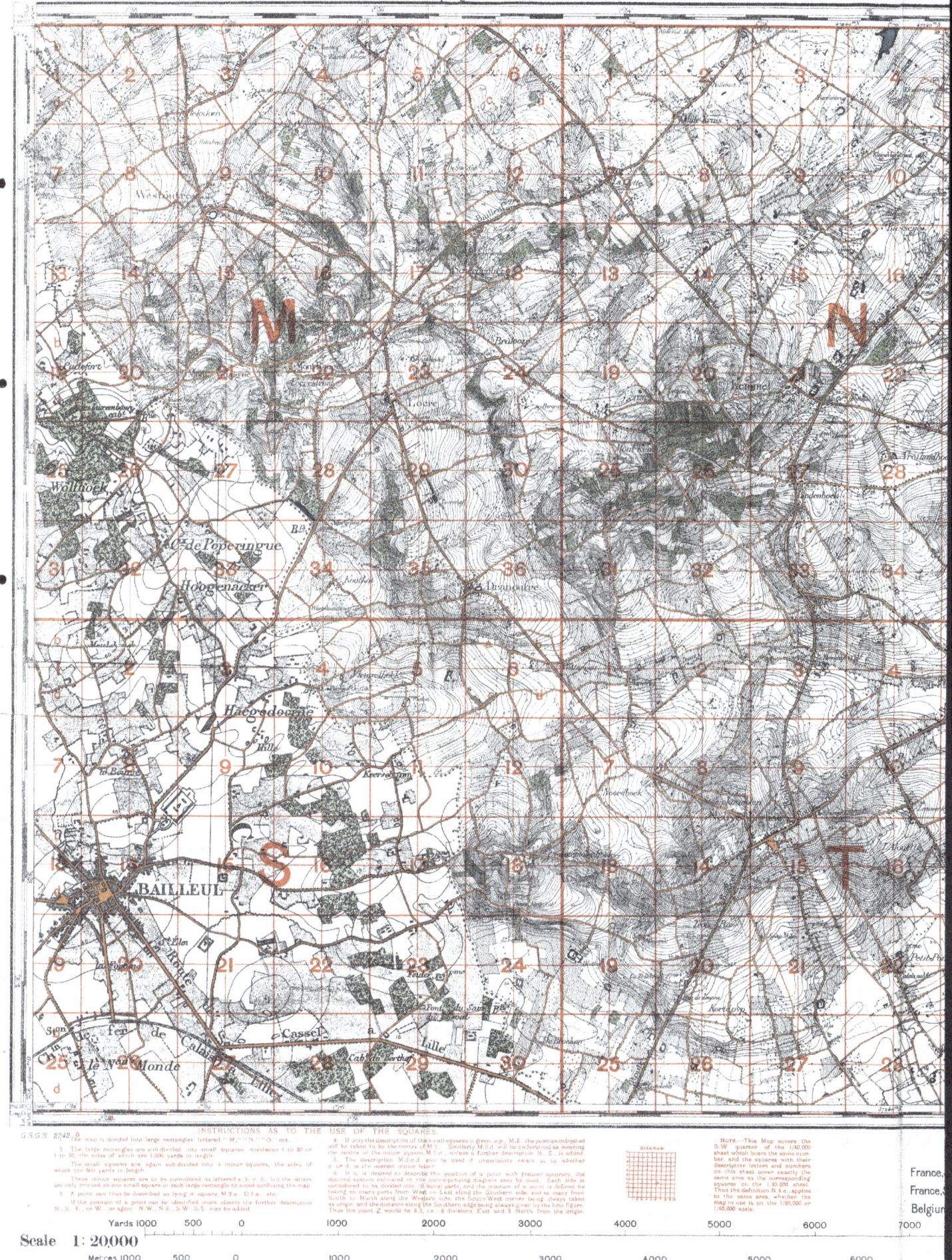

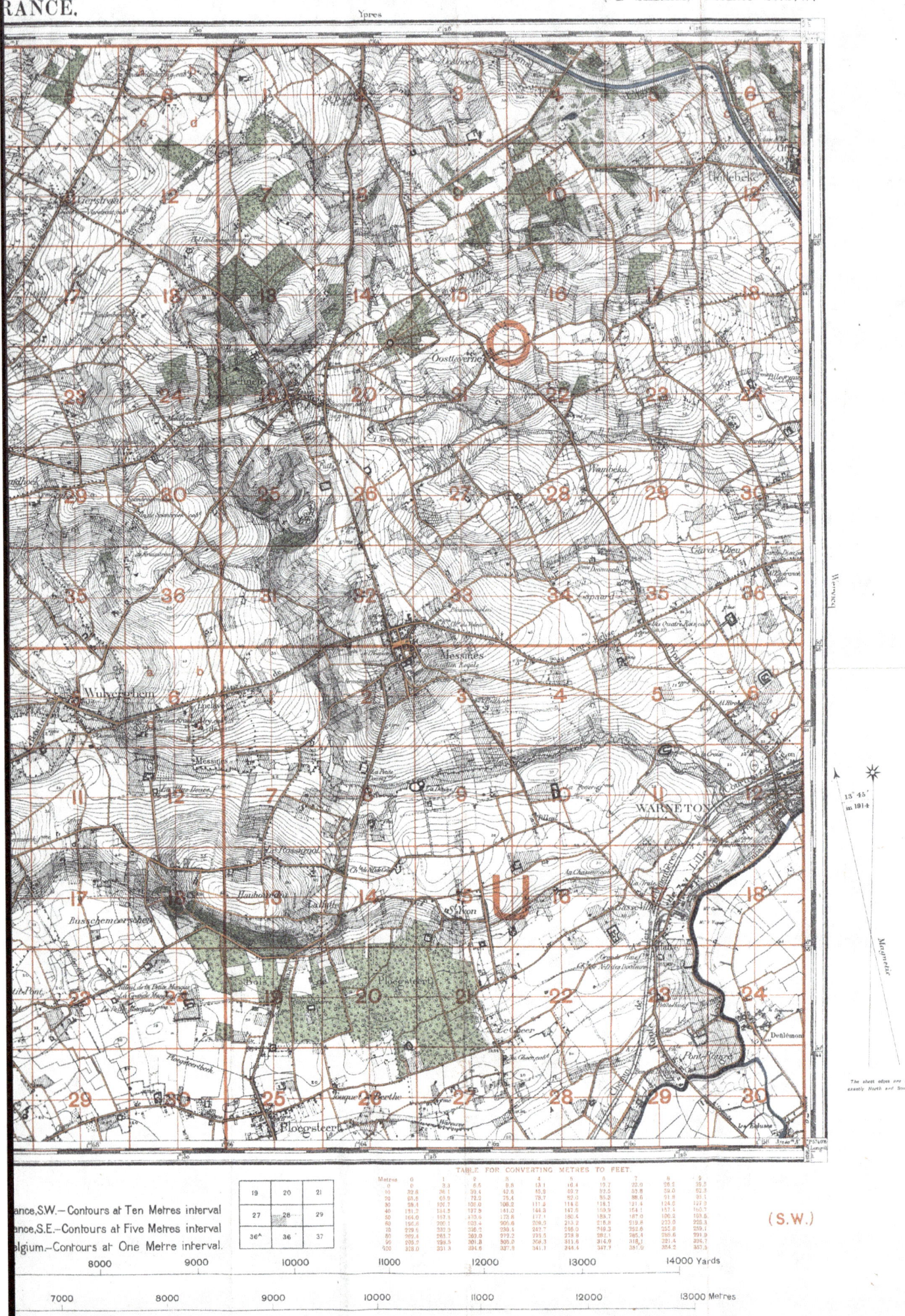

TRANSLATIONS.

Auberge, Aub^ge	Inn.
Bac	Ferry.
Cabaret, Cab^t	Inn.
Carrière	Quarry.
Cheminée	Factory Chimney.
Déversoir	Weir.
Écluse	Lock.
Étang, E^g	Pond.
Fontaine, Font^e	Spring.
Gué	Ford.
Marais	Marsh.
Moulin, M^in	Mill.
Nacelle	Ferry.
Puits	Well, Shaft.
Source	Spring.

BELGIUM AND FRANCE.
("B" SERIES).
SHEET 28.S.W.

19	20	21
27	28	29
36ᴀ	36	37

Scale 1/20,000.

"A" series — 136/137
"B" series — 40

SUBJECT.

No.	Contents.	Date.

G.S.,
4TH DIV,
MAR., 1915

LE TOUQUET

& FRELINGHIEN

Appendix

Bond Delivery
L. Davis

April 1915

Appendix (A)

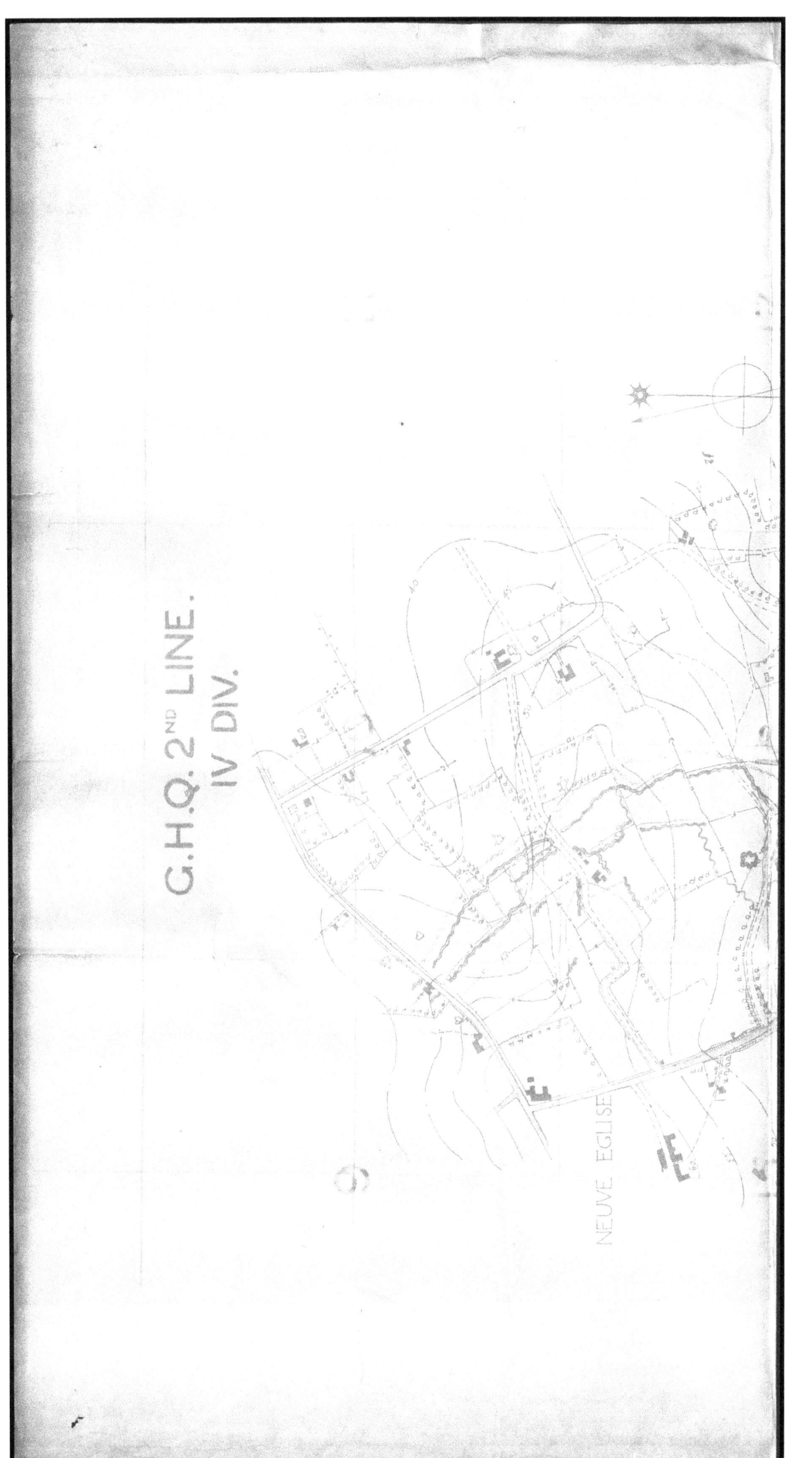

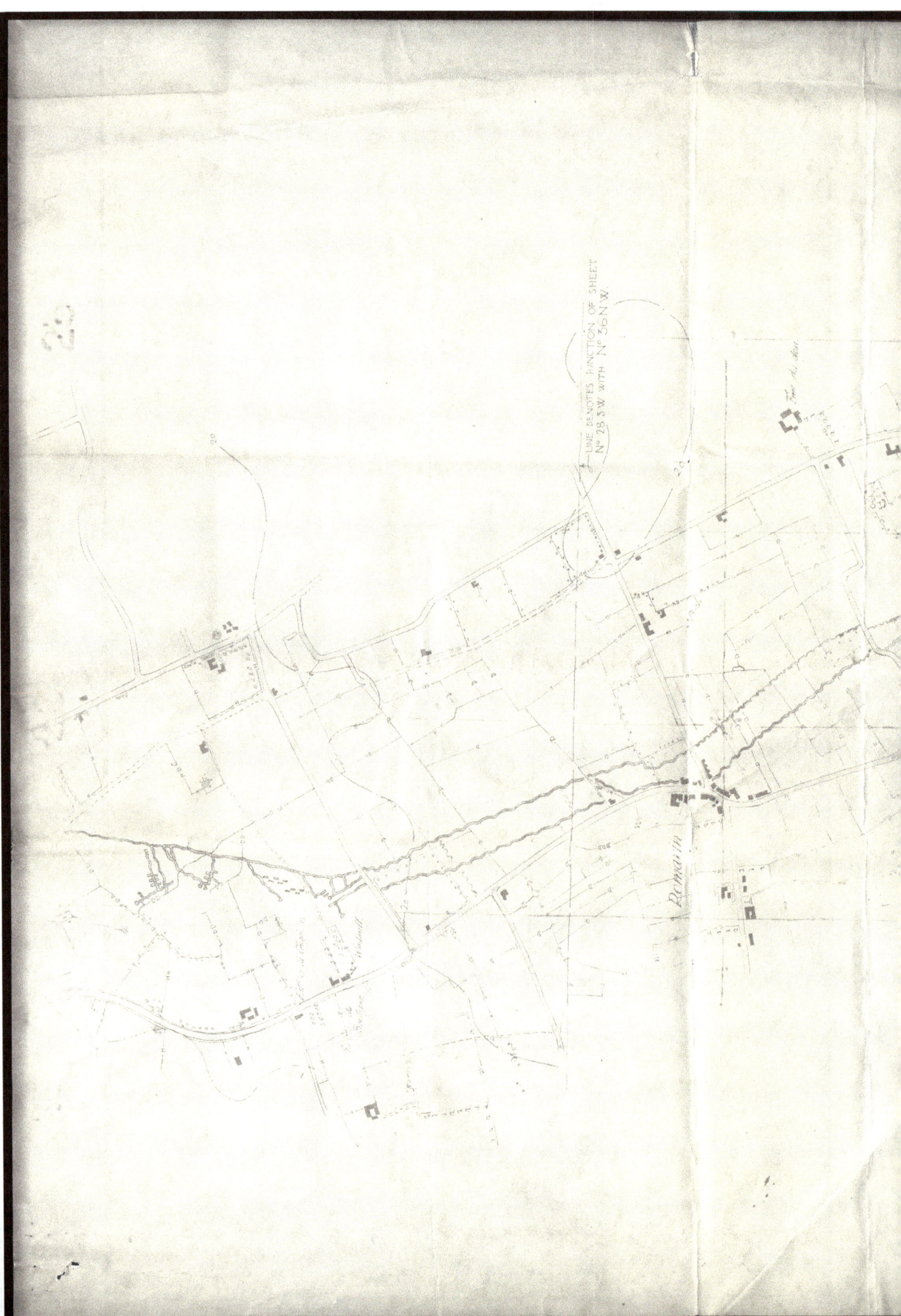

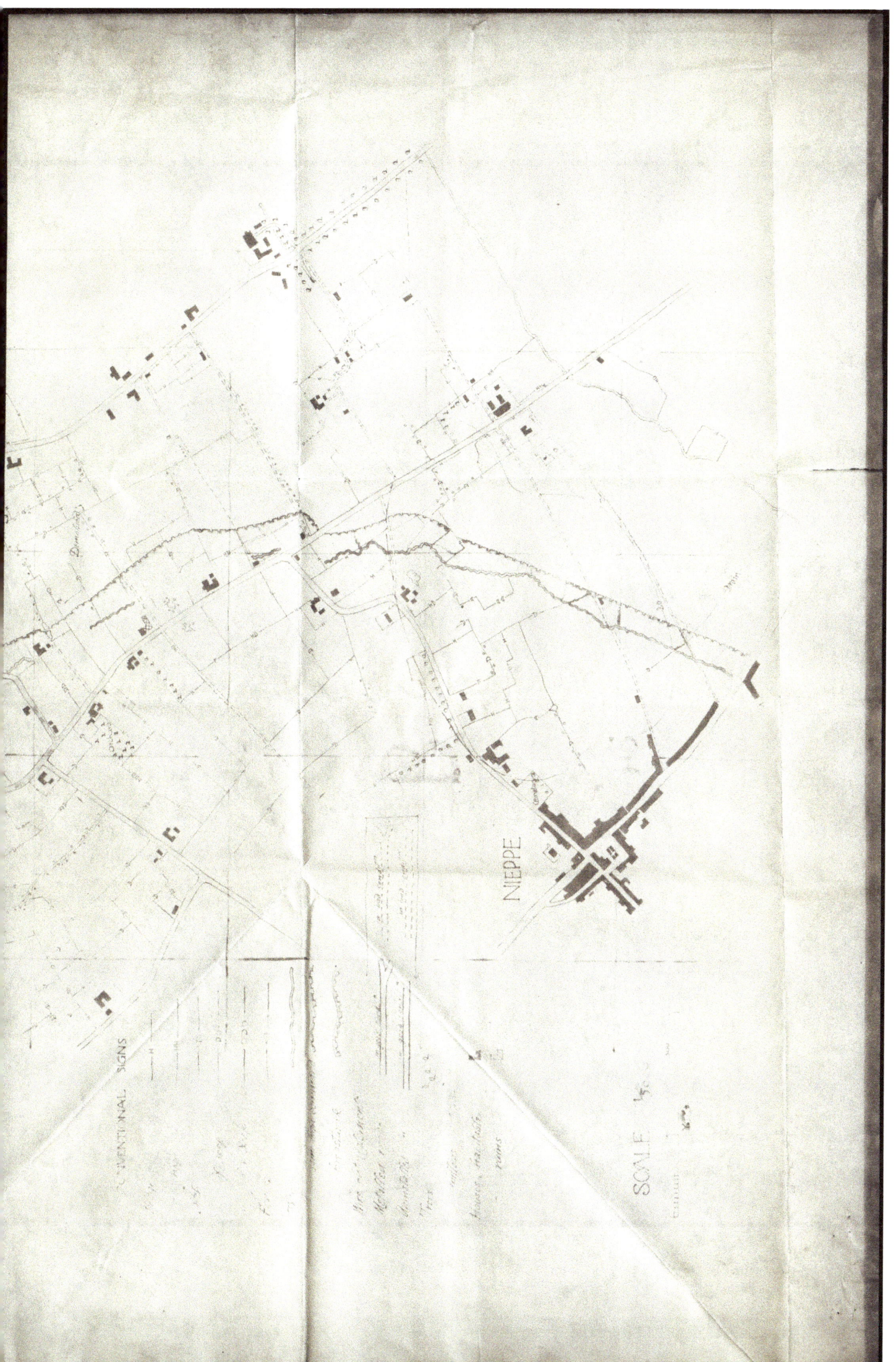

Sind
4th Div.

Some further information about the move
is forwarded.

WRRtTmf? Carter
for Brig Gen.

12 Rugfeld

4th Division

War Diaries

General Staff

APRIL 1915

War Diary
4 Div.
April 1915.

Appendix (B)

Sketch in two portions
showing the Section
of G.H.Q. 2nd Line
for which 4 Div.
was responsible
until Mid-April
1915.

III. Corps.
Second Army.

GENERAL STAFF

4th DIVISION

APRIL

1915

(Note: The Messages referred to in the Diary will be found in a separate box marked "Messages".)

Attached:

1. Report by G.O.C. 11th Inf.Bde. on Operations 24th April/3rd May.
2. Papers relating to explosion of Mine at Le Touquet.
3. Weekly & Progress Reports.
4. Div. O.Os. Nos. 23 to 25.
5. Distribution of Infantry.
6. Casualties for April & May.
7. Maps.

WAR DIARY
NIEPPE 1st April 1915.

Slight frost during night, bright cold day.

4-40 am. Quiet night reports to 3rd Corps (H/228, J/2, BM/84, G/1, G/92, G/963)

12-29 pm. 11th Brigade report Sausage Balloon up, bearing 48 degrees ~~true~~, true, from 11th Brig Hdqrs.--Forwarded to 3rd Corps. (BM/87, GG/2)

12-43 pm. Air reconnaissance 8-40 to 10-0 am. Area Armentieres - Deulemont - Commines - Menin - Halluin - Roncq - Bondues - Lille - Lods - Wavrin - Fromelles clear of all movement. IG/43

1-44 pm. 10th Brig report Germans shelling Steenbecque, No 7 trench, U/1/a, with howitzers, and asks for co-operation from Hows. Petite Douve with 27 FAB. 7th Siege Batty were instructed to turn on their guns.
(H.231, GG.3, G.648, G.650, G.649)

5-45 pm Evening report to 3rd Corps and exchanged with 5th and 6th Divs. Quiet day. Very little shelling and sniping.
(BM.11, BM.88, G.667, G.975, GG.6, BBM.10 & 12, GG.5)

7-30 pm Hostile shelling report from 4th Div. Arty. forwarded to 3rd Corps. BBM.13

9-45 pm 12th Brig. report Germans appear to be celebrating Bismark Centenary. Light shown on parapet, seven bonfires in direction of Pont Rouge, bugles blown and much cheering. Reported to 3rd Corps. BM.14 GG.7

9-45 pm 10th Brig. report three red lights sent up from German trenches just before their trenches were shelled this afternoon. H.234 GG.7

9-55 pm Receipt to 3rd Corps for their Confidential No. G.651 (Line of Demarkation of 4th and 6th Divisions) GGG.161 G.10

WAR DIARY - 2nd April 1915.

MESSPE.

          Fine night, bright morning. Rained at 8-30 pm and at intervals throughout the night.

4-45 am   Night reports forwarded to 3rd Corps and exchanged with 5th and 6th Divs. Left Sector (10th Brig) report that on two occasions enemy opened with shrapnel followed by heavy rifle fire on party working on new breastwork   BBM.20
joining Douve - Steenbecque trenches - evidently pre-   G.12
concerted. Also rafale of 6 shrapnel later at 1-50 am.   G.979
Red lights all over the place (G.11, H.236, BM.16, BM.99   GA.31

10-25 am   12th Brig. report transport heard to and from   G.14
Frelinghien and Pakenham, 8-15 to 1 am. To 3rd Corps.   BM.17

10-50 am   11th Brig. report illumination of German trenches with fairy lights South of Le Pelerine in U.21.B.7.3. Men in this area yesterday were dressed in green and some in   G.15
grey.   BM.104

12-55 pm   3rd Corps inform us that an aeroplane resembling   IG.445
Maurice Farman type will be flying from Bailleul. Units   G.16
warned.   G.17

4-16 pm   3rd Corps inform us that an aeroplane would be flying round Bailleul at 3 am, 3rd April. This flight was afterwards cancelled owing to unfavourable weather conditions. (G.24, G.25, IG.450, IG.449, GS.9, G.664)

5-55 pm   Evening report to 3rd Corps. Little sniping or shelling. Various uniforms observed by 11th Brig. and Arty.   BM.117.
(G.997, G.735, BBM.29, GG.10, BBM.25, G.20, H.239, BM.38,

7-25 pm   32nd F.A.B. report a column of German Infantry moving in fours, N.W., on road in O.24.C at 5-50 pm. This column took 4½ minutes to pass a given point. 3rd Corps informed.   G.22

8-30 pm   Rif. Brig. report several Germans wearing brown   G.22/4
uniform at Prowse Point, U.14.b.   BM.121

CASUALTIES FOR THE MONTHS OF APRIL & MAY 1915.

(Note: The Lists of Officer Casualties
referred to appears to be
MISSING).

WEEKLY AND PROGRESS REPORTS.

2/4/15

WEEKLY REPORT.

1. RESUME. In the Right Sector work for the week has chiefly consisted in improving communications and providing a retrenchment round the Snipers' Houses; in the Centre Sector in improving and retrenching the ST. YVES defences; in the Left Sector in burying dead animals, cleaning up the lines and commencing works designed to make the line continuous.

2. RIGHT SECTOR. 12th Inf. Brig.

(a) In the LE TOUQUET Section a trench has been dug in front of the OLD SNIPER'S Ho. and provided with large bombproofs. There are now 12 of these in the little gardens on the North side of the SNIPERS' HOUSES. The trench running out from LUKER'S HOUSE towards CARTERS Farm mentioned last week has been continued.
The communication trench from DESPIERRE Farm to the ESSEX CENTRAL Farm is now completed and boarded the whole way.

(b) It is proposed to prolong the above communication trench to the rear until it joins the Divisional Supporting Line; also to make a communication trench from DESPIERRE Farm to the left of the ESSEX Line about the WARNAVE.

(c) German artillery on one day shelled LYS Farm with 40 Little Willies and also shelled de la RABEQUE Farm from time to time. Rifle Grenades active and sniping as usual.

(d) Saxons called out that they were to be relieved by Prussians, but no further evidence to show that this has taken place.

3. CENTRE SECTOR. 11th Inf. Brig.

(a) LE GHEER Section. Work on covered ways from the KEEPER'S COTTAGE to cross roads and communications generally in LE GHEER improved. More accommodation made in Hants trench.
PLOEGSTEERT WOOD SECTION. Accommodation at Argylls and angle of Somerset left trench made for garrison to be immediately on the spot. Communication trench in rear of Somerset left trench completed.
ST.YVES Section. Work on the front line breast works at the corner N.E. of ST.YVES is still continuing. Communication trench completed from ST.YVES to SUNKEN Road (E.Front) Fire trench on the North and East of ST.YVES begun and nearly finished. A cover trench approximately between PROWSE Point and wood north of MOATED Farm is half finished. Communications for use by support improved. Wire improved on whole front.
WORK PROPOSED.

iii. ST.YVES Section. Make communication between right of SUNKEN Road and SOMERSET left trench. Continue work on closing of gaps and supporting line about ST.YVES village.
ii. PLOEGSTEERT Wood Section. Improvements to parados on left trench. Lengthening communication trench towards the wood.
i. LE GHEER Section. Continue work on communications and supporting points.

(c)

Progress Report on 2nd Line, 1st April, 1915.

(a) R.LYS to LE TOUQUET Road.

Trench complete, revetted and floored. Three communication trenches dug, partly screened and floored. Double wire fence being improved. 7 emplacements for Machine Guns made.
Supporting Points. LYS Farm and FLEPEQUE farm practically complete. Motor Car corner entrenched and partly wired.

(b) LE TOUQUET - WARNETON Road.

Trench complete except 200 yards flooring. Three communication trenches in hand.
Supporting Points. GRAND RABEQUE farm, nearly completed, wiring finished, M.G. emplacement and loopholes made, barricade started. LITTLE RABEQUE Farm completed.

(c) WARNETON Road - LE GHEER Road.

Trenches completed and floored. Communication trenches in hand, also road barricades. Drains deepened throughout section. M.G. emplacement completed.
Supporting Points. LONDON SUPPORT Farm and MILLFUL Farm completed.

(d) LE GHEER Road - ROSSIGNOL.

Trench and breastworks line almost completed. Head cover for 9 breastworks still to be done. Wire entanglement completed. Hedge screen between breastworks not yet started.
Supporting Points - completed.

(e) ROSSIGNOL to 5th Division Boundary.

Details under consideration. An old trench is usable should it be required.

(c) Shelling occasional. Sniping intermittently fairly active.
(d) No information of note available re enemy.

LEFT SECTOR.   10th Inf. Brig.

CIS-DOUVE Section.   Communication trenches are now completed as follows:-
Boarding of (ii) and (iii) not yet finished.

(i) Point 150 yards North of Forward Estaminet to point South of Seaforth Farm.

(ii) Point 400 yards North of Forward Estaminet on Messines Road to Seaforth Farm.

(iii) Along Messines Road to front barricade. A support trench in rear of Seaforth Farm 100 yards in length has been completed and provided with numerous bombproofs.

TRANS-DOUVE Section. The fire trenches on the right of the line, and the one next to it, are being joined up by a breastwork 150 yards in length. All along the line the parapet and wire has been improved and firing platforms provided.

(b) It is proposed to construct supporting points some 300 yards in rear. These cannot be accurately explained until the production of a corrected map which is now in course of being done.

(c) Shelling more pronounced than usual.-Seaforth Farm, La Hutte and Trans Douvia shelled on several occasions and some damage inflicted. Sniping as usual.

(d) Nothing of special interest noted concerning the enemy.

Maj-General,
Commdg. 4th Division.

2/4/15.

War Diary, Gen.Staff, 4th Divn.
3rd April, 1915.

NIEPPE. Raining at intervals throughout night and day.

4.45 a.m.   Night reports from Brigs. forwarded to 3rd A.C. and
            exchanged with 5th and 6th Divs. Quiet except that
            10th Brig. report 20 H.E. shell between LA PLUS
            DOUCE Farm and NEUVE EGLISE, between 10 and 11 p.m.
                (G.26, H.242, B.M.124, B.M.33, G.755, G.3, G.27).

8.15 a.m.   Acknowledgment to 3rd A.C. of Secret G667 (Allotment   G.G.15.
            of Arty.Ammunition.)

9.40 a.m.   Hamps report loud explosion 9 p.m. last night south   G.G.17.
            of LA BASSE VILLE. Engine working south end German   B.M.125.
            barricade, and hammering of metal same place.

1.32 p.m.   4.2 How. fuzes fired yesterday are 1915 date, makers   G.28.
            name SIMSON. One fuze has steel nose. All brass   C.10.
            type.

5.56 p.m.   Evening report. No shelling. Sniping brisk in centre
            sector, otherwise quiet.
                (G.32, B.M.41, B.M.135, H.247, G.12, G.785, B.M.37).

6.48 p.m.   Hostile shelling report from 4th D.A. forwarded to   G.33.
            3rd A.C.   B.M.39.

6.55 p.m.   32nd F.A.B. report work of wiring various places recently G.34.
            carried out by Germans. To 3rd A.C.   N.13.

9.30 p.m.   32nd F.A.B. report movements of 20 2-horsed vehicles   G.37.
            with certain number dismounted men at 5.15 p.m. going N.14.
            North in P. 27. d, also 2 or 3 supply wagons going
            North West on road in U.5.b.

 NIEPPE.

War Diary - 4th April 1915.

Rain at intervals during night and early morning. Cleared up for a short while about 10 am but was dull for rest of day.

4-45 am   Quiet night reports forwarded to 3rd Corps and exchanged with 5th and 6th Divs. (BM.47, H.251, BM.1, GG.19, G.17)

9-50 am   27th Brig. observed yesterday two Germans in trench N. of Messines - Wulverghem road about U.2.a, wearing grey blue tunics and caps - no greatcoats. Also one German in trench about U.2.a.c. South of Wulverghem - Messines road wearing dark blue cap - no great coat. Forwarded to 3rd Corps.   GG.21

10
6-45 pm   Evening report to 3rd Corps and exchanged with 5th and 6th Divs. Right Sector - no change. Centre Sector - 45 Little Willies against Rif.Brig., sniping brisk. Enemy digging on a trench behind barricade at Le Gheer. Black & white and blue and white flags exposed from Avenue. Left Sector - no shelling, sniping heavier than usual. Red lamp waved twice at 1 am. White flag exhibited in Avenue 10am to 5-15 pm. Artillery quiet. (G.39, BM.55, BM.15, H.254, G.28, G.849, G.40, BBM.51)

6-45 pm   Hostile shelling report from Div.Arty. forwarded to 3rd Corps.   BBM.55

7-05 pm   32nd F.A.B. and 11th Brig. report various uniforms observed. Also a battalion seen marching North near Zandvoorde (P.3). At 5-30 pm four ammunition wagons with eight horse teams seen moving N. along road parallel to and E. of Warneton - Ypres road. At 5-50 pm a battery of four guns and four wagons were seen marching N.W. along Commines - Ypres road.
(GG.29, BM.17, N.19, GG.33)

10-10 pm   3rd Corps inform us that a Zeppelin passed over Calais moving Eastwards and may be expected over our lines. Circulated. The dirigible was not seen by any of our units.   IG.456
GG.31

10-50 pm   6th Div. report that their 17th Brig. saw an aeroplane over their lines going towards Armentieres about 9-10 pm. Circulated. The King's Own heard sounds of an aeroplane about 10-15 pm.

Col. Hankey, Sec. Imperial Defence Committee was shown round our lines and taken to places of interest this afternoon.
(GG.32, IG.459)

3rd Corps Secret G.600/1 received and acknowledged.
(Subject - preparation for offensive operations. 4/Div.GGG.169) GG.27

LB.

WAR DIARY
5th April 1915.

NIGHT.

Rain at intervals during night and throughout the day.

4-25 am.   Quiet night reports to 3rd Corps, and exchanged with
           5th and 6th Divs. (BM.60, BM.20, H.258, GG.34, Y.A 34, G.39)

12-34 pm. Rifle Brig Sunk Road Trench, report at 12-15 pm., enemy laying   N.27
           communication wire across front from S. to N. at about 1000 yds. GG39
           Forwarded to 3/Corps.

1-50 pm.   Artillery report wagon carrying planks seen at noon, moving
           N.E. in O.24.D. At 12-10 pm, 3 men (Black uniform white
           brassards) disappeared behind La Potterie farm. Two men in
           grey were also seen same place. Persistent shelling of
           Douve trenches, Retaliated, but shelling continues.   N.28

12-55 pm. 3/Corps were asked if any new German formations were known   GG/40
           to be on 10th Brigade front.? Replied--No information.   IG/463
                                                                         GG/44.

5-50 pm.   Evening report to 3/Corps and exchanged with 5th and 6th
           Divs.-Little shelling or sniping of Right and Centre Sectors
           Left Sector received about 160 shell, mainly about Douve. No
           casualties. Arty retaliated effectively. Germans busy plank- G/41
           ing second line trenches in U/10/A. Sandbags on Avenue trenches GG/47
           Many odd men of the enemy observed behind German lines, nearly G/921
           all wearing grey uniforms. (GG/46, BM/31, BM/67, H/274, N/29, G/44, BBM/72

5-5 pm.   11th Brigade report E.Lancs have distinctly heard sounds of
           mining, under front house at Le Gheer. Passed to 12/Brig &
           C.R.E. (BM/27, BM/26, BM/31, G/42, G/43)

7-5 pm.   Detailed report of Hostile shelling received from Div Arty
           and forwarded to 3/Corps.   BM/73

8-40 pm.   32/Arty report 2 men near Belheen, one wearing long light   N/31
           grey coat, and one putties and breeches. Forwarded to 3/Corps. G/45

10-45 pm. 10th Brigade report German seen in Petite Douve Farm today   H/278
           in light blue grey coat, and peaked cap with red on it.   GG/53
           Forwarded to 3rd Corps.

9-16 am   Acknowledgment to 3/Corps of G/700 (Revised mining register) G/37
5-10 pm   Acknowledgment to 3/Corps of G/706 (Instructions re Secret)
                                             (Correspondence.) (GGG/174) GG/45
              "   "   IR/175 (Guides)   (GGG/172)
9-55 pm.   Acknowledging receipt of G/713 (Discussion of Secret Matters) GGG/174

              "   "   IR/21 (Map Dranoutre-Voormezeele.   GGG/56

10-55 pm.   "   "   G/632/27 (Amm for S.Mid.Div) GG/38.48, BBM/74
                                                                         G/716

W A R   D I A R Y
6th April 1915.

Wet night, bright morning, turning to rain in afternoon and evening accompanied with a high wind.

4-45 am. Quiet night reports to 3/Corps and exchanged with 5th and 6th Divs. (H.282, BM/38, BM/73, G/47, G/049, G/47, GG/54)

11-20 am. 10/Brig inform us that new trench joining the left of Douve left to centre Steenbecque No.2 will be called Steenbecque No.2 No.1.--D.Arty and Div Engrs informed.   GG/59   H/284

5-46 pm. Evening report to 3/Corps and exchanged with 5th and 6th Divs. German aeroplane dropped 4 bombs about 12-10pm. about South-End of Le Bizet, otherwise very quiet day. Arty fired on working parties, apparently with effect.   G/49   BM/45   BM/86   H/293
(G/51, N.36, G/50, BBM/82)

6-30 pm. 27 FAB report Germans seen wearing grey uniforms.
32 FAB report that trenches near La Potterie farm considerably strengthened with loopholes and wire, etc, during last 2 days. At 1 pm. 3 companies paraded in P.27.d, near what is thought to be a balloon shed, and were still there at 2 pm. At 3 pm howzrs and limbers seen going South in O/24/C, and later 20 led horses seen going NE in O/24/C
At 5 pm 2 Officers seen walking from Messines along Warneton Road, one dressed in light grey, the other wore a black cloak. Both wore round black caps. Forwarded to 3/Corps.   G/52

6-5 pm. Arty forwarded Hostile Shelling Report--practically nil. Forwarded to 3/Corps.   BBM/83

9-25 pm. 29 FAB report at 5-20 pm, 6 rounds shrapnel fired by a Fd Gun at No.1 trench. At 5-30 pm one 15 cm howzr, fired 13 rounds H.E. into Square U/13/B no damage.(3 of these were blind) At 6-40 pm a loaded G.S. wagon, with team of 6 horses seen moving along Warneton-Messines road in Square U/3/15 near Messines. A batty to the right of 29 FAB fired at it.   GG62   C/7

3-52 pm. Acknowledgment to 3/Corps for IR/50 (Secret)   G/48

10-25 pm. Acknowledgment to 3/Corps for G/632/31 (Secret) Scale of Arty ammunition) passed to Div Arty.   GG/57

A conference was held at 2 pm. and was attended by Br-Gen F.G.Anley, Commdy 12th Brig. and by C.R.A. and C.R.E. 4th Div. Plans for local offensive action were discussed.

A Section of the 7' Siege Bty ordered under command of 4' Div   G709

WAR DIARY
7th April 1915.

NIEPPE.

High wind during night, dull day with occasional showers.

4-30 am. Quiet night reports to 3/Corps, and exchanged 5/6th Divs.
(1,2,3,4,5.)

10-30 am. 32 FAB report an explosion (in P.28.C, or P.31.D) was noticed, near enemy's parade ground. Men seen running on several occasions, apparently practising an assault after exploding a mine. About 15 men in grey seen leaving 2nd line trench near Point 27 in U/10/A carrying sacks, but no rifles.
----Repeated 3/Corps.--   6, 7

11-41 am. Forwards report from Lt Hutton, 32 FAB, to 3/Corps, movement of Vehicles in O/24/C at 5-35 pm also Platoon at 5-55pm A Company at 6-20 pm, then half battn followed by ¾ battn, again followed by another column, size of which could not be judged owing to darkness. All these parties were moving N.W.   8

In O/24/C at 6-10 pm. one platoon with some cookers moving S.W. In U/6/A three GS wagons, one limbered wagon, and one ~~unusual~~ unusual shaped wagon, possibly a gun, all going N.
In U/6/b or V/1/A, one batty moving South. In O/33/D several individuals in black dress seen, moving about.   9, 10, 11, 12, 13

6-0 pm. Evening report to 3/Corps and exchanged with 5th and 6th Divisions. Centre Sector 2 Little Willies near Som. Ho. and 2 shrapnel near L.R.B. Hdqrs. About 40 very heavy shell at Chateau de la Hutte. Trench Mortar fired at enemy's barricade at Warneton road. Enemy believed hit. Left sector little shelling, less sniping. Arty shelled several working parties, and engaged guns at O/34/d, which considerably damaged La Hutte Chateau, destroying the Howitzer's observatory there.   14, 15, 16, 17, 18, 19, 20

9-50 pm. 32 FAB and 12 Brig again report considerable movement behind German lines, wiring and planking of trenches. Forwarded to 3/Corps. The G.O.C. 3/Corps complimented the Observing Officer of the 32 FAB on the valuable report.   21-22, 23,24, 25,26, 27,28, 29,30

7-0 pm. Hostile Shelling report for the day, received from Div Arty and forwarded to 3/Corps   31

3/Corps notify us that 7th Fd Coy R.E. will be transferred to South Mid Div on 18th April next.

WAR DIARY
8th April '15.

NIEPPE.

Fine night, rain at intervals during the day, clearing up at night.

1,2,3

4-40 am. Quiet night reports to 3/Corps and exchanged with 5/6th Div. 4,5.

8-40 am. Air reconnaissance 60 M.T. in C/11/C at 7 am this morning 6
whole column W of River, halted on South side of road, just 7
clear of Frelinghien pontoon bridge. A later reconnaissance 8
reports no transport seen on any road within a radius of 9
2000 yards of Frelinghien bridge at 10-40 am. 10,11

9-20 am. Major Symons, 7Fd Co R.E. requested to meet Corps Commdr 12
at Div Hdqrs in connection with Mining Operations. 13

11-40 am. Som L.I. report enemy, apparently wearing black overcoats 14
were seen on parapets, opposite S.L.I. Right Trench, were 15
fired at, several being hit. 16
17

5-45 pm. Evening report to 3/Corps and exchanged with 5/6th Divs. 18
Quiet day, Right and Centre Sectors. Left Sector persis- 19
tent sniping of working parties on Steenbecque No.1 last 20
night. Enemy's patrol encountred at Ruined House in 21
U/8/c/N.E. Avenue reported to be strongly held. Arty 22
report much movement of transport and pedestrians.in 23
U/29/A/C, & U/6/a. 24
25

6-20 pm. 12th Brig inform us that Monmouths intended testing search- 26
light tonight about 9 pm. All concerned notified. 27.

6-45 pm. Arty report of enemy's hostile shelling during the day.
Forwarded to 3/Corps. 28

9-30 pm. Further Arty report of movements and general intelligence. 29

7-53 pm. Arrangements made with 12th & 18th Brigs, also 6th Div for
consultation in connection with Scheme for firing Mine.
(30,31,32,33,34,35,36,37,38,39,40,41)

5-5 pm.   Acknowledgment of Secret papers from 3rd Corps........... 42

3/Corps No/G.751
G.754---Offensive Operations.
G.755---Command--

WAR DIARY
9th April 1915.

NIGHT. High wind during night and morning. Heavy thunder storm just before noon with rain, clearing about 5 pm.

4-30 am. Night reports forwarded to 3/Corps and exchanged with 5/6th Divs. — 1,2,3,4, 5 & 6.

8-30 am. Arrangements concerning the explosion of a mine in Le Touquet, which was successfully carried out. Further particulars as to this Operation are attached as an addenda. — 7,8,9, 10, 11, 12, 13, 14.

9-23 am. E.Lancs report a sentry saw a Railway train, with lights in it, pass northwards on line within German posts about 11-30 pm last night. — 15.

10-10 am. 29 FAB, estimated that two battns were seen in O/29/c at 9-55 am, marching towards Gappard — Reported to 3/Corps.
A later report states that at 10-7 am, the force halted, and were drilling in O/27/d, or O/27/b. 7th Siege were asked to turn on to them, but the party had gone before they were able to do so. — 16. 17.

11-10 am. Air reconnaissance 6 to 7 am. All roads clear, no rolling stock or trains seen. — 18.

12-16 pm. Som L.I. report Germans fired 17 Little Willies at their Centre trench. 135th Batty retaliated. — 19 20

1-30 pm. 32 FAB report Villas at Northend Warneton on Ypres road, still apparently used as H.Q. as telephone wires lead to them. Wagons seen moving N. on Ypres-Warneton loaded with planks. — 21 22 23

5-55 pm. Evening report. Situation unchanged. Centre Section, 30 Little Willies in N.E. salient of Som L.I. section. Left Sector, 48 shell at trenches N. of Douve, by night and 32 during day. Sniping against Douve, left, heavy at dawn. — 24, 25 26 27 (31, 30, 29, 28

7-30 pm. Report from Left Sector, re uniforms seen, forwarded to 3/Corps. — 32.

6-45 pm. Arty forward hostile shelling report, forwarded to 3/Corps. (33,34)

8-50 pm. Lancs Fus report 27 Germans wounded, seen crossing Frelinghien bridge, as result of the explosion this morning. Our casualties one killed, 4 wounded. — 35, 36.

9-50 pm. 32 FAB forward Intelligence notes from their observing officer. Forwarded to 3rd Corps. — 37, 38 39.

11-30 pm. 3/Corps inform us a Zeppelin reported to have passed over Bethune between 7 and 7-30 pm. — 40

Receipt ackd to 3/Corps of Secret Letters............ 41.
G/761 Duties Arty Advisors.----- 4/Div Bo. GGG/184
G/762 Employment of Cavalry..... 4th Div GGG/185.

WAR DIARY
10th April 1915.

NIEPPE.

Fine night, dull day.

4-30 am.	Night reports from Brigades forwarded to 3/Corps and exchanged with 6th and N.Mid Divs.----All quiet, except with 10th Brigade who report--Enemy shelled working party in Steenbecque No.1, and indulged in several bursts of fire, stopping work.	1 2 3 4 5
12-35 pm.	Lan. Fus report last night party of Germans, wearing helmets, relieved about 13 Germans wearing ordinary caps at Le Touquet--Forwarded 3/Corps.---	6 7
1-25 pm.	32/FAB report movements of horses in U/12/B, and a lorry in O/36/D. Reported 3/Corps.	8 9
2-0 pm.	Instructions received from 3/Corps re relief of 10/Brig by Warw. Brig on night 12/13th. The 10th Brigade to take over billets at Bailleul vacated by Warw. Brig.--10/Brig informed.	10 11 12 13
6-0 pm.	Evening report to 3/Corps--Right and Left Sectors received a few shells. Our Arty retaliated, searching in O/32/C for hostile guns. Also six rounds were fired at guns reported by R.F.C. in O/32/B,NE. 31st Heavies put 40 rds into Frelinghien this morning.	14 15 16 17 18 19
6-50 pm.	Hostile shelling report received from Div Arty and forwarded 3/Corps	20
6-10 pm.	12/Brig--Are 2 Trench Mortars lent from 6/Div still with you ?--They replied that mortars had been returned.	20 A 21 22
9-25 pm.	Intelligence information from 32/FAB & 10th Inf Brig, forwarded to 3/Corps. (23,24,25,26,27)	
9-45 pm.	Mon. Regt. report a bright green and a red light, sent up by enemy at 8 pm. in direction of Square U/28. To 3/Corps.	28 29

3/Corps Secret letters acknowledged.

G/771 (Re Artillery Ammunition Allce)   30

G/774 (   )   31

WAR DIARY
11th April 1915.

NIEPPE.

Fine night and day.

4-25 am. Quiet night reports forwdd 3/Corps and exchanged with 6th
Div and N.Mid. Divs.   (1,2,3,4,5)

9-30 am. Op. Order No.23, issued-For the withdrawal of units of 10/
(1) Brigade on the night of 12/13th (less Arg. & Suthld. Highrs,
to be withdrawn on the 18th April) and to be relieved by units
of the Warwickshire Brig.
(2) For the withdrawal of Units of 11th Brig (less Lon Rif Brig,
to be withdrawn later) on the night of 15/16th April and to be
relieved by 1st S.Mid Brig.- Attached.-

11-0 .m 10th Brig report movements of troops and horses, with and
without wagons, heard last night from midnight till 2-30 am   6
this morning. Almost continuous on Messines- Warneton road.   7
The 11th Brig were asked to try and confirm, but the replies   8
were contradictory.

5-45 pm Resume of evening reports from Brigades forwarded to 3rd Corps
and exchanged with 6th and N.Mid.Divisions. Right Sector reports
houses in Le Touquet - Bizet road shelled with incendiary shells
and one house in North Block set on fire. Centre Sector - sniping
brisk but little shelling. Left Sector - heavy sniping at dawn,
little shelling.
(9, 10, 11, 12, 13, 14, 15)

6-10 pm Items of Intelligence forwarded to 3rd Corps. (16 & 17)

7-25 pm Left Sector report yellow sausage up from 12-45 pm to 2 pm
and again from 3 pm to 4-10 pm. Another one seen at 6-50 pm.   18,19,20

9-50 pm 32 F.A.B. report working party busy all day near Sucrerie.
15 men carrying sacks dispersed by 135 Batty. At 6 pm 50
mounted men, a supply wagon, one platoon and one battn seen
going N.E. in O.24.C. Four wagons seen on road U.6.a N.E.
Party of 20, probably civilians, seen on Gard Dieu - Holleneke
road. Five four-horses wagons seen S. of Warneton - Quesnoy
road loaded with what appeared to be parts of aeroplane.   21,22,23.

10th Brig. report their H.Q. in Bailleul will be at
No. 23 Rue de Lille.   24

War Diary - 12th April 1915.

NIEPPE   Fine day and night.

4-25 am   Quiet night reports to 3rd Corps and exchanged with 6th
           and N.Mid.Divs.   (1, 2, 3, 4, 5 & 6)

9-30 am   Air reconnaissance 5-30 to 7 am. Much timber stacked in
           centre of Messines. One train, some rolling stock and 4 M.T.
           wagons seen in Commines.   (7)

9-30 am   Centre Sector reports rather more transport than usual
           heard last night, direction uncertain, believed to be North
           to South. A band was playing in Warneton direction about
           11-30 pm. Two red lights were fired simultaneously from a
           point about 400 yards due South of White Estaminet at 1-50 am.
                                        (8, 9, 10 & 11)

11-55 am   Left Sector report that Little Willis has been shelling the
           road junction 200 yards S.W. of their H.Q. persistently since
           10-10 am. War.Inf.Brig. halted at safe distance. Seaforths
           just missed being shelled.   (12)

5-45 pm   Evening report to 3rd Corps. Right Sector reports about
           20 shell fell in Snipers Houses causing considerable damage
           to front line. Centre Sector normal. Left Sector - more
           shelling than usual. (13, 14, 15, 16, 17, 18, 19, 20, 21 & 22)

6-19 pm   S.Lan.R. report seeing working parties carrying planks near
           R.Lys this morning opposite Brewery at Frelinghien.   (23 & 24)

7-15 pm   Hostile shelling report from Div.Arty. forwarded to 3rd Corps.
           Considerable shelling of Petit Pont during the morning by 10·5 cm
           howitzers and one 10 cm gun, probably from about O.32.b or d.
           These same guns shelled Douve trenches between 4 and 5 pm.   (25)

8-56 pm   32nd F.A.B. report 6-50 pm that 134th Batty. observed saw
           what looked like ¼ battn in U.11.a. Flash again seen this
           evening at old position in U.12.c.   (26 & 27)

10-50 pm   R.Ir.Fus. report between 5 and 6 pm enemy opened fire with
           a new gun heavier than any used against that Sector before.
           It fired 19 rounds, one of which was blind. It open N.W. of
           Deadcow farm and shortened range till it found the trenches.
           The Div. Arty. think these are probably 15 cm howitzers believed
           to be near Gapaard or O.32.b.d. and th inform us that R.F.C.
           would search for them tomorrow.   (28 & 29)

           3rd Corps were informed that the 19th Hussars would leave
           Nieppe at 7-30 am on 14th inst. and proceed via Bailleul to
           St Sylvestre Cappell.   (30, 31, 32 & 33)

           Receipts to 3rd Corps for Secret Nos :-
           I.R..190   (Falcons) - GGG.177
           G.928   (Kite flying) - GGG.190

           Readjustment of our front ordered by Op. Order No. 23 of
           11th, giving changes of address of 10th Brig. and War.Brig.
                                        (35, 36, 37, 38, 39 & 40)

           The Warwick Inf Brig relieved 10th Inf Brig (less 7/A.& S.Highrs)
           in their trenches this day, and came under orders of GOC 4th Div.
           The 10th Inf Brig went into billets at Bailleul on relief.

NIEPPE.
WAR DIARY
17/4/15.

Fine night and day.

4-45 am Night reports forwarded to 3rd Corps and exchanged with 6th and
         4th Divisions.   (1, 2, 3, 4, 5, 6, 7, 8 & 9)

9 am   3rd Corps ask how battns of War.Brig. are disposed in trenches.
         Replied - 5th Warwicks were South of Douve with one Coy North of
         Douve in line formerly occupied by 1/R.Ir.Fus. 7th Warwicks are
         North of Douve with left on Wulverghem - Messines road in line
         formerly occupied by 2/R.Dub.Fus.   (10, 11 & 12)

11-10 am 27th F.A.B. report sentry heard airship or aeroplane over Neuve
         Eglise at 11-50 pm - 20 bombs were dropped. 3rd Corps informed.
                                                            (13)

1-20 pm 3rd Corps inform us that War.Brig. and S.Mid.Brig. (latter from
         15/16th) will be under G.O.C. 4th Div. till midnight 17/18th.
         After midnight (17/18th) the command of the line from River Warnave
         to Wulverghem - Messines road will devolve upon Gen. Heath, Commdg.
         South Midland Division. All concerned informed.   (14, 15 & 16)

6-15 pm Evening report to 3rd Corps. Right Sector - 60 Little Willies
         around Barkenham Fm at 9 am. During the day a few more shell fell
         around Carters Fm and Touquet Houses. Small breach made in Railway
         Barricade. About 35 shell fell in Monmouths trench H.Q. Centre
         Sector - a little shelling. Left Sector - quiet. Artillery
         dispersed working parties in Birdcage and O.34.D. and shelled
         enemy's haystack observing station and knocked down Pont Rouge
         Chimney.   (17, 18, 19, 20, 21, 22, 23 & 24)

6-45 pm Various items of Intelligence from 32nd F.A.B. forwarded to
         3rd. Corps.   (25)

7-10 pm Hostile shelling report from Div. Arty. passed to 3rd Corps. (26)

8-55 pm Further intelligence notes from 32nd F.A.B. and War.Inf.Brig.
         forwarded to 3rd Corps.   (27, 28 & 29)

10-13 pm A small concentrated searchlight observed in U.2.c by artillery
         observing officer in Left Sector trenches. 3rd Corps and Inf.
         Brigs. informed.   (30, 31 & 32)

11-17 pm Communication by wire re-established between 5/War.R. and A.& S.
         Highrs. after short breakdown.   (33, 34 & 35)

         11th Brig. new Hd. Qrs. will be Farm at cross roads in Square
         F.12.a 9.7. Sheet 36 A.   (36)

12 mn   S.Lancs. report 2 guns near Greytown in Frelinghien. Magnetic
         bearing 100 degrees from end of Carters farm. Passed to Div.Arty.
                                                            (37)

11 pm   Acknowledged receipt of Secret No. G.774/4 to 3rd Corps.

WAR DIARY
14th April 15.

NIEPPE.   Fine night. A little rain in morning, clearing early until evening, when rain again fell, intermittently.

4.35.   Quiet night reports to 3/Corps and exchanged with 5/6th Divs.
(1,2,3,4,5 & 6)

11th Brigade report their Headqrs will be at School, 2 miles S.by W. of Bailleul, after their move 17/18th.instants.   7.

1-20 pm.   The gun now at Petit Pont to be sent to No.5, Squadron, aerodrome this evening. Captain Mortimore to report to 3/Corps H.Q. with reference to arrangements for dealing with airships.   8.

5-45 pm.   Evening report to 3/Corps. Right Sector--Situation normal,   9
King's Own received several Little Willies round one of   10
their trenches last night, and they were also shelled today.   11
Centre Sector -- No shelling, little sniping. Left Sector,   12
6 shell fell near Cha. la Hutte, and 3 near Le Rossignol,   13
apparently from Gapaard. More wire was erected opposite left
of 7th Argtll & Suthd Highrs.   14
Arty report enemy were shelled at Avenue Farm by 32nd FAB   15
from whence snipers were firing, also retaliated on enemy   16
at Douve trenches and dispersed working parties near Sucerie.   17
South Midland Howzrs shelled Snipers House in U/28/D; 6/9.
7th Siege Batty fired at hostile battery near Gapaard.
29th FAB shelled working party near Sucerie U/17/D last night,
also working party in enemy's front libe trench.
(18

6-15 pm.   Lt H.S.Ellis 29 FAB detailed to attend Course in Observation   (19
and communication between aircraft. Name forwarded 3/Corps.   (20
(21

6-45 pm.   Hostile shelling report from Div Arty forwarded to 3/Corps
--Little Shelling.   22

6-45 pm.   32 FAB report two wagons loaded with planks seen going S.
on road E.of Sucerie.   23

9-50 pm.   Suspicious looking officer seen at Bethune and Laventie   24
yesterday.--All Units informed if seen, he is to be arrested.   25

9-26 pm.   The South Mid. Brig. RFA forward a report concerning suspicions being aroused on account of knowledge of the dispositions of our troops and guns, displayed by an Estaminet keeper, and the movements of a white horse belonging to him, which   26
coincided with shelling from the enemy. Forwarded 3/Corps and S.Mid. Brig asked to avoid any action te likely to arouse suspicions of the suspect.

8-35 pm.   Zeppelin reported to have passed over Ypres 7-45 pm, going   27
South. All Units informed.   28

South Midland Division report that their H.Q. will move to Nieppe on Friday 16th April.   29.

"B" Squadron 19th Hussars left the 4th Division this day & One Squadron Northampton Yeomanry arrived to take their place as Div Mounted Troops.

NIEPPE.
WAR DIARY
15/4/15.

Heavy mist at night, clearing at 8 am. Fine day.

5-0 am. Quiet night reports to 3/Corps and exchanged with 6th & (1,2,3,4,═══)
N.Mid Divs. (5, 6 & 7)

12-10 am. The 3/Corps inform us that the 4.7 inch battery S.Mid Div   8
will come under orders 4th Div Group from midnight 17/18th   9
--4th Div Arty informed.--

1-0 pm. To S.Mid. Div suggesting 27th and 134 batteries RFA be   10
relieved night of 16/17th, and 135th and 127th batteries   11
night 18/19th. S.Mid.Div agreed

3-27 pm. 3rd Corps suggest that now anti-aircraft are reduced to
2 guns, they be turned on to different positions on alter-
nate days---Passed to Div Arty.   12.

2-16 pm. Requested 3rd Corps to loan us the services of M.G.Officer   13
══Approved.══ for 13th Brigade who are without an experienced   14.
M.G.Officer.---Approved.   15

5-50 pm. Evening report to 3/Corps and exchanged with 6th & N.Mid
Divs. Right sector little shelling. Centre Sector. Little   16
shelling or sniping. Left Sector little shelling or sni-   17
ping. Several rockets, with red white and blue stars sent   18
up from Messines. Arty report shelling of working parties   19
N.of Railway by 14 FAB, at La Basse Ville, Sucerie, Birdcage, 20
and E. of St Yves. 4th S.Mid Howzrs shelled Sniper's House   21
in U/28/D, also Sniper's House in Avenue. Considerable acti- 22
vity on the part of the enemy observed today in Birdcage.   23
(24,25,26,27,28)

6-25 pm. Intelligence items re uniforms and transport forwdd 3/Corps.

7-0 pm. Hostile shelling report from Div Arty forwarded 3/Corps:-
15 cm. Howitzers fired 5 shell at Le Touquet. 10th Fd Howrs
shell fell near Le Bizet. 8th Fd Gun shell fired at Le Touquet 29
2 Fd Gun shell at Ploegsteert. 8 Fd Gun shell at Douve tren-   30
ches and also 8 rounds from Fd Howzrs.

8-0 pm. 11/Brig report their Hdqrs to be at School in F/12/A, East   31.
Reference Sheet 36/A.

7-9 pm. South Mid Inf Brig Hdqrs established in farm vacated by
11th Inf Brig. (T/29/D)   32

9-30 pm. 32 FAB report flashes again visible this evening in U/6/c
and undoubtedly were from anti aircraft guns. Germans   33
appear to be duplicating their communication trenches in   34
U/9/D and U/9/C. Intelligence notes, movements and uniforms. forwarded to 3 Corps.

Ackd receipt of Secret letters to 3/Corps (G/828)   35
(G/822)   36

1/S.Mid Brig relieved 11th Inf Brig (less Lon Rif Brig) in their
trenches this day, the latter moving into billets in the area--
Steenwerck - Noote Boom.
One 15 in gun, the 114th Battry RFA, and S.Mid Heavy Batty
arrived in the 4th Division area and came under the orders of
~~these 4th Div~~., this day.

WAR DIARY

NIEPPE.
16/4/15.

Fine night and day.

Time	Entry	No.
12-1 am.	3/Corps inform us that German L.V.G. aeroplanes observed yesterday was marked with white cross on large black disc. --Our Units informed.--	1, 2
2-30 am.	Lon Rif Brig heard mining sounds in close proximity, from direction Birdcage. S.Mid Brig ordered to still continue "listening patrols".	3, 4
4-40 am.	Quiet night reports to 3/Corps and exchanged with N.Mid & 6th Divs.	(5,6,7,8,9,10,11, 12)
7-50 am	S.Mid Div inform us that our 11th Brig Units in second line and billets were relieved by Units of S.Mid Brig.	13
12-42 pm.	Air reconnaissance 10-20 to 10-40 am. No movements. Increased digging along the River Lys.	14
1-0 pm.	Amended Table "C" Nos 2 & 4 received from S.Mid Div. (No 4 forwarded 12th Brig)	15, 16, 17
1-0 pm.	3/Corps were told Armoured Train should go to old position in H/5/C.	18
1-5 pm.	6th Div requested to hand over 12th Siege Battery guns to us, ~~ai from~~ the vicinity of Road Junction H/18/b and B/10/11 centre, during the night 17/18th.	19.
5-55 pm.	Evening reports to 3/Corps--Right Sector 54 Little Willies and White Hopes fired at cottage in coppice, near Le Touquet, only 8 hits. Convent in East End of Le Bizet shelled with Little Willies and White Hopes this morning. Centre Sector, -No change. Left Sector- A little shelling.	20, 21, 22, 23, 24
7-30 pm.	Germans with green caps and grey uniform seen in U/22/D and with grey uniform and grey forage caps with red bands opposite Essex trenches. Essex Regt received 30 rifle grenades at trenches in front of Cross Roads C/4/a	25, 26, 27 (28,29,30)
7-20 pm	Div Arty forward Hostile shelling report, forwarded to 3/Corps--About 60 field gun shells fell behind Le Touquet support trenches during morning. --10 Fd Howr shells near Le Bizet. A few single shots, Fd Howr fell near St Yves. 80 Fd Gun Shells near Douve trenches, also some against trenches on Messines-Wulverghem road.	31
9-45 pm.	32/Brig RFA report several men seen passing along Communication trenches from right end of Avenue to La Potterie, all dressed in grey and apparently strange to the neighbourhood.	32, 33
	Ackt sent to 3/Corps for Secret papers:- G/844) G/847) Moves of Royal Arty.	34
	G/848 (Allotment of guns and Ammunition) G/849 (Distribution of Units to 4th,6th & S.Mid Divs.)	35

The 3rd Siege (6 inch Howr) battery arrived in 4th Div Area and comes under the orders of G.O.C. 4th Div this day.

War Diary - 17th April 1915.

NIEPPE.

Rain during night - fine day.

10-40 am   The War. Inf. Brig. asked that 2 Coy. of A. & S. Highrs. may
            march to Bailleul, starting at 11-45 am in order to clear the
            road for 4/Oxfords. We replied that there was no objection
            and the relief was finally completed at noon.   (1, 2 & 3)

4-40 am   Quiet night reports to 3rd Corps and exchanged with 6th and
            N.Mid. Divs.   (4, 5, 6, 7, 8, 9, & 10)

11-45 am   Air reconnaissance 7 to 8 am. Movements of horsed and M.T.
            vehicles observed. 2 new pontoon bridges constructed between
            Frelinghien and Pont Rouge, both North of old pontoon bridge.
            Div. Arty. and 12th Brig. informed.   (11, 12 & 13)

2-50 pm   Air reconnaissance 2 am. No movement observed in or around
            Quesnoy and Armentieres - Lomme road also clear.   (14)

6-5 pm   Evening report to 3rd Corps. Right Sector received 18 bombs
            at railway barricade, all of which missed, and replied with 12
            which landed in trenches. Seven bombs fired at Snipers Houses.
            E.Lancs. retaliated with 11. Centre sector received 12 shell
            at 8/War. H.Q. Left Sector - one Little Willie hit Hulls Burnt
            Farm. With assistance of aeroplane observation the 31st Heavies
            found the range of and shelled hostile battery in C.33.D. and
            a battery in D.1.c. S.Mid. Arty. shelled German trenches in
            retaliation for shelling of 8/War. H.Q. and silenced German
            battery.   (15, 16, 17, 18, 19, 20, 21, 22 & 23)

7-12 pm   Hostile shelling report received from Div. Arty. and forwarded
            to 3rd Corps.   (24 & 25)

7-30 pm   War. Brig. report that from 4 to 5 pm, 16th, about 60 shell
            at Douve trenches from direction of Gapaard. From 5-15 to
            5-15 pm about 25 shell were fired at Dead Cow farm and cottages
            between that place and La Hutte Chateau. 3rd Corps informed.
                                                       (26 & 26a)

9 pm   Messages from War.Inf.Brig. says that at 8-17 an airship was
            reported South of Wulverghem going S.W. 3rd Corps and units
            informed.   (27, 28 & 29)

9-3 pm   12th Brig. ordered to render morning and evening reports to
            4th Div. from midnight 17/18th.

10-35 pm   3rd Corps inform us that a mine under Hill 60/ I.29.c.d. was
            satisfactorily exploded by 5th Div. Arty. officer reports
            enemy's position captured. German prisoner states "Enemy's
            losses heavy" our casualties few. Later report from 3rd Corps
            states we now occupy a position beyond mine crater and that
            German artillery fire has now practically ceased. A German
            aeroplane was brought down near Elver - Dinghe, the pilot being
            killed and the observer and machine captured.
            At Nieppe we had heard very heavy firing from 7 pm onwards.

11-47 pm   Right Sector reports heavy horse transport heard between
            Le Touquet and Warnave from 8 to 11 pm. The movement is more
            than usual.   (34 & 35)

            Receipt to 3rd Corps for Secret No. G.849/1 (Arty. moves)

            The S.Mid.Div. relieved our 7/A.& S. Highrs., L.R.B. and
            2/R.Ir.R. in their trenches to-day. These units went into

            billets with their respective Brigades.

W A R   D I A R Y
18/4/15.

NIEPPE   Fine night, sunny day.

4-50 am.   Quiet night reports to 3rd Corps and exchanged with 6th & South Mid. Divs.   (1,2,3,4,5,6)

9-26 am.   Air reconnaissance 6 - 6.45 am. No movement in area Armentiers - Lille - Menin - Frelinghien.   7.

10-25 am.   12/Brig report that S.Lancs heard transport moving in a North Easterly direction to the N.E. of Frelinghien continuously from 9 pm to 3 am. 3/Corps informed.   8 9

2-25 pm.   3/Corps inform us ~~that~~ of successful explosion of mine by 5th Div on Hill 60, followed by fierce fighting through night, and hand to hand fighting from 5-30 - 7 am. It is believed 150 Germans were buried in trench when mine exploded. Our M.Guns did good work in the counter attacks made by the enemy. Our positions are being strengthened. All Units informed.   10 11

4-50 pm.   Evening report - 12/Brigade received 6 Little Willies and 12 bombs, all of which were misses. Monmouths claim several hits with trench mortars. A few White Hopes were fired at at Convent in East end, Le Bizet this morning, no damage Reported. 18/Brig. report Estaminet, Au Bon Coin, Frelinghien burning nicely all day. Artillery report 14 FAB fired 10 rds in retaliation and 31/Heavies shelled batteries in U/30/D/6,4, and O/30/D/H,W.   12 13 14 15 16 17

7-55 pm.   Artillery forward Hostile Shelling Report for the day, forwarded 3/Corps:-
9-30 am 20 Fd Guns shell fell at Houplines from direction L'Aventure.
10-30 am 4 howr,5.9 (2 blind,2 shrapnel) fell at Le Bizet from Les Ecluses (U/30/d/N.W)   5 light Howr shell, one at a time, fell near Convent and Church, Le Bizet, from Les Ecluses.
1-0 pm. 1 light Howzr shell on Le Bizet - Warneton road.   18
4-30 pm. 6 howzr shell 5.9, fell at Le Bizet from Les Ecluses.   19

8-7 pm.   18/Brig state it is difficult to question all persons desirous of proceeding along the Frelinghien road at C/22/A, and request all officers be provided with passes.   20 21

At midnight 17/18th the command of the front from the Messines - Wulverghem road to the river Warnave passed from GOC 4th Div. to GOC, S.Mid Div, and G.O.C., 4th Division took over command of 18th Inf Brig, and the front on the River Lys held by them, and of certain other troops (See attached) 22 ABC. and also large map, App" A and note thereon).

WAR DIARY
19/4/15.

NIEPPE.-

Fine night and fine day.

4-40 am.   Quiet night reports from Brigades forwarded to 3/Corps
              and exchanged with 6th and S.Mid Divs.   (1,2,3,4,5,6)

8-50 am.   18th Brig report that Westminsters consider more trans-
              port than usual was heard, up to midnight, moving South on a   7
              road further in rear of enemy's lines than transport usually   8
              moves on.--Forwarded to 3/Corps.--

9-30 am.   12th Brigade report that Le Bizet is being shelled by
              Little Willies and Heavy Shells, and this has being going   9
              on for an hour. Requested an aeroplane be sent up, as it
              might stop the shelling. Aeroplane was sent up.   10

9-52 am   18th Brigade report 15 heavy transport wagons moving
              along the Perenchies - Frelinghien road in direction of Fre-   11
              linghien.--3/Corps informed.--   12

12-56 pm.   Air reconnaissance 10 - 10.40 am.--No troops seen in
              Area Fleurbaix - Ennetieres - Perenchies - Bondues - Roncq
              - Messines.   At Bois Blancs wood planks are close to the
              East side of the road--O/2/A, N.W.---   13.

2-25 pm.   18th Brig informed a party of gunners is going to
              bury communication wires behind their front tonight.   14

2-50 pm.   3/Corps requests that two batterys of 29th Brig RFA
              be allowed to remain under S.Mid. Div, as at present.--
              Div Arty informed.   15

5-50pm.   Evening report to 3/Corps. Very little shelling in
              18th or 12th Brigades.   (16,17,18,19,20,21,22)

9-55 pm.   12th Brigade report Monmouths think the Germans to   23
              their front are strange, as they are behaving differently   24
              and stand on their parapets. They quickly jumped back into
              trenches on Monmouths opening fire---To 3/Corps.

10-10 pm.   Aeroplane heard by S.Lancs (12/Brig) to the south of   25
              Lys farm at 9-20 pm. Forwarded to 3/Corps.   26.

WAR DIARY
20th April 1915.

Fine night and fine day.

4-35 am. Quiet night reports to 3/Corps, and exchanged with 6th &
S.Mid. Divs.   (1,2,3,4,5)

4-30 pm. Air reconnaissance - Roads clear. A column of smoke seen
for several hundred yards, along the enemy's trench line,
towards Neuve Chapelle   6.

5-45 pm. Evening report to 3/Corps--Quiet day.--A German aeroplane   7
dropped four bombs into Armentieres.--20 Little Willies   8
fired at Lys section, about midday.   9
                                        (10,11,12,13)

6-45 pm. Hostile Shelling Report from Div.Arty, forwarded 3/Corps.
Light gun fired 6 rds at Le Touquet. Little Willie
shelled Estaminet Du Bon Coin in C/4/a, for an hour.
Fd Guns shelled trenches N.of Le Touquet and the village
itself. Fd Guns fired 30 rds at Le Touquet. A few field
gun shells directed at the Le Touquet trenches running from
village to railway.   14.

9-27 pm. 18/Brig forward report from W.Yorks that enemy are throwing
lights, high up, in air along front from Perenchies to Road
Junction 600 yards S.E. of Quatre Hallots. About 20 or 30   15
appeared in ¼ of an hour. Forwarded to 3/Corps.   16

9-50 pm. 12/Brig report that the Germans have blown up a mine at
Railway Barricade. No damage to our lines. No attack
followed. One casualty.   17.

7-5 pm. 3/Corps notify us that a party of 13 Cadets will be attached

to us on the 23rd for 24 hours instruction in the trenches.

---6 Cadets will be sent to 12th Brigade Area, and 7 Cadets

to 18th Brigade.

NIEPPE.   War Diary - 21st April 1915.

　　　　　　Dull night - little rain in early morning - afterwards fine.

4-30 am   Quiet night reports exchanged with 6th and S.Mid. Divs. and
            forwarded to 3rd Corps.   (1-2-3-4-5 & 6)

12-45 pm   3rd Corps message directs that an officer of 11th Brig. be
            detailed to instruct S.Mid.Div. in bomb-throwing. 2/Lt.A.E.Stevens
            Hamps. R. was detailed for this duty.   (7, 8 & 8)

5-49 pm   Evening Report. Very quiet day. Some light shelling in 18th
            Brig. area.   (10,11,12,13,14,15 & 16)

7-15 pm   Hostile shelling report received from Div. Arty. and forwarded
            to 3rd Corps. About 40 shell reported to have fallen near
            Le Bizet.   (17)

            3rd Corps order one section of 6" Hows. and one 9.2" How. from
            4th Div. to be placed at disposal of 5th Div. Arrangements made
            to move these guns at midnight 21/22nd and they were expected
            to be at Vlamertinghe at 5 pm 22nd.   (18,19,20 & 21)
                                                           26 & 27.
            3rd Corps order move of remainder of 6" Hows. and one section
            Mountain Battery to 5th Div. Arrangements were made for move
            of remainder of 6" Hows at 10 am 22nd and for move of section of
            Mountain Batty. at midnight 21/22nd.   (22,23,24 & 25)

11-50 pm   18th Brig. report that the right of No. 2 Section heard enemy's
            transport sounding like heavy motors moving from North to South
            from 10 to 10-20 pm. Forwarded to 3rd Corps.   (28 & 29)

            Major Symons R.E. reports strong indications of German counter-mine
            against our left gallery at Snipers House mine.
            A charge was prepared for exploding our mine early tomorrow.
                                                           LB

NIEPPE.

War Diary - 22nd April 1915.

Fine day - cold wind.

4-30 am   Quiet night report to 3rd Corps and exchanged with 6th
          and S.Mid.Div.   (1,2,3,4,5,6)

8-30 am   The mine at Le Touquet, mentioned in yesterday's diary was
          successfully fired at 7-15 am. The Germans afterwards retaliated
          by shelling Snipers Houses with Heavy guns. (7,8,9,10,11,12 & 13)

1-2 pm   Air reconnaissance report 9-10 am. Considerable movement of
          individuals in village of Premesques. Horse transport moving
          South on Perenchies - Lomme road. In Lomme 30 M.T. vehicles
          standing on either side of street. 15 M.T. vehicles were seen
          leaving village on Pont Roube road.   (14)

2-32 pm   18th Brig. report that Durhams heard troops, estimated at several
          hundred men, marching on road in direction of Frelinghien,
          apparently stopping near half thatched cottage. Singing and
          extra wheeled traffic heard off and on between 11 pm and 1-15 am.
          3rd Corps informed.   (15 & 16)

6-50 pm   Evening report. The mine fired this morning destroyed part of
          enemy's front walls and about 20 yards of ground between the lines.
          The Snipers Houses were first shelled this morning with Field guns
          and afterwards with Heavy guns. Considerable damage - no casualties.
          Farm Delmotte in C.19.b shelled about 11 am with incendiary shell
          and caught fire - now extinguished. Railway barricade shelled
          with about 45 heavy shell about noon - some damage done.
              18th Brig. report enemy busy on parapets - otherwise quiet.
              Artillery report: 31st Heavies shelled Batty. in U.30.d N.W.
          and two heavy batty positions in U.30.d. Also shelled T.16 in
          Frelinghien and set on fire a factory. This was in retaliation for
          shelling of Le Touquet.   (17,18,19,20,21,22,23 & 24)

7-15 pm   Hostile shelling report from Div. Arty. passed to 3rd Corps.
          200 shell at 12th Brig - about 80 of which were 15 cm Howr. shell,
          and 30 Fd. Howr. shell - the remainder were from field guns. (25)

9-15 pm   3rd Corps inform us a Zeppelin was seen over Fleurbaix at 8-50 pm
          flying in a westerly direction. Circulated.   (26 & 27)

4 pm   4th report remaining section of 6" How. Batty. left at 10-30 am,
          section Mtn. Batty. at 1 am and 9.2" How. at 4-35 am.   (28)

9-20 pm   Receipt to 3rd Corps for their Secret G.934 (Dumping Artillery
          Ammunition)   (29)

                                                              LB

WAR DIARY
23rd April 1915.

Fine day, with cold piercing winds.

4-50 am Night reports to 3/Corps.--Enemy exploded a mine in Le Touquet section about 1 am, between our Sniper's Houses and his. No damage to us. Enemy was working on Brewery again all first part of night and what sounded like metal rails and timber were being unloaded.
Motor horn heard at Frelinghien at 9-30 pm. Wheeled transport heard from Hobbs farm moving forwards and backwards, across 18th Brig front all night.

8-55 am. 18th Brig report Sounds of heavy guns and limbers moving Northwards about midnight. After about ¼ of an hour sounds were drowned by lighter transport also moving north.

9-50 am. 3/Corps report - Heavy bombardment yesterday evening at Hill 60. Heavy attack delivered against Junction Canadian and French. Asphyxiating gas forced French back to Canal. Early morning attacks against Broodseine and right of 27th Div. repulsed. Canadian counter-attacks on left, drove enemy back through wood C/10/D, towards Kaeselaere and farm from YPRES have marched C/20/A.C. French counter attack not yet developed. Enemy digging in on line Boesinghe canal, crossing Beesclare. Circulated to all concerned.

1.40 p.m. 12 Brig. report our guns have set Pond House on fire reducing it to ruins and exploding ammunition.

3 p.m. 3rd A.C. inform us columns of hostile infantry reported by N.M.Div. moving S.E. on YPRES-WARNETON road at 11.35 am, but nothing observed by S.Mid.Div. of this movement.

5.45 pm Evening reports to 3rd A.C. Quiet day, except for incidents mentioned above.
  (13, 14, 15, 16, 17, 18, 19).

7.30 pm Hostile shelling report from D.A. forwarded to 3rd A.C. Little shelling.

10.12 pm Various information re use of poisonous gases received from 3rd A.C. and circulated.

10.41 pm 3rd A.C. inform us that 5th Corps counter attack astride the YPRES-FILCKEN road progressing favourably against stubborn resistance. 13th Brig. believed to have gained ridge C.15.c to C/11/c, S.E. of BOESINGHE. French and Belgians made attack on Bridge head at Steinstratz at 6 pm. Hill 60 heavily shelled.

At 11 a.m. warning orders were received to hold our 10th and 11th Brigs. in readiness to proceed to support units fighting on our left, the former by march route, the latter by rail. Arrangements were made and orders finally received at 7 p.m. for 10th Brig. and 10th Fd. Ambce. to proceed tonight to LOCRE and DRANOUTRE. The Brig. marched at 7.30 p.m. and notified us their H.Q. would be DRANOUTRE.

WAR DIARY
24th April 1915.

NIEPPE.

Fine night and fine day. Rather cold wind.

4-40 am   Quiet night reports as usual.   1,2,3,4,5.

7-25 am   18/Brig report that transport was heard continuously between   6
          8-11 pm last night, about Quesnoy, N.W. and along R. Deule.   7
          Some of it sounded like a Fd Battery at the trot. To 3/Corps.

5-57 pm. Evening report to 3/Corps--12/Brig report Le Bizet shelled
          this morning for 2 hours. 12 Little Willies at Left High
          Command on Le Touquet section, 6 at Avenue trenches and several
          at Cross Roads barricade. No damage.
              18/Brig report Germans are sapping new trench in front of
          Brewery, and have made 2 M.G. emplacements low down among debris 8
          in face of Brewery. Hobbs Farm shelled between 5-30 and 6-30 am   9
          and again at 11 am. Our 14/FAB shelled M.G. House, Le Touquet and
          the Triangle. 29/FAB shelled trenches opposite our left.   10
          Heavies shelled batteries at D/7 a, C/12 a, D/2 d, and D/13 d,   11
          setting fire to farm behind latter and D/25 a,b, North.   12
          Siege Group retaliated against Quesnoy.   13
                                                                           14
6-58 pm   Hostile shelling report from Div Arty forwarded 3/Corps.   15
          --Intermittent shelling by Fd Guns, 15 cm Howrs and 15 cm
          gun, L'Epinette receiving many shell from 4 pm onwards.
          Le Bizet, Le Touquet and E. of Bizet were shelled at intervals.

8-33 pm   18/Brig report Westminsters say Germans are digging a new trench
          from Burnt Farm in a Southerly direction, apparently with a view 16
          to connect up with 4 Hallots--Forwarded to 3/Corps.   17

          Reports of the situation of the battle to the North of Ypres   18
          were received from 3/Corps during the evening and are attached. 19
                                                                           20

9-6 am.   Warning orders received for 11/Brig to entrain 2 hours later.

10-25 am 3/Corps notify us 10/Brig marched at 7 am from Locre to Ouderdom,
          and are under orders 5th Corps.

          12/Fd Ambce are to provide Bearer Subdivisions to accompany 11th
          Brig, strength 3 Officers, 105 men, and will entrain at Steenwerck.
              Five trains provided for 11/Brig and 12/Fd Ambce:-
                      1st from Bailleul
                      2nd "   Steenwerck
                      3rd "   Bailleul
                      4th "   Steenwerck
                      5th "   Bailleul (for M.Guns)

11-45 am 12th Fd Motor Ambces ordered to accompany transport--march route

11-45 am 3/Corps notify us 11th Brigade proceeded to Poperinghe, and are
          under orders of Cav Corps, for operations towards Elverdinghe.

12-12 pm. 3/Corps notify us transport of 11th Brigade to march Bailleul -
          Locre - Zevaton - Poperinghe, and will park about 1½ miles short
          of Poperinghe.

                    ZEVECOTEN

                                                              LB

WAR DIARY
25th April 1915.

NIEPPE.

Fine night and day, with change of wind for a short time, which veered round again to the N. and N.E.

4-30 am.	Quiet night reports as usual.	1,2,3,4,5,6,7 & 8
1-45 pm.	18/Brig report Germans appear to have removed greater part of their wire from Burnt Farm to Half Thatched Cottage, which is opposite Sher.Foresters.	9 10
5-55 pm.	Evening report forwarded to 3rd Corps---12/Brig received 12 Little Willies at Left High Command and Centre Trenches on Le Touquet section this afternoon. No damage done. --18/Brig report-Enemy have shelled our working parties a good deal, otherwise quiet. Arty report -About 2 pm Our Fd Guns and Howrs shelled Grand Verquin, Les Oursins and Chastel Farms in retaliation for their shelling of our working parties.	11 12 13 14 15 16 17
7-0 pm.	Arty Hostile Shelling Report from Div Arty, forwarded to 3/Corps.--Little shelling.--	18
9-55 pm.	18/Brig report large amount transport heard moving in a Northerly direction through La Houlette at 9 pm. Forwarded 3/Corps.	19 20

Reports of the situation to the North of Ypres, sent us from 3/Corps, circulated to our Brigades and are attached. (21,22,23,24,25,26,27)

W A R   D I A R Y
26th April 1915

        Fine night and day. Light N. and N.E. wind still blowing.

4-40 am.	Quiet night reports to 3/Corps and exchanged 6th and S.Mid Divs. (1,2,3,4,5)
1-35 pm.	Air reconnaissance:- Column of 50 Carts observed Le Chien (D/12/D) moving N.W. at 10-30 am. Div Arty informed.. (6)
4-50 pm.	Evening report 20 Little Willies at Le Touquet trenches, 6 Rifle Grenades near Rly Barricade. Arty shelled Blanchisserie in C/15/c getting two direct hits on southend of building. Also shelled trench on Rly line(C/4/a), Deulemont church and retaliated on batteries in D/1/c, U/30/D,N.W. and C/12/a,causing cessation of hostile fire. (7,8,9,10,11,12,13)
7-22 pm.	Hostile shelling report from Div Arty forwarded 3/Corps.-- Little Shelling. 14
8-15 pm.	18/Brig report Sherwood Foresters observed a body of Infty with transport,estimated 1 battn, moving in a southerly direction, towards Le Falot at 7-5 pm. 16
9-25 pm.	West Yorks report considerable movement of transport along road from 4 Hallots to Aventure, probably reliefs. The movement ceased at 10.45 p.m. 17 18
9.25 p.m.	6th Div. report ~~had~~ heavy transport sounds like M.T. followed by lighter transport, moving North near Perenchies starting at 7 and ceasing at 7.40 p.m. 19 20
10.21 p.m.	Monmouths report heavy wheeled transport heard to their front between 8 and 9 p.m. - direction uncertain, but noise very loud. 21 22 23

      Reports of the situation, to our north, forwarded from Third Corps, circulated to all concerned and are attached.
        (24, 25, 26, 27, 28, 29, 30, 31.)

War Diary, General Staff, 4th Division.
27th April, 1915.

NIEPPE.   Fine night and day.   Rather cold.

4.45 a.m.   Night reports as usual.   (1, 2, 3, 4, 5, 6).

4.35 p.m.   Arty.Officer, Hill 63, reports Very Lights are being sent   7
up in line with Hill 63 and Pont Rouge. Fwd.3rd A.C.

2.14 p.m.   18 Brig. report enemy's miners are very close to our mine   8
at Sheet 36 C.16.d. and working fast. R.E. Officer will not blow
up our mine until absolutely necessary.

5.44 p.m.   Westminsters in 18 Brig. think enemy are ignorant of the   9
fact our mine is so close to theirs as they make a deal
of noise.

5.46 p.m.   Evening report - 12 I.B. received 60 Little Willies at   10
trenches and Sniper's Houses also 40 rifle grenades on   11
LE TOUQUET section. Monmouths were also shelled with   12
Little Willies. 29th F.A.B. shelled working party in   13
C.4.a. 4.7 Bty. shelled Les Oursins farm and set fire   14
to haystacks in C.23.b. 2nd F.A.B. shelled guns in D.4.a & 15
and Chastel Farm.

7.5 p.m.   Div.Arty. forward hostile shelling report forwarded to   16
Third Corps.

11 p.m.   12 I.B. report R. Ir. heard sounds like enemy's horse   17
transport moving South of the Warnave between 7.45 and   18
8.15 p.m. - forwarded to 3rd A.C.

   Acknowledges receipt of Secret G990 (Order of Battle)   19
and G988/2 (Operations orders for move).

   From 3rd A.C. - Operation order No. 25 attached, ordering
withdrawal of units 12 I.B. from R.Lys to R. Warnave section
night 28/29th April and of proceeding to area Bailleul-Meteren-
Fletre-Merris preparatory to marching on 30th to rejoin 10th
and 11th I.Bs.
~~Amb=9th=Fd.=Co=oRp=Hope=Uds=as=above=Fd.=Co.=R.E.=and=11th=Fd.====~~
9th Fd.Co.R.E., West Lancs. Fd.Co. R.E. and 11th Fd.Ambce.
will also proceed as above.
Div.Arty. to remain in its present position for the present.

Various messages from the North circulated and attached.
   (20, 21, 22, 23, 24.)

WAR DIARY
28th April 1915.

Fine night and day.

4-35 am.	Quiet night reports as usual.	1,2,3,4,5.
7-10 am	3rd Corps order that the relief of 4th Div by 6th Div be postponed until further instroutions, but shortly afterwds. notified us that previous orders would hold good.	7 8
5-55 pm.	Evening reports to 3rd Corps -- No change.--	9,10,11,12
10-35 pm	12/Brig inform us of reliefs of their units.	13,14.
11-7 pm.	A warning order for the march of 31st (H) Battery tomorrow, received from 3/Corps and passed to Arty. 3/Corps were informed the Battery would be ready to move at 8 am.	15.

W A R   D I A R Y
29th Apr 1915

NIEPPE.

Fine night, sunny day.

3rd Corps order route for the march of the 31st Heavies, in support of action of "Up North". Acknowledged and passed to 1. Div Arty.

7-15 am.   Quiet night report from 6th Div, also from our 10th Brig.   2
9-0 .m   --The Brig was successful in bringing down a German aero-   3
plane just before sunset.

9-0 am.   12/Brig inform us last Battn reached their billets at 4 am.   4.

2-0 pm.   Warning orders received for E.Lancs to rejoin 11/Brigade,   5
           starting at 6 pm. and to reach a point west of Vlamertinghe   6
4-25 pm.   on the Poperinghe road at 7-30 pm. --Motor busses were de-
           tailed for the conveyance of this Regiment.

    The regimental transport to march by Locre - Zevecoten - Reninghelst, Cross Roads in G/17/c - H/7, and to arrive at regimental billet not later than 10-30 pm.

    Warning orders and several messages received for the move   7
    of 12th Brig, 9th and W.Lancs Fd Co's R.E. to take place   8
    at 8 pm., but afterwards amended to read 8 am tomorrow.   9
       The 12/Brig to arrive at Ouderdom huts at 10-30 am and   10
    the Fd Co's R.E. to arrive at Dickebusch at 10-15 am.   11
                                      (12,13,14,15,16,17, 18)

10-58 pm. 3rd Corps report Zeppelin seen in Area Ypres - Poperinghe.   19
           It was afterwards seen at Bailleul.   20

    Acknowledgment sent to 3/Corps for receipt of
       Secret G/1010.
          (Counter measures against asphyxiating gases)

WAR DIARY
30th April 1915.

Fine night, warm day

8-9 am	3/Corps order One G.S. and One Administrative Offr 4th Div to visit Hdqrs 5/Corps at level crossing 1 mile West of Ypres, to get in touch with situation. Lt-Col Butler (GSO 2) and Capt Smyth-Osbourne (DAA&QMG) proceeded.	1.
10-45 am	3/Corps notify us 12/Brig is at disposal Canadian Div this evening.--Brigade to be disposed in huts along Vlamertinghe Ouderdom road. Head of column to reach Ouderdom 10-30 am.	2
11-0 am.	10/Brig inform us they have had a quiet night. The enemy shelled St Jean and set village on fire in several places -_Owing to Hdqrs being shelled, transport moved ½ mile further back. All well with 10/Brig and things working smoothly with transportation of supplies, etc.	3
3-40 pm. *when*	3/Corps notify us that 12/Brig *come* under Canadian Div. at 6-30 pm, the Head of Brigade to be at Pottenhoek. To be ready to move on Brielen.	4
3-45 pm.	9th and W.Lancs Fd Co's R.E. to be attached 27th Div.	5.

SECRET

38

Work on the main gallery of the mine on LE TOUQUET Road (No 1 in Mine Register) has been stopped since yesterday as it seems certain that the enemy is driving a mine across our front and further advance in our gallery will lead to detection. Our exact distance from the enemy's gallery cannot be guaged but it is a significant fact that the air in our gallery has got much purer.

In accordance with your instructions I am placing a charge and tamping it and will report probable time of completion this evening. It is hoped that the firing of this charge will not damage our branch gallery. Further details attached.

H B Jones Lt Col RE
CRE 4th Divn.

8/4/15

SECRET

LE TOUQUET Mine – 8-4-15

From shaft to head of main gallery.	190 ft
From head of main gallery to left branch gallery	64'
From head of main gallery to nearest point of German barricade	36'
From head of main gallery to centre of barricade (approx)	50'
Depth of bottom of gallery below ground level.	17'
Line of least resistance (measured fr centre of charge)	16'
Proposed charge, gunpowder	1200 lbs
Calculated diameter of crater	41'
do Horizontal radius of rupture	35'

I do not consider it advisable to increase the charge

H.B. Jones Lt Col R.E.
CRE 4th Divn

NIEPPE
8/4/15

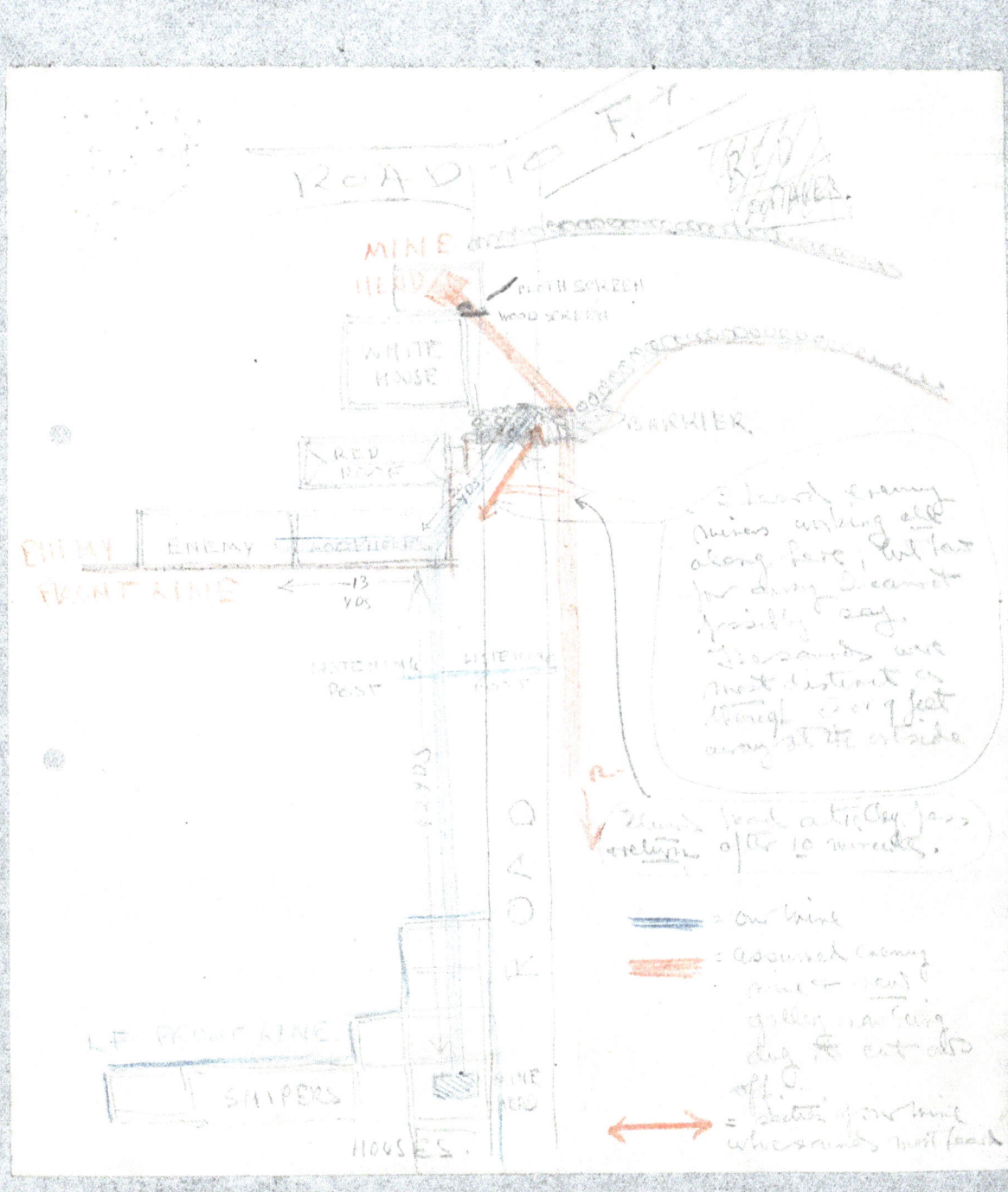

Sketch labels:
- KHAKI GROUND SHEET STRETCHED IN FRONT OF SHOP DOORWAY.
- NEW BOARD SCREEN WHERE TO HIDE HOLE ROPE HOIST WAS ORIGINALLY SEEN.
- NEW DOUBLE LINE OF SANDBAGS ON TOP OF WOOD SCREEN
- WHITE HOUSE
- SCREEN
- ENEMY BARRIER
- ROAD.

Enemy appears to have put up a board screen over the shell hole where 10 days or so ago we observed the rope hoist working also a cloth screen low down in the road outside the shop (?) the latter I cannot account for. Have reported above to Edwards.

Maurice James 2/8

2.45 P.M
P. 4.15.

To The Adjutant
2 Lancs Fus
8/4/15

I forward enclosed report
& sketch made by Mr
Jamon at my request.
It appears important as
if correct shows that
enemy have done much
more than simply
countermine. May I also
note observation of Capt
Edwards that trolley
which passed in direction
of Packman's Farm
did not return for

ten minutes.

I forward report
for what it is worth

O.C. Arch F.C.
C.C.C

I presume that one would
not use trolleys in a
small countermine

SECRET.

Subject:- Report on Operations 9-4-1915 - Explosion of mine.

12th Infantry Brigade No. G. 64.

Head Quarters,
    4th Division.

    I forward herewith my report on the explosion of the mine carried out by this Brigade in LE TOUQUET this morning and operations relating thereto.

9-4-1915.

Brigadier General,
Commanding 12th Infantry Brigade.

OPERATIONS AT LE TOUQUET 9TH APRIL 1915.
EXPLOSION OF A MINE.

1. Owing to the fact that the enemy were on the point of discovering the mine by means of a counter mine, it became necessary to fire it prematurely, and at a time when the explosion could not be the prelude to an infantry attack.

   In these circumstances all that could be hoped for was

   (1) Kill a number of Germans.

   (2) Weaken the enemy's defences, and ascertain his dispositions with a view to facilitating an attack on LE TOUQUET in the future.

   (3) Learn by experience the effect of a heavy explosion on the defending troops and the precautions necessary for the safety of the attackers.

2. THE PLAN.

   The mine was fired at 8-30.a.m., the earliest moment possible after the discovery of the approach of the German Counter Mine.

   Previous to the explosion the enemy's trenches and defended houses in the neighbourhood of LE TOUQUET were subjected to a bombardment by Artillery and trench mortars, and to bursts of fire. The bombardment lasted for twenty minutes; there was then a pause of ten minutes.

   During the night some gaps were purposely made in our barbed wire entanglements.

   In the early morning two companies of Infantry were extended and advanced towards the subsidiary line of trenches to the West of LE TOUQUET. By this means it was hoped that the enemy would anticipate attack and man his defences in strength during the pause before the mine was exploded.

Immediately after the explosion the Artillery were ordered to turn their fire onto the approaches leading towards LE TOUQUET with a view to attacking the enemy's reinforcements should he attempt to bring any up. The Infantry were ordered to cheer and open a rapid fire on the trenches and houses in front of them.

The programme was carried out as ordered.

3. THE EFFECTS OF THE EXPLOSION.

The effect in material was considerable. The "White House" was practically demolished, and other defended houses were badly damaged. The full value of the damage done cannot at present be estimated, but it is hoped that further advance has been facilitated.

The enemy's casualties are unknown. It is thought that the whole of the garrison within a radius of 20 yards of the centre of the explosion must have perished besides any men working in the enemy's mine. A few wounded men were observed crawling away, and between 1.p.m. and 5.p.m. twentyseven men on stretchers were carried away.

The enemy's wire entanglements in the immediate neighbourhood of the explosion was destroyed. No large crater appears to have been made, but a large mass of debris was formed which would have been a more or less difficult obstacle to a rapid advance.

The force of the explosion threw a large number of bricks and stones into the air. It appears necessary for all troops within a distance of 250 yards at least, to be provided with overhead protection.

4. The ENEMY'S DISPOSITIONS.

There is nothing to indicate the strength of the enemy holding LE TOUQUET and the trenches near the village. In the morning the smoke of the usual number of fires were observed.

The

The enemy's Infantry holding the hostile front line only fired a comparatively few rounds. Usually in our trenches in this portion of the line it is unsafe to show above the top of the parapet; directly after the explosion the troops opened a heavy rifle fire from over the top of the parapet and suffered practically no casualties. It seems possible that the surprise of the explosion to the enemy may have given our men the advantage of a start in the opening of fire, and that once that fire was started, he found it impossible to fire back.

A hostile machine gun and a considerable rifle fire opened from FRELINGHIEN. The Machine Gun was located. If in the future a further advance is attempted, it would seem necessary to arrange a heavy rifle fire, as well artillery fire against the village.

The enemy's artillery fired a few rounds but did little damage. Accurate shrapnel fire was opened after the explosion, on the houses in our possession in LE TOUQUET, but not until after a delay of sufficient length to have enabled our troops to have crossed the ground between the opposing defences without loss. The majority of rounds appeared to have been fired against the houses at some distance from the front line apparently with a view to preventing the arrival of reinforcements.

In the evening the enemy opened a heavy bombardment on LE TOUQUET Ry. Station and Battalion Head Quarters with 5.9" Howitzers. They did comparatively little damage.

EXPLOSION OF MINE AT LE TOUQUET.   GGG/180

This mine of which you have been given details in the mining report, had on the 8th instant reached a distance of 190 feet with the main shaft, as reported in my GGG/180 of the 8th instant.

From the noise of trollies moving and other signs it was evident that either a German mine was being run close to the head of our mine shaft, or else that the Germans had discovered our mine, and were preparing a counter mine. In either case no time was to be lost, and orders were issued that all work should cease in our mine, and that 1200 lbs of gun powder should be placed in it and well tamped, so that, if possible the side gallery should be saved.

It was calculated that the head of our mine was within about 40 to 45 feet away from the enemy's barricade, which was it's main objective, and it was calculated that if the explosion was successful the crater would reach just short of the barricade, but that it would bring down the nearest German House and loopholed wall, facing our Sniper's Houses.

With the object of blowing up as many Germans as possible it was decided to make a demonstration with infantry and artillery so as to cause the Germans to man their defences, and orders with this object were issued by G.O.C., 12th Brigade.

The time of the explosion was settled between Major Symons R.E. in charge of the mine, and the Brigadier Commanding 12th Brigade, and depended entirely on how long the tamping, etc., took.

Major Symons' report giving these times was sent to you this morning.

It was finally decided to blow up the mine at 8.30 a.m. and at 8 oclock demonstrations began.

A member of the Divisional Staff went down to witness
                                                              the resul

2.

the results of the explosion, from the forward trench about 200 yards from the end of the mine, just in front of Barkham Farm.

He reports as follows:-

"Bombardment commenced at 8 am., the 5 inch howitzers firing at Pond House, and the 18 prs at the trench north of Le Touquet. The trench mortar situated in the corner of the Sniper's Houses bombed the breastwork in front of the Estaminet House with considerable success. The infantry opened fire all along the line, in the neighborhood of Le Touquet.

The enemy's rifle fire was completely subdued by ours, but one or more Machine Guns opened fire from the Houses in Frelinghien, south of the Lys.

At 8.30 am., precisely an enormous explosion took place, a cloud of smoke shot upwards, and with it, timber, bricks and earth, and it is hoped some Germans. Some of the bricks were thrown as far back as our own barricade and Barkham Farm, that is to say, about 250 yards from the mine.

Most of the men were under cover, but the anxiety to see the explosion caused some of them to expose themselves, and a few of them were hit by falling bri bricks."

It is impossible to say how many Germans were hit blown up, or injured, by the explosion, but the result was apparently satisfactory.

The main object of exploding the mine was to blow up the enemy's mine and there is every probability that this object was achieved.

The force of the explosion apparently just reached the barricade, but did not seriously damage it. On the other hand, it blew down a large part of the
                                    loopholed

loopholed wall, facing the Sniper's Houses, which had been much strengthened by the Germans, and must have been held by them at the time of the explosion.

After the smoke had drifted away a huge mass of rubble and a large crater could be seen.

Only one German body was seen and this was that of a wounded man, which was pulled in by his comrades out of the crater. Two or three other Germans who were apparently attempting to dig something up in the crater, were fired at and disappeared.

So far as can be ascertained, the calculation as to the position of the head of our mine was correct, as the edge of the crater reached just about where it ~~exploded~~ was expected to.

It will probably not be safe for anyone to enter the mine for 36 hours, and so it has been impossible to ascertain so far whether our side gallery has been damaged. This will, however, be done as soon as possible.

There was little retaliation by the Germans in the shape of gun fire, but they fired at certain points of our communication trench, leading up to Le Touquet, with Little Willies and Rifle Grenades, thus indicating what they considered to be our vulnerable points. These places can be easily rendered bomb proof, and this information will be of great value to us.

It is hoped shortly to forward to you the names of certain officers and men who have carried out to a successful finish a very difficult task. Not only was mining carried through very difficult soil and much hampered by water, but during the last 48 hours they have been carrying out a very dangerous task, in close proximity to the enemy, and liable to be blown up at any moment, as there is no doubt that the Germans were working extremely hard in order to anticipate us.

Since writing the above, a report has been received which

which shews that 17 German wounded have been seen crossing Frelinhien bridge, from Le Touquet.

9/4/15.

[signature]

Major-General,
Commanding 4th Division.

4th Division.

At 8-30 am I exploded the mine in LE TOUQUET. Charge 1200 lbs was taken from barrels and put in sandbags. These were then taken by trolly up to the junction and then by hand up to the chamber prepared before. The filling of sandbags from barrels took 2 hours, loading 2 hours and tamping 12 hours. I tamped 70 feet with air spaces. I did not see the result but bricks were thrown as far back as our Barricades. A few of our men have been hit with these bricks. The mine appears to have brought down most of the wall facing Snipers' Houses. Owing to gas I do not think it will be safe to investigate our galleries for 36 hours, but judging from reports I am afraid they must be damaged. Captain Edwards and two men were "gassed" during the tamping but have recovered. I think considerable damage must have been done to whatever was behind the front German walls although the barricade itself did not appear to be much damaged. It is quite sure that with large charges under brickwork one must be under cover or a considerable distance back.

9/4/15.

Sd. C.B.O.Symons, Major,
Commdg. 7th Fd. Co. R.E.

3rd Corps.

Forwarded.

Sgd A.A.Montgomery

Colonel,
for Maj-Gen. Commdg. 4th Div.

4th Division.

Following report received from Major Symons :-
"I had a good look at the crater, etc., made by the
mine yesterday. It seems to have blown up some gallery
across the road and considerably shaken the barricade.
This tends to prove that we have blown in the listening
gallery of the Germans which we thought they were making
diagonally across our front. The centre of the crater
is just where I expected, about 9 ft from the edge of
the road and quite close to the house with the porch
whence their barricade seems to start. At the other
end the wall and house has been shaken down up to within
about 25 ft of the corner nearest the salient trench.
A huge mass of debris of course is left which might
be a considerable obstacle to an attacking force.
About one hundred feet of wire entanglement was destroyed
across the front. The mine is too full of water to
enter; it is above the knees at present, so I will have
it pumped out and report tomorrow."

10th April, 1915. Sgd. H.B. Jones. Lt.Col.R.E.
C.R.E. 4th Division.

4/Div. No. 1

3rd Corps.

60.

In continuation of my message No. 59 of this morning, I have the honour to report that a mine was exploded at Le Touquet at 7-15 am this morning.

Information was received from a listener in the mine gallery yesterday evening that the Germans could be heard working at about 6 yards distance from the head of the gallery and it appeared likely that they were running another counter-mine against us. As we were now already practically inside their front line it was decided that it was best to blow up our mine at once and orders to this effect were issued yesterday evening. A charge of 500 lbs was put in the end of the gallery and well tamped. No artillery or other demonstration was made as it was feared that this might give the enemy warning of an approaching explosion. On the 8th April when the first mine at Le Touquet was exploded, a demonstration was made to draw them into the front line. A different course of action was therefore, adopted on this occasion. The mine exploded at 7-15 am and debris were thrown for a distance of 200 or 300 yards back, but without damage to our men. The damage to the enemy has not yet been definitely ascertained, but a good deal of their defences must have been blown away, judging by the violence of the explosion.

The accompanying sketch shows the position (a) of the crater of the mine exploded on the 8th April, (b) of the crater of the mine exploded this morning, and (c) of the head of our mine shaft.

No-one has been able to go down the mine shaft yet, but it is still hoped that further mining operations in this direction will be possible and also that the moral effect of the successful explosion of these 2 mines has been considerable.

A.H. Montgomery
Col for
Maj-Gen
Commdg. 7th Div.

22/4/15

12th Inf. Brig. (RIGHT SECTOR).

Date - nights of :-	CONVENT SECTION.	WARNAVE SECTION.	LE TOUQUET SECTION	LYS SECTION	In Billets.			
31/1	2 Coys R.Ir.R.	Essex.R.	Lan.Fus.	2 Coys 5/S.Lan.R.	K.O.	Mons.	2 Cos R.Ir.	2 Cos 5/S.L.
1/2	"	2/Mon.R.	"	"	"	Ex.R.	"	"
2/3	"	"	"	"	"	"	"	"
3/4	"	"	Kings.O.	"	L.F.	"	"	"
4/5	"	"	"	"	"	"	"	"
5/6	"	Essex.R	"	"	"	Mons.	"	"
6/7	"	"	"	"	"	"	"	"
7/8	"	"	Lan.Fus.	"	K.O.	"	"	"
8/9	"	"	"	"	"	"	"	"
9/10	"	Mon.R.	"	"	"	Ex.R.	"	"
10/11	"	"	"	"	"	"	"	"
11/12	"	"	Kings.O.	"	L.F.	"	"	"
12/13	"	"	"	"	"	"	"	"
13/14	"	Ex.R.	"	"	"	Mons.	"	"
14/15	"	"	"	"	"	"	"	"
15/16	"	"	Lan.Fus.	"	K.O.	"	"	"
16/17	"	"	"	"	"	"	"	"
17/18	"	Mon.R.	"	"	"	Ex.R.	"	"
18/19	"	"	"	"	"	"	"	"
19/20	"	"	Kings.O.	"	L.F.	"	"	"
20/21	"	"	"	"	"	"	"	"
21/22	"	Ex.R.	"	"	"	Mons.	"	"
22/23	"	"	"	"	"	"	"	"
23/24	"	"	Lan.Fus.	"	K.O.	"	"	"
24/25	"	"	"	"	"	"	"	"
25/26	"	Mon.R.	"	"	"	Ex.R.	"	"
26/27	"	"	"	"	"	"	"	"
27/28	"	"	Kings.O.	"	L.F.	"	"	"
28/29	"	"	"	"	"	"	"	"
29/30	"	Ex.R.	"	"	"	Mons.	"	"
30/1	"	"	"	"	"	"	"	"

TABLE "A".

UNIT.	PRESENT BILLETS	DESTINATION.	TIME OF ARRIVAL.	TIME OF DEPARTURE.	ROUTE	REMARKS.
Warwicks.	La Creche	Bailleul.	Midday.		A4c - S27a.	
Seaforths.	Pt. 63.	"	12.30 p.m.		Romarin-Rabot.	To be clear of Rd. Junc.T28b North by 10.15 and not to pass Rd Junc.in B8b before 11 a.m.
R.Dub.Fus.	Steenbecque Trenches.	"		After relief.	Neuve Eglise Cross Rds.B1.	
R.Irish Fus	Douvé Trenches	"		"	Ploegsteert-Romarin-Rabot.	Head not to pass Rd.Junc.T28b North before 10.20 a.m.
1/Warwick-shire Btn.	Bailleul.	Pt.63 Billets for Douve Trenches	11 a.m.		Crossroads B1-T25d-T28c-T28b.N Petit Pont.	Move out of 63 Billets in relief at 6.45 p.m.
2/Warwick-shire Btn.	"	Pt.63 Billets for Steenbec-que Trenches.	11.15 a.m.		"	Move out of 63 Billets in relief at 7.15 p.m.
3/Warwick-shire Bn.	"	Pt.63 Billets	7.30 p.m.		"	
4/Warwick-shire Bn.	"	Romarin.	3 p.m.		Crossroads B1-T25d-T28c.	

G.S.O.11.

SECRET.   Copy No. 5

OPERATION ORDER NO.24
by
Maj.Gen. H.F.M. Wilson, C.B. Commdg. 4th Div.

14/4/15.

1. In continuation of Operation Order No. 23 of 11/4/15, the following alteration as regards command will take place as shown below.

(a) G.O.C. South Midland Division will take over command of the section of 3rd Corps line from River WARNAVE (junction with 12th Infantry Brigade) to WULVERGHEM-MESSINES road (junction with North Midland Division) from midnight 17/18th instant.

(b) The following artillery, now under 4th Division, will come under the orders of G.O.C. South Midland Division from above hour :-

    29th F.A.Brig. (less 126th Battery).
    32nd F.A.Brig.
    1/South Midland Brig. R.F.A.
    South Midland Howitzer Brig. R.F.A.

(c) The following R.E. of 4th Division will also come under the orders of G.O.C. South Midland Division from above hour :-

    9th Field Company, R.E.
    West Lancs Field Company, R.E. (T).

2. Table 'B' referred to in Operation Order No. 23, has been issued to all concerned.

Issued at 11.45 a.m.

                                      Colonel,
                            General Staff, 4th Division.

Secret.

Copy No. 1

OPERATION ORDER No. 25
by
Maj-Gen. H.F.M.Wilson, C.B. Commdg. 4th Div.

NIEPPE.
28/4/15.

1. The 12th Brigade will be withdrawn from their present line on the night of 28/29th, handing over from the LYS to the RAILWAY BARRICADE (inclusive) to the 6th Division, and from the RAILWAY BARRICADE (exclusive) to the WARNAVE to the South Midland Division.

2. The W.Lancs. Fd.Co. R.E. will return under command of 4th Division.
   The 7th Fd.Co. R.E. will be concentrated with South Midland Division.
   The 9th Fd.Co. R.E. will be concentrated with the 4th Division.

3. The 12th Brigade, 9th Fd.Co. R.E. and W.Lancs. Fd.Co. R.E. and 11th Fd.Ambce. will march during the night of 28/29th April, via NIEPPE and BAILLEUL, to the area :- BAILLEUL - METEREN - FLETRES - MERRIS and be billeted according to a table to be issued later.
   The above troops will be prepared to move on the morning of the 30th instant to rejoin the 10th and 11th Brigades.

4. The 4th Div. Arty. will remain in its present position pending further orders.

5. ~~The above troops will be prepared to move~~
   The remainder of 4th Divisional troops not included in paras 3 and 4 will be prepared to move at short notice.

6. Billeting parties from the units mentioned in para 3 will assemble at the bridge at PONT-DE-NIEPPE at 9 am, where motor lorries will meet them and convey them to the Square at BAILLEUL where they will be met by the D.A.Q.M.G. 4th Division.

Colonel,
Gen. Staff, 4th Div.

Issued at 12-30 am

DISTRIBUTION OF INFANTRY.

4th DIVISION.

DISTRIBUTION OF INFANTRY.

Month of APRIL.

10th Inf. Brig. (LEFT SECTOR).

Date – Nights of :–	DOUVE trenches	STEENBEQUE trenches	Point 63 Brig.Res.	LA CRECHE Div.Res.
31/1	2/Sea.Hghrs.	1/R.War.R.	2/R.Dub.Fus.	1/R.Ir.Fus.
1/2	"	"	"	Sea.Highrs.
2/3	R.Ir.Fus.	R.Dub.Fus.	R.War.R.	"
3/4	"	"	"	"
4/5	"	"	"	"
5/6	"	"	"	"
6/7	Sea.Highrs.	R.War.R.	R.Ir.Fus.	R.Dub.Fus.
7/8	"	"	"	"
8/9	"	"	"	"
9/10	"	"	"	"
10/11	R.Ir.Fus.	R.Dub.Fus.	Sea.Highrs.	R.War.R.
11/12	"	"	"	"
12/13	"	"	"	"
13/14	"	"	"	"
14/15	Sea.Highrs.	R.War.R.	R.Dub.Fus.	R.Ir.Fus.
15/16	"	"	"	"
16/17	"	"	"	"
17/18	"	"	"	Sea.Highrs.
18/19	R.Ir.Fus.	R.Dub.Fus.	R.War.R.	"
19/20	"	"	"	"
20/21	"	"	"	"
21/22	"	"	"	"
22/23	Sea.Highrs.	R.War.R.	R.Ir.Fus.	R.Dub.Fus.
23/24	"	"	"	"
24/25	"	"	"	"
25/26	"	"	"	"
26/27	R.Ir.Fus.	R.Dub.Fus.	Sea.Highrs.	R.War.R.
27/28	"	"	"	"
28/29	"	"	"	"
30/1	"	"	"	"

Starting Point for reliefs – COURTE DREVE.

2 Coys of 7/Argyle & Sutherland Highlanders in trenches on right of DOUVE section.
H.Q. and 2 Coys in reserve at PIGGERIES.

7/A. & S. Highrs. relieve the night previous to other reliefs.

11th Inf. Brig. (CENTRE SECTOR)

Dates - Nights of :-	ST YVES	PLOEGSTEERT WOOD.	LE GHEER	In Support	In Reserve.
31/1	Rif.Brig.	Lon.Rif.Brig.	Hamps.R.	E.Lan.R.& 1 Co. L.R.B.	Som.L.I.
1/2	"	"	"	"	"
2/3	"	"	"	"	"
3/4	"	"	"	"	"
4/5	"	"	E.Lan.R.	Rif.Brig.& 1 Co. L.R.B.	Hamps.R.
5/6	Som.L.I.	"	"	"	"
6/7	"	"	"	"	"
7/8	"	"	"	"	"
8/9	"	"	"	"	"
9/10	"	"	"	"	"
10/11	"	"	"	"	"
11/12	Rif.Brig.	"	Hamps.R.	Som.L.I.& 1 Co. L.R.B.	E.Lan.R.
12/13	"	"	"	"	"
13/14	"	"	"	"	"
14/15	"	"	"	"	"
15/16	"	"	"	"	"
16/17	"	"	"	"	"
17/18	Som.L.I.	"	E.Lan.R.	Hamps.R.& 1 Co. L.R.B.	Rif.Brig.
18/19	"	"	"	"	"
19/20	"	"	"	"	"
20/21	"	"	"	"	"
21/22	"	"	"	"	"
22/23	"	"	"	"	"
23/24	Rif.Brig.	"	Hamps.R.	E.Lan.R.& 1 Co. L.R.B.	Som.L.I.
24/25	"	"	"	"	"
25/26	"	"	"	"	"
26/27	"	"	"	"	"
27/28	"	"	"	"	"
28/29	"	"	"	"	"
29/30	Som.L.I.	"	E.Lan.R.	Rif.Brig.& 1 Co. L.R.B.	Hamps.R.
30/1	"	"	"	"	"

Copy No. 22

OPERATION ORDER No 23
by
Maj.Gen. H.F.M. Wilson, C.B., Commdg. 4th Div.

NIEPPE.
11/4/15.

1.   The 10th Infantry Brigade, less 7th Argyll & Suthd. Highrs, will be relieved by the Warwickshire Brigade from Bailloul on the night 12/13th April.
   The 10th Inf. Brig., less 7th Argyll & Suthd Highrs., will take over the billets of the Warwickshire Brigade in Bailloul.
   The moves of these two Brigades will take place as shown in Table "A".
   The 7th Argyll & Suthd Highrs. will continue to hold their present trenches, and will come under orders of the Officer Commanding Warwickshire Brigade from midnight 12/13th.

2.   The 1st South Midland Brigade, from the area Steenwerck,-(excl)- Noote Boom, will relieve the 11th Brigade, less London Rifle Brigade on the night 15/16th April.
   Preliminary arrangements for this relief will be carried out on the night of the 14/15th.
   The 11th Inf. Brig., less Lon. Rif Brig. on relief by 1st South Midland Brig. will move to the area Steenwerck (excl)- Noote Boom.
   Movements for this relief will take place as shown in Table "B". (To be issued later.)

3.   On the 17th April the Gloucester and Worcester Brigade will move from Merris Area to billets, to be notified later, in the Rabot - Nieppe - Ploegsteert - Petit Pont Area.
   On the night 17/18th, the line held by the South Midland Division will be readjusted in such a manner as to admit of the 7th Battn. Argyll & Suthd. Highrs and the Lon Rif Brig being relieved by Units of the South Midland Division.
   The 7th Argyll & Suthd Highrs and Lon Rif Brigade will rejoin 10th and 11th Brigades, respectively, as shewn in Table "B" (To be issued later.)

4.   La Croche will be reserved for the South Midland Divisional Train.

5.   Until further orders are issued the South Midland Howitzers and F.A. Brigades, now with 4th Division, will remain with the 4th Division. The artillery of 4th Div. will remain in its present position.

6.   The 7th Fd Coy R.E. will remain in 4th Division, for the present, and will not be transferred on the 18th, as arranged.

7.   Orders will be issued later as regards the movements of the 10th Fd Ambce.

Issued at 9.30 am.

Colonel,
Gen. Staff, 4th Division.

DIVISIONAL OPERATIONS ORDERS NOS. 23, 24 & 25.

4/Div. GGG.28 23/4/15

3rd Corps.

WORK REPORT.

12th Brigade Sector.

(a)   Machine gun emplacements have been made as follows :-

    2 between LYS FM and CARTER'S FM.
    2 close to CARTER'S FM.
    2 in fire trench in front of BARKENHAM FM.
    2 in front of SNIPER'S HOUSES; one of these was
        knocked out by shell fire yesterday and
        repairs should be completed to-night.
    3 in fire trenches North of SNIPER'S HOUSES (known
        locally as Coppice, Salient and Dreadnought
        trenches).

Emplacements for 2 guns have been begun close to LONDON FM and almost completed.

Shell trenches have been dug between ESSEX CENTRAL FM and the ESSEX CROSS ROADS.

A new supporting work to hold one platoon has been begun on the South bank of the R. WARNAVE. This work has been joined up by a short communication trench with the communication trench that runs from OBSERVATION FM to ESSEX CROSS ROADS.

A communication trench has been dug along the HOUPLINES - LE TOUQUET railway line to connect with the trench that runs up from the LE TOUQUET Station to the SNIPER'S HOUSES. It joins this trench just East of the Station buildings.

Screens have been put up behind LE TOUQUET Station to prevent the road being observed from the direction of DEULEMONT.

A communication trench has been dug from the support trench South of LUKER'S HOUSES to BARKENHAM FM.

(b)   It is proposed to continue the work on communications and support trenches at LE TOUQUET.

(c)   Both at LE TOUQUET and at the Railway Barricade the increased hostile shelling reported last week has suffered some diminution, but it is still more pronounced that it had been before the blowing up of our mine on the 9th instant.
The SNIPER'S HOUSES, the Railway Barricade and LE BIZET have all been shelled in turn, but except for the burning of Fme de la MOTTE in LE BIZET no material damage has been done.

Sniping has been less than usual.

(d)   No change in the enemy's dispositions has been noticed.

23/4/15.

Maj-Gen.
Commdg. 4th Divn.

4th Division.

Progress Report - Supporting Line.

15/4/15.

R.Lys to Le Gheer Road.

Completed except for a small length of communication trench and the supporting point at Motor Car Corner.

Le Gheer Road to Le Rossignol.

Practically completed. 2 supporting points behind Touquet Berthe not quite finished and a small amount of communication trench near Hoysted House to be done.

Le Rossignol to Wulverghem Road.

Trenches in the 4 grass fields West of Le Rossignol, one third completed and drained.

Work in hand on Plus Douce Farm defences. Decimal of progress .2. Work on North side of river Douve not yet started.

The line was inspected yesterday by C.E. 2nd Army who expressed himself as very pleased with the work done.

4. LEFT SECTOR. (10th. Inf. Brig.).

With the relief of the 10th Brig. impending nothing new was undertaken.
(c) The enemy has been very active during the past week in shelling our trenches in trans-DOUVIA. Working parties were frequently obliged to stop work. Retaliati by our guns put a stop to the nuisance.
(d) No information of interest was obtained about the enemy. Uniforms seen show that the troops in front of us have not been relieved.

16th April, 1915.
Major General,
Commanding 4th. Division.

2. **RIGHT SECTOR.** (12th Inf. Brig.).

(a) The communication trench from LA FLENQUE Farm to LE TOUQUET Station has now reached the H.Q. of the Sector and and not more than 200 yards remains to be done. It is not yet boarded.

The work of retrenchment in rear of the SNIPER'S HOUSES continues. A fire trench has been made running south from the North Block. Its primary object is to give shelter to the reserve platoon stationed there in case the Houses are shelled.

Carter's Farm has been much strengthened and converted into a strong supporting point with a good field of fire towards FRELINGHIEN.

On the left of this Sector a communication trench from OBSERVATION Farm to the left of the ESSEX line has been dug through and boarded. Near the forward end it forks, one branch going to the Estaminet DU BON COIN at the Essex cross roads and the other towards the R. WARNAVE. Great praise is due to the Monmouth and Essex Regts. for the exceptional skill and rapidity with which they make communication trenches. Both these regiments are remarkably good at digging and vie with each other in the amount of work they do during their periods of 4 days in the trenches.

Short lengths of trench connecting several isolated trenches on the left of the Essex line and also joining up with the R.Irish across the R. WARNAVE are now completed.

(b) It is proposed to continue work in hand, i.e. LA FLENQUE Farm - LE TOUQUET communication trench and retrenching LE TOUQUET.

(c) There has been a great increase of shelling about LE TOUQUET, due, no doubt, to the successful explosion of mine there and to the fact that our Artillery has been shelling the BREWERY across the River very severely. A good many H.E. Shell were dropped into the station, North Block (setting 2 houses on fire) and the SNIPER'S HOUSES. The damage has been inconsiderable.

(d) It is not believed that any change has taken place in our front, Saxon uniforms are daily seen by our observation officers.

3. **CENTRE SECTOR.** (11th Inf. Brig.)

(a) At LE GHEER a high command has been completed which enables one to pass from RUTTER LODGE along the front to the PICKET HOUSE. Work has continued on the covered way from the KEEPER'S COTTAGE to the front edge of the wood.

The communication trench from the Hampshire T. trench to the wood via PALK VILLA has been reopened and boarding is almost completed.

Between PALK VILLA and GERMAN HOUSE the 2 advanced breastworks have been connected by a fire trench to accommodate 1 platoon.

At ST.YVES the retrenchment covering the salient is now completed. It runs from N.W. corner of ST.YVES round close in front of the East edge of the village and down the slope in a southerly direction towards the THREE HUNS Farm.

(c) Shelling has been as usual and sniping rather more active than recently due to the "lively lot" taking their turn in the trenches opposite this part of our line.

(d) Except for normal reliefs there is no reason to suppose any change in the units to our front has taken place.

4/Div. GGG.28   16/4/15

3rd Corps.

WEEKLY REPORT.

1. RESUME.

During the past week work in the Division has been affected by the relief of the 10th and 12th Brigades.
In the sectors held by these 2 brigades practically nothing fresh was undertaken, though several works in hand were completed.
In the 12th Brigade sector the work of improving communications and strengthening retrenchments was continued.

Now that the 4th Division is for the first time relinquishing a large part of the line it has held since last October, it may be of interest to recapitulate the progress - described week by week in these reports - that has been made since the incessant wet weather at the end of last year reduced our trenches to such a state that it became almost doubtful whether the infantry could continue to hold them.
During the winter the front line could not be reached by day except in 2 small sections, one South of Le Gheer and the other in the middle of Ploegsteert Wood. The fire trenches themselves consisted largely of short lengths cut off from those on either flank. Wire entanglements were in many places dangerously scanty: at very few points could the parapet be described as bullet-proof: dugouts and barricades had mostly fallen in: a second line close in rear can hardly be said to have existed.
As a contrast to this state of affairs, it is possible now to walk along the front line trenches from Le Touquet to the R.Douve, except for two short gaps at the Dreadnought Trench (Le Touquet Section) and just North of the Birdcage.
The following communication trenches are to-day available.

(a)	La Flenque Fm - Le Touquet	800 yards
(b)	Le Touquet Station - Carters Fm.	300 "
(c)	" " - Snipers' Houses	800 "
(d)	" " - Railway Barricade	1200 "
(e)	Despierre Fm - Essex Central Fm.	800 "
(f)	" " - Essex Cross Roads.	600 "
(g)	Le Gheer - Hampshire Trench	200 "
(h)	Ploegsteert Wood - Hants Trench	300 "
(i)	St Yves - Sunken Road Trench.	120 "
(j)	Point 63 - Seaforth Fm (trench)	600 "
(k)	" (alternative trench beyond Forward Estaminet)	300 "

The whole front has practically a complete double row of wire and in some places there is a zone of entanglements from 40 to 50 yards broad.
There is a second line and here and there a third and fourth, at close supporting distance behind the front line, and finally the dugout accommodation is now almost sufficient for all men off duty by night and in many places for the much larger number off duty by day.

2. Right Sector.

(b) It is proposed to continue the work in hand.

(c) The enemy shelled and destroyed an observation station in LA COUR Chateau. Our working parties were also fired on several times but with small result.

(d) All observation tends to show that there have been no changes in front of us.

9th April, 1915.

Major General,
Commanding 4th Division.

4th DIVISION.

PROGRESS REPORT - SUPPORTING LINE.

General.

River LYS to LE GHEER Road. Front line trench completed, floored and wired.

(a) LYS to LE TOUQUET Road. Three communication trenches dug, two boarded. 8 machine gun emplacements made. Railway barricaded.

(b) LE TOUQUET to WARNETON Road. Two communication trenches completed, one half finished. 8 machine gun emplacements completed. WARNETON Road barricade completed.

(c) WARNETON Road to LE GHEER Road. Two communication trenches dug, one partly so. Machine gun emplacements in farms in hand. Skeleton barricade for one road in hand.

Points d'appui in above sections completed as regards trenches and wiring.

(d) LE GHEER Road to ROSSIGNOL.

Front line of defence completed throughout except a proportion of the head cover, half the breastworks have parados constructed. Machine Gun emplacement and wood paths still in hand.

(e) ROSSIGNOL to WULVERGHEM Road.

Trenches West of ROSSIGNOL marked out and being started tonight, work on LA PLUS DOUCE Farm and Farm South of it in hand.

CENTRE SECTOR. (11th Inf. Brig.)

(a) ST YVES Section. Work on front line breastworks at N.E. corner progressing. Firing steps improved. Fire trench made from N.E. of ST YVES round by east end of village to the Three Huns Farm. This makes a retrenchment to the salient and gives cover from shell fire for garrison of ST YVES.

Junction of Sunken Road and Somerset Left trenches completed.

PLOEGSTEERT Wood. Accommodation in Left Trench improved. Breastwork at ROPE Corner given accommodation and occupied in place of detached posts between Left Trench and Wood. Extra wiring put out. Room made for 12 additional men in Left Trench.

LE GHEER Section. Communication within LE GHEER completed. Covered way into LE GHEER and along edge of wood is progressing. Fire trench and machine gun emplacement made, joining the two outworks, north of PAU Villa.

(b) ST YVES Section. Revetting and wiring new trenches round ST YVES. Close gaps in front line. Make machine gun emplacement at Three Huns Farm to protect new St. YVES trenches.

PLOEGSTEERT Wood. A low wall of sandbags to be put up so that "crawling" communication can be established by daylight with Left Trench. Trench will be dug as soon as ground drys.

LE GHEER Section. Continue covered way in the Wood. Additional revetment and wiring to the outwork trench. A communication trench with this outwork trench will be made.

(c) There has been very little shelling in this Sector during the past week and practically no sniping.

(d) No movements of the enemy have been observed. A new piece of German trench is reported opposite the salient of L.E. corner - ST YVES Section. This joins up the enemy's trenches across a space of about 100 yards, where formerly the defence consisted of trenches flanking the gap. By a conversation which took place between some Germans and some officers it is almost certain that the enemy in front of this Sector are Saxons. Some men who spoke from the trench to the north of the BIRDCAGE were talking with a different brogue, probably not Saxon but still South German. The Saxons apparently had men who came from ALSATZ in their ranks.

LEFT SECTOR. 10th Inf. Brig.

(a) The chief work has been :-

(i) Construction of JOLIEVILLE in the new huts for the reserve battalion in F.26.b.
(ii) The breastwork that is to join up the two front trenches on the right of the Trans-ROUTE section. The original gap of 150 yards has already been referred to as a source of danger. This work when completed will also act as a covered communication between the two fire trenches.

In addition the work of boarding the various communication trenches already dug has been continued and the second trench from the forward Estaminet to Seaforth Farm is now completed.

9/4/15

WEEKLY REPORT.

1. Resume. During the past week progress has been made in the direction of increasing means of communicating with the front line and in completing retrenchments close behind certain points. LE TOUQUET, the Railway Barricade and ST YVES may be cited as instances of where both the above descriptions of work have reached completion.

There are now very few parts of the line that cannot be reached by day and this enables wounded men to be got out quickly. There are still an insufficient number of communication trenches to enable reinforcements to be moved rapidly forward under cover to any desired point and consequently this work will continue for some time to come.

The action of the enemy during the week has been normal. Our Arty. observation station in LA HUTTE Chateau was destroyed, but otherwise no damage has been done by hostile Arty. fire.

There is no reason to suppose that units in our front have been changed.

2. RIGHT SECTOR. (12th Inf.Brig.)

(a) In order to enable reinforcements to reach LE TOUQUET from the neighbourhood of LE BIZET a communication trench is being made from the Divisional supporting line near LA FLENQUE Farm to connect with the trench already made from the Railway Station. About 400 yards of this has now been dug.

In the WIPERS Houses the following work has been done -
(i) 3 Mountain Gun emplacements immediately behind the front wall. (see plan attached).
(ii) 32 bomb proof shelters have been made in the little back gardens - 20 of these during the week. They still require flooring.
(iii) The walls facing FRELINGHIEN have been strengthened in anticipation of possible bombardment from this quarter.

At CARTER'S Farm a support trench 50 yards in length has been made (a).

During the winter the most advanced fire-trench North of the SNIPERS Houses has been isolated. The old communication trench has now been reclaimed and boarded. (b).

At the Railway Barricade the retrenchment mentioned last week has now been completed by the joining of the left semi-high command of the LE TOUQUET section with the right semi-high command of the WARNAVE section (c). It is now possible to proceed direct from LE TOUQUET Station as far as the Essex Cross Roads.

(b) It is proposed to continue the work in hand mentioned above and in addition
(i) to dig a communication trench from OBSERVATION Farm to the WARNAVE (d).
(ii) to construct a support trench close in rear of the front line between Essex Cross Roads and the River WARNAVE.

(c) Sniping and shelling have been rather less than usual especially on Easter Sunday.

(d) The uniforms observed show that the Saxons are still in front of this Sector.

War Diary
HQ 4th Div
April 1915.

Appendix C

Sketch showing the
position of the Arty
supporting 3 line.

4th DIVISION.

CASUALTIES.

The total casualties for the months of APRIL and MAY, 1915 are as follow :-

OFFICERS.			OTHER RANKS.			TOTAL.		
K.	W.	M.	K.	W.	M.	K.	W.	M.
87	224	36	1566	5476	3470	1653	5700	3506

The names of officers are in attached lists.

www.ingramcontent.com/pod-product-compliance
Lightning Source LLC
Chambersburg PA
CBHW080841010526
44114CB00017B/2350